HOME MADE BASICS

FOR OMAR

HOME MADE BASICS

Simple Recipes, Made from Scratch

YVETTE VAN BOVEN

PHOTOGRAPHY BY
OOF VERSCHUREN

Abrams, New York

CONTENTS

INTRODUCTION

I began to help out in the kitchen and around the house from a very young age. My mother thought it was important that we kids knew how dangerous appliances could be, so we wouldn't try to use them without her permission and get hurt in the process. So, at four I had already learned how to sew on a sewing machine: my mother gently pushing the pedal, me holding the fabric underneath the needle. I found out how the lawn mower worked by helping to push it across our large Irish garden, and, whenever it got jammed, by carefully removing tough branches or wads of wet leaves from in between the sharp blades. I learned to always grab the hedge trimmer by its handles, with *both* hands.

And I learned how the stove worked.

Soon, I stood on a chair next to my mother at the kitchen counter, jotting down her every move. When I didn't know how to write the words, I drew them: a pan, a spoon, a whisk, sketching arrows to indicate her actions. (I do pretty much the same thing today.)

I learned to roll meatballs, to make a stew, to bake cookies and soda bread and lasagna.

When my mother gave me a children's cookbook with step-by-step instructions, I moved from picture to picture, from one step to the next. And that's how I still make my books: step by step. Nothing here is too complicated, because you can't cook something complex until you've mastered the basics.

This project began as a book aimed at a child like the little chef I once was. But I quickly realized that this should be a book for *everyone* who likes to cook, but who also feels a little intimidated in the kitchen from time to time.

And even experienced cooks need tried-and-true recipes like these in their arsenal—foundational and satisfying food that they can make without a lot of fuss.

I wrote *Home Made Basics* for anyone who wants to put a cozy meal on their dining table each day with methods that aren't much more challenging than heating up some leftovers or assembling a few quality ingredients.

So remember: whatever your comfort level in the kitchen, all you have to do to make delicious food is to follow the instructions, step by step.

x Yvette

in the dunes near the beach in Inchydoney, West Cork

SOME INFO TO GET STARTED

YIELD

All recipes serve four, unless indicated otherwise.

PREPARATION TIME

Each recipe mentions a preparation time, which starts the moment the onions are chopped, the beans shelled, or any of the other ingredients listed are prepped. This preparation time might vary from cook to cook, depending on your skill level.

Don't forget to ALWAYS read the whole recipe first, so you won't encounter any surprises. In each recipe I also mention whether you should marinate for an hour ahead of time or if you should wait one day before you can dig in.

MEASUREMENTS

1 tablespoon = 15 ml
1 coffee (dessert) spoon = 7 ml
1 teaspoon = 5 ml

OVEN

I have a gas oven as well as an electric convection oven. I use both for testing.

I always give an average temperature in my recipes.

Puff pastry, for example, bakes at a high temperature: at least 400°F (200°C), but sometimes 425°F (220°C). On the other hand, a slow-roasted cut of Boston pork butt calls for a lower temperature, 300°F (150°C) and— depending on the weight—a long time to cook, about 5 hours. Ovens vary in temperature, even those from the same brand. You can use my stated temperatures and baking times as reliable estimates, but make sure to adjust them to your own oven if necessary.

Always use an oven thermometer; they cost next to nothing and are easy to find. The only temperature you can trust is the one you measure yourself *inside* the oven. The dial on the front may indicate the desired temperature but not necessarily the *actual* temperature of your food. Always properly preheat the oven and carefully measure the temperature.

And because every oven is different, the indicated cooking times are approximations. Always check your dish or baked good around the stated cooking time to see whether it's ready.

Once you really begin to get the hang of your oven, you'll start using it more. I cook more than half of my dishes in it, often more than one dish at a time. That way I keep my hands free for doing other stuff in the meantime.

BROTH

I won't mention this in every recipe, but home made broth always tastes best. Simple dishes are greatly improved by the intense, full-bodied flavor of home-steeped broth. Bouillon cubes are an easy substitution (not everyone has the time to make broth from scratch!) but it isn't always the tastiest solution.

I use bouillon cubes sparingly and freeze my home made broths in small batches to use for different dishes. Besides, the smell of a pot of broth, gently simmering on the stove, is amazing!

My broths often give a chicken carcass and some leftover celery, carrots, and leeks from the produce drawer a second life. I give recipes for making broths in the "Soup" section (pages 107–109).

EGGS

I prefer to use medium eggs. Farmers' market eggs can greatly vary in size. If you think your eggs are very small, use two instead of one. It can really make a difference in a recipe if there isn't enough egg in it.

MILK/DAIRY

Always opt for whole milk, yogurt, or heavy cream. The high fat content is where the flavor is. This is true for *all* dairy: more fat = more flavor. Just so you know.

BUTTER

I never use margarine. Yes, I know, butter is fat. But if you eat healthfully, a buttered slice of whole-wheat bread won't hurt.

OLIVE OIL

I always use delicious, good-quality olive oil. "Extra-virgin," it usually says on the bottle. I use it for cooking as well as in salads and baked goods. I can taste the difference.

Unless explicitly stated otherwise, every recipe that calls for olive oil means: extra-virgin, of good quality.

MEAT

Everyone should decide for themselves what kind of meat they buy. But my motto is: eat meat less often, and *if* you choose to eat it, buy organic and grass-fed products whenever possible, sourced from animals that lived an honest life.

In this book I give you plenty of recipes for dishes without meat and in the others I suggest where you can leave it out. However, there is a short chapter with recipes in which meat or fowl takes center stage because I love those as well.

FISH

I eat fish more often than I eat meat. I try to stay away from farm-raised fish and to buy only seasonal, wild-caught fish. Each fish species has its own season in which it is at its best. At the fishmonger, always let yourself be guided by what's on offer instead of the recipe. Fish rarely arrives on demand; that's just how nature works.

Connemara, Ireland

PARTICULAR INGREDIENTS EXPLAINED

ACACIA HONEY

Honey is a product of nature. Almost all honey crystallizes over time, except for acacia. So, if you don't use honey very often, this one will always be liquid, even after sitting on the shelf for a long time. Of course, supermarket honey in one of those squeeze bottles also stays liquid, but do know that it has been processed and lacks the health benefits of natural honey. Instead, buy raw honey from an apiary or an organic food store.

PEARL BARLEY & ALKMAAR BARLEY

Barley is sold as polished, hulled barley grain, with different degrees of polish. Hulled but only partly polished barley is called pot barley or Scotch barley. In the Netherlands it's also sold under the name "Alkmaar barley." If the barley is polished even further, into almost round pearls, it is called pearl barley. Nowadays you can find (pearl) barley in almost any supermarket. Some stores place it near the superfoods, others in the special diet food section, and sometimes it's in the aisle with the rice and other cereals. So it might take some searching. But it is very tasty and very nutritious.

MIRIN

Sweet Japanese rice wine. Can be replaced with sweet or sugar-based sherry or white port.

MISO

In short: miso is a paste made from fermented soybeans, salt, and koji. Koji is fermented soy or barley with the addition of a fungus. If this sounds very unusual, just think of a blue cheese: also made by adding a fungus.

There are all kinds of misos for sale; the white and red ones are the most common. White miso is a good entry-level miso if you are still unfamiliar with the ingredient. This flavoring is used for everything—hot or cold—and is best explained as "umami," or the fifth flavor. It's extremely addictive!

NIGELLA SEED

Nigella seed is also commonly called black onion seed, black cumin, or kalonji and isn't readily available at the supermarket. But you will certainly find nigella seed at Middle Eastern and Indian supermarkets, and I regularly buy it online, too. These are the black seeds on Turkish bread (pide), and which are also widely used in Indian cuisine. I am slightly addicted to them. They taste like toasted onions.

RICE VINEGAR

A somewhat milder vinegar than the regular vinegar from the supermarket. It is made from fermented glutinous rice and water. The color can range from transparent to dark brown, depending on the type of rice used and whether the rice grains are polished or not. There is Chinese and Japanese rice vinegar—wheat or sake is often also added to the latter. I like to use Japanese brown rice vinegar myself.

SZECHUAN PEPPERCORNS

Szechuan peppercorns are a particularly delicious and aromatic spice with a hint of lemon flavor. In addition, they contain a special molecule that sends a signal to your brain to cause tingling on the sides of your tongue and on your lips, which is why it is often described as a numbing pepper.

TAHINI, WHITE OR DARK

Tahini is a paste made from crushed sesame seeds. Nothing new so far, because you probably knew that already. However! Be aware that there are two types: white (or light) and dark. The white tahini is made from lightly roasted sesame seeds; the dark one is made from dark roasted sesame seeds and is somewhat fuller in taste. The latter is more like peanut butter and can also be used as a substitute (if someone has a peanut allergy, for example). I prefer to use white tahini.

BLACK GARLIC

Black garlic is ordinary garlic that has aged in an oven for weeks until it turns black. The result is a milder flavor—subdued but penetrating, a little licorice-like, but still savory, a flavor called "umami." It no longer has the sharpness and intensity of raw garlic.

SHOPPING FOR LESS COMMON INGREDIENTS

ASIAN INGREDIENTS
like gochujang, gochugaru, miso, rice vinegar, and mirin: Asian markets, good supermarkets, hmart.com

SPECIALTY BEANS
waldfarming.nl (for Frisian forest beans) and ranchogordo.com

QUALITY MEATS
such as beef, leg of lamb, or pork: farmers' markets, local producers, natural foods stores

GOLDEN SYRUP
good supermarkets or online

DRIED HIBISCUS AND ROSE PETALS
Latino and Middle Eastern markets, natural foods stores (in the bulk herbs and teas section)

SPECIALTY RAW HONEYS
such as acacia honey: good specialty supermarkets and natural foods stores

MASA HARINA
good supermarkets and Latino markets

SPECIAL FLOURS LIKE MALT FLOUR
Bob's Red Mill; Amazon.com

HERBS AND SPICES
such as nigella seed: Indian markets, penzeys.com, and foodsofnations.com (Kalustyan's)

BLACK GARLIC
good specialty supermarkets, natural foods stores, and foodsofnations.com (Kalustyan's)

the West Cork kitchen

MORNING

ochtendwandeling in de Ierse tuin, West Cork

BAKED BREAKFAST SAVORY SCONES, SAVORY SC
ZUCCHINI BREAD, DUTCH SPICE CAKE, MAKING C
(DUTCH FRENCH TOAST) WITH GRUYÈRE & TOMA
SANDWICH WITH FIGS & TAPENADE, SALMON ME
GRILLED GOAT CHEESE SANDWICH FRESH BREAK
RICOTTA, RADISH TARTINE, BRUSCHETTA WITH CEL
WITH LIGHTLY TOASTED GRANOLA, STRAWBERRY,
WATERMELON, ALMOND MILK & GINGER SHAKE
ÇILBIR WITH PAPRIKA POWDER, ÇILBIR WITH PAPRI
ASPARAGUS, SWEET OMELET SOUFFLÉ, GREEN SH

ONES WITH DOUBLE EGG SALAD, QUICK
RUMPETS, POTTED CRAB, WENTELTEEFJES
TO, INDIAN WENTELTEFJES, GRILLED TALEGGIO
LT TOAST, JALAPEÑO GRILLED SANDWICH,
FAST BRUSCHETTA WITH FAVA BEANS &
ERIAC REMOULADE, JAM, BREAKFAST SYLLABUB
YOGURT, GREEN TEA & CARDAMOM SHAKE,
BREAKFAST WITH EGGS POACHING AN EGG,
KA BUTTER, CELERY CARAWAY YOGURT & GRILLED
AKSHUKA

making breakfast with Guus

SAVORY SCONES

(For sweet scones add ½ cup/50 grams confectioners' sugar)

Preheat the oven to 425°F (220°C). THAT'S HOT!

!

In a large bowl, combine all of the ingredients briefly but thoroughly to resemble coarse grains.

½ tsp salt

4 tsp baking powder

3½ c (450 g) all-purpose flour

½ c + 2 tsp (125 g) cubed cold butter

Pour in 2 beaten eggs and about 10 tbsp (150 ml) buttermilk and knead everything into a cohesive ball. You may need less liquid, but maybe more.

DON'T ADD ALL OF THE LIQUID AT ONCE!

Dust the countertop with flour. Press the dough ball into a slab ¾ inch (2 cm) thick.

With a cookie cutter or a glass, cut out 8 scones. Knead the leftovers of the dough over and over again into a slab and keep doing this until all of the dough is used.

Brush the scones with buttermilk and place on a greased baking sheet or a sheet of parchment paper in the hot oven. Bake them for about 15 minutes, depending on their size, until golden brown and done. Let cool slightly.

HA!

SAVORY SCONES WITH DOUBLE EGG SALAD

PREPARE: 35 MINUTES
BAKE: 15 MINUTES
SERVES 6 TO 8 FOR
BREAKFAST OR LUNCH

8 eggs
5 to 6 tablespoons
   mayonnaise (page 129)
2 tablespoons very finely
   chopped green herbs,
   such as chervil, chives,
   dill, parsley, plus extra for
   garnish
2 heaping finely chopped
   tablespoons cornichons or
   other small, sour pickles
1 tablespoon red wine
   vinegar
a few drops of home made
   hot sauce (page 141)
   or green Tabasco sauce
   (optional)
1 (1¾-ounce/50 g) jar
   fish eggs (see headnote)
splash of lemon juice
sea salt and freshly ground
   black pepper
8 to 10 savory scones
   (page 21)

I don't like fake. I really dislike the taste of cheap truffle oil, for example. It has nothing to do with real truffles. Bags of cheap grated cheese: you don't taste cheese, it's all congealed salt rennet. Just grate a chunk of real farmhouse cheese. Now *that* is grated cheese.

There's one fake ingredient, however, for which I'll make an exception: in this egg salad I don't use real caviar. Instead, it's a beautiful imitation product that looks like it, but in fact consists of gelled balls of fish stock. Almost all fish eggs, including salmon eggs, flying fish eggs and so on, are dyed: just turn the jar and check the ingredients list. All fake—unless you buy real wild salmon eggs, but that might be a bit expensive for such a simple salad.

A simple egg salad will look dignified after adding some fake caviar. And those salty balls lend this recipe a really cool taste and texture. So just this once I'll let go of my principles, okay?

Place the eggs in a large saucepan filled with ample cold water. Bring the water to a boil, let it boil for 1 minute (time it!), then cover the pan with a lid and let stand for 12 minutes. Drain the eggs, shock them with cold water, and peel them in cold water. Chop into pieces.

Put the mayonnaise in a bowl and using a spatula, loosely fold in the green herbs, cornichons, red wine vinegar, home made hot sauce, and the eggs. Add the fish eggs. Season the salad with a few drops of lemon juice. Let the salad stand as long as possible so that the flavors can absorb. Taste and add salt and pepper as needed.

Halve the scones, spoon some salad onto each half scone, and serve immediately.

This is delicious with some of the leek oil from page 187 drizzled on top. Oh, and it's also lovely with the home-smoked fish on page 393.

QUICK ZUCCHINI BREAD

PREPARE: 20 MINUTES
BAKE: ABOUT 40 MINUTES
MAKES 1 LOAF

3¼ cups (400 g) self-rising
    flour, plus extra for dusting
2 zucchini, coarsely grated
heaping ½ cup (50 g)
    rolled oats
⅓ teaspoon baking soda
    (or 1½ teaspoons baking
    powder; see below)
1 teaspoon salt
1 bunch (½ ounce/15 g)
    thyme, leaves only
1 egg, beaten
1¼ cups (300 ml) buttermilk
½ cup (50 g) finely grated
    Parmesan or other
    aged cheese

BAKING SODA

Also commonly called sodium
bicarbonate, sodium hydrogen
carbonate, bread soda,
cooking soda, bicarbonate, or
bicarb, baking soda is many
times more powerful than
baking powder. But if you
don't have it on hand, please
substitute 1 teaspoon baking
powder for each ¼ teaspoon
baking soda.

Baking soda reacts to acidic
additives in your batter, so
you should add sour dairy
such as buttermilk, sour cream,
or yogurt (or simply some
lemon juice) to recipes in
which it is used.

Beware of addictiveness! With its crunchy cheese crust and the mildly sweet flavor of the grated zucchini, this bread is extremely binge-able.

Preheat the oven to 425°F (200°C). Dust a small baking sheet with flour and set aside.

Spoon the grated zucchini into the center of a clean tea towel and fold the ends of the cloth together. Twist the cloth as tightly as you can—do this over the sink. Squeeze as much water as possible from the zucchini.

In a large bowl, combine the flour with the oats, baking soda, and salt. Add the thyme and zucchini and mix until everything comes together nicely.

Beat the egg with the buttermilk and pour it—except for 2 tablespoons!—over the flour mixture. Stir with a wooden spoon until the dough comes together. Spoon the dough onto the counter and knead until just cohesive. This dough should not be kneaded through and through, otherwise the bread will not leaven.

Shape the dough into a ball, place the ball on the baking sheet, and brush with the 2 tablespoons egg-buttermilk mixture you set aside. Sprinkle the bread with the grated cheese. Using a sharp knife, carve a deep cross in the top.

Bake the bread for about 40 minutes, until it is nicely golden brown and the bottom sounds hollow when you tap it.

Eat the zucchini bread warm, spread with a lick of butter, or add a fried egg. This bread is also delicious with a stew or a bowl of soup.

Oof

BREAKFAST COOKIES

PREPARE: 7 MINUTES
BAKE: 25 MINUTES
MAKES 8 PIECES

scant 1 cup (150 g) steel-cut
   oats (not rolled oats)
pinch of sea salt
1 teaspoon ground cinnamon
⅔ cup (170 g) nut butter or
   peanut butter
3 tablespoons honey or
   maple syrup
1 banana (preferably overripe,
   because sweeter), mashed
about 7 ounces (200 g) of
   a mixture of your choice:
   raisins, dried cranberries,
   pepitas, puffed quinoa,
   millet, chopped or roasted
   nuts, flaxseeds, and/or
   chopped dried fruit

tool
stand mixer

These are a kind of muesli cookies. They hardly contain any sugar, just a bit of honey, and no egg. So vegans will be happy too (as long as you use maple syrup instead of honey).

On weekdays I am not much of a breakfast person. Somedays I might eat some fruit. A biscuit like this one is always welcome, though, especially when I'm busy. I might bring one to eat on my way to my first appointment of the day.

Preheat the oven to 325°F (160°C). Line a large baking sheet with parchment paper.

Combine all the ingredients in a large bowl in a stand mixer. Use a mixer with a dough hook, as this is a firm dough.

Using 2 tablespoons, scoop large dollops of dough onto the baking sheet and flatten with clean hands. The cookies don't spread during baking, so you need to shape them yourself.

Bake the cookies for about 25 minutes, until the edges start to brown. Let cool completely on the baking sheet. The cookies will keep for a week, if packed in an airtight container. They can also be stored in the freezer.

BAKED BREAKFAST

MAKING CRUMPETS

YOU'LL NEED:
2 TO 4 CRUMPET RINGS OF ABOUT 3¼ INCHES (8 CM) IN DIAMETER;
OR 2 ROUND ALUMINUM CANS (ABOUT 6 OUNCES/ 170 G) CRABMEAT: FIRST CUT
OFF THE LID, SCOOP OUT THE CONTENTS NEEDED FOR THE RECIPE ON PAGE 31,
AND THEN CUT OUT THE BOTTOM. THOROUGHLY WASH.

In a large bowl, mix 1 c plus 2½ tbsp (275 ml) lukewarm milk with ¼ c (60 ml) water. Add 1 envelope (¼ oz/7 g) yeast and ½ tsp sugar. Let stand for 10 minutes.

Using a whisk, stir in 1¾ c (225 g) all-purpose flour in batches, then add 1 tsp salt. Whisk out the lumps and you'll end up with a thick batter that slowly runs off your whisk in a thin stream.

Cover the bowl with plastic wrap and let the batter rise for 1 to 1½ hours in a warm place until it has doubled in volume and you see air bubbles appear on top.

Heat a skillet (a well-seasoned pan or a nonstick one) over low heat.

Thoroughly grease the inside of the rings. Place them in the skillet.

Spoon the batter into the rings up to about one-third from the top.

Cook the crumpets over low to medium heat until the tops are dry and riddled with small holes. If the heat is too high the bottom of the crumpets will burn quickly. SO BEWARE!

CRAB

Carefully remove the rings. If you have trouble doing this, cut the crumpets out of the rings. This works best if you wear an oven mitt and use a regular dinner knife with a round tip. But as long as you greased the rings well, you won't need to do this.

CRAB

Now very briefly brown the crumpets on the other side.

ALWAYS SERVE CRUMPETS WARM, FRESHLY BAKED OR REHEATED
IN A WARM SKILLET, PREHEATED OVEN, OR A TOASTER,
PREFERABLY DRIPPING WITH MELTING (SALTED!) BUTTER.

POTTED CRAB

PREPARE: 20 MINUTES
SOLIDIFY: AT LEAST 1 HOUR
SERVES 4 FOR BREAKFAST
OR LUNCH

1 cup plus 1⅔ tablespoons
   (250 g) butter
juice of ½ lemon
2 canned anchovies, minced
½ teaspoon freshly
   ground mace or freshly
   grated nutmeg
½ teaspoon white pepper
2 (6-ounce/170 g) cans
   quality crabmeat, drained;
   or 8¾ ounces (250 g)
   cooked shrimp
pinch of cayenne pepper

Besides being one of the most delicious things you can serve on a warm crumpet, potted crab is also delicious on crackers and served with some drinks. Feel free to substitute shrimp for the crab. For extra flavor, let the shrimp shells steep in the melted butter too. If you do, make sure to strain the butter before pouring it into the jars.

In a saucepan over low heat, melt the butter and heat until the sediment (the milk protein) on the bottom turns dark, and the clear, yellow liquid turns a light tea color. Pour the clarified butter through a sieve, lined with a paper towel, into a bowl.

Wipe the pan clean and add the lemon juice, chopped anchovies, mace, and white pepper to the pan. Pour the clarified light brown butter from the bowl into the pan and heat the butter over low heat for a few minutes until the anchovies have completely dissolved.

Turn off the heat and add the crab or shrimp to the butter. Fill small bowls or glasses with the butter mixture, sprinkle with a pinch of cayenne pepper, and allow the butter to solidify. The potted crab will keep in the fridge for months, provided the fish and shellfish are fully covered in the butter.

You can also let the potted crab set somewhat and then spoon it directly, lukewarm, onto freshly baked hot crumpets (pages 28–29) or warm toast. Afterward, your life will never be the same.

BAKED BREAKFAST

Dutch French toast with Gruyère & tomato

WENTELTEEFJES (DUTCH FRENCH TOAST) WITH GRUYÈRE & TOMATO

PREPARE: 15 MINUTES
BAKE: 7 MINUTES
SERVES 4 FOR BREAKFAST
OR LUNCH

about 10 ounces (300 g)
   cherry tomatoes on
   the vine
1 to 2 tablespoons olive oil
sea salt and freshly ground
   black pepper
5 eggs, beaten
⅓ cup (75 ml) milk
5 ounces (140 g) Gruyère
   cheese, grated
4 slices of country bread
about 4 tablespoons (50 g)
   butter
a few sprigs chives or
   2 scallions, chopped
handful (1¾ ounces/50 g)
   of watercress, nasturtium,
   mustard leaves, and/or
   garden herbs such as fresh
   chervil, tarragon, dill, or
   fennel flowers

Bread that is a little past its prime is actually better for making
wentelteefjes. This way, you turn something that is a little stale into a
completely joyous dish!

Heat the broiler until it's nice and hot, at least 400°F (200°C).

Put the cherry tomatoes, preferably still on the vine, on a rimmed
baking sheet, lightly coated with olive oil. Drizzle a splash of olive
oil over the tomatoes and sprinkle with salt and pepper. Roast
the cherry tomatoes for 5 to 7 minutes, until they are tender and
beginning to brown. Set the tomatoes aside.

In a large, deep plate, beat the eggs along with the milk, Gruyère
cheese, salt, and pepper. Place the slices of bread—cut large ones in
half—one by one in the deep plate. Let soak for up to 5 minutes.

In a large frying pan over medium heat, melt a knob of butter. Place
as many slices of Dutch French toast as will fit in the hot pan and
scrape the remaining cheese off the plate onto the bread. Fry the
French toast for 3 to 5 minutes on each side or until crisp and golden
brown, turning with a sturdy spatula, as the cheese tends to stick.
Repeat the previous steps until all the *wentelteefjes* have been toasted.

Serve the *wentelteefjes* with the cherry tomatoes, sprinkled with chives
or scallions to taste and with a handful of watercress, mustard leaves,
fresh garden herbs, or some edible flowers like nasturtium on the side.

INDIAN WENTELTEEFJES

PREPARE: 15 MINUTES
SERVES 4 FOR BREAKFAST
OR LUNCH

In a shallow bowl, beat 4 eggs along with 3 tablespoons low-fat yogurt
and 2 teaspoons mild curry paste.
   Soak 2 thinly sliced red onions with 1 finely chopped green
(jalapeño) pepper in 2 tablespoons red wine vinegar mixed with
1 tablespoon ginger syrup, sprinkle with 1 teaspoon toasted cumin
seeds, and season with salt and pepper.
   Soak 4 slices of bread one at a time in the egg mixture.
   In a skillet, heat some ghee or butter. Fry the bread in batches until
nice and brown on both sides. Serve with the onion and pepper and
sprinkle with a handful of fresh cilantro leaves.

grilled taleggio sandwich with figs and tapenade

PREPARE: 10 MINUTES
MAKES 2 LARGE GRILLED
SANDWICHES

4 slices of sourdough bread
2 tablespoons butter
4 tablespoons (60 ml)
 kalamata olive tapenade
 (for home made tapenade,
 see page 89, or use
 ready-made)
7 ounces (200 g) taleggio
 cheese,* sliced, or brie
freshly ground black pepper
3 to 4 fresh figs, sliced

*Taleggio is a cheese
produced in a valley of the
same name in the Bergamo
region of Italy. It is creamy,
slightly sweet, and melts very
easily when heated.

GRILLED TALEGGIO SANDWICH WITH FIGS & TAPENADE

In my opinion, bread fried in butter and filled with melted cheese is about the most delicious thing there is. Nothing made in an electric panini press—however ingenious—beats a good old grilled sandwich. The edges of the bread straight and crunchy, the bread itself greasy and crispy, the filling creamy and always too hot. You almost want to get a hangover just so you're allowed to eat them all day (if you want to actually do this, I'll give you some ideas in the drinks section).

Butter all 4 of the sourdough slices. Turn the slices over so the butter is on the bottom. Spread 2 slices of bread with a thick layer of olive tapenade. Divide the taleggio on top and sprinkle generously with black pepper. Place the figs on top of the cheese. Put the 2 remaining bread slices on top (the buttered side facing up!) and press them slightly.

Place the sandwiches in a hot skillet over medium heat. If you want, you can weigh them down with a plate upon which you can place a can of tomatoes or something heavy like that. Grill the sandwiches until they are golden brown, turn them over, and fry the other side until crispy.

PREPARE: 10 MINUTES
MAKES 2 LARGE GRILLED
SANDWICHES

1 (6- to 6½-ounce/170 to
 185 g) can boneless salmon
 in oil, drained (look for the
 MSC certification)
4 tablespoons (60 ml)
 mayonnaise (page 129)
2 scallions, sliced into rings
2 stalks celery, cut into
 small cubes
1 teaspoon spicy mustard
½ teaspoon curry powder
sea salt and freshly ground
 black pepper
4 slices whole-wheat bread
2 tablespoons butter
4 thick slices of aged
 Cheddar cheese
pinch of paprika

SALMON MELT SANDWICH

Combine the salmon, mayonnaise, scallions, celery, mustard, curry powder, and salt and pepper into a creamy salad.

Butter the bread slices. Turn the slices over so the butter is on the bottom. Cover the first slice of bread with half of the salmon salad, top with a slice of cheese, sprinkle with paprika, and press the next slice of bread, butter side up, on top. Repeat this with the other bread slices and the remaining toppings.

In a skillet over medium heat, grill the sandwiches on both sides until golden brown: while grilling, push the sandwiches down with a spatula so the filling sticks together nicely. Halfway through cooking, partly cover the pan with a lid so the cheese gets hot and melts more easily.

PREPARE: 10 MINUTES
MAKES 2 LARGE GRILLED
SANDWICHES

2 tablespoons pickled
  jalapeños, from a jar
1 tablespoon finely chopped
  fresh cilantro leaves
1 clove garlic, grated
2 tablespoons fresh
  goat cheese
5¼ ounces (150 g) aged
  Cheddar cheese, grated
1 piquillo pepper, from a jar,
  finely chopped
4 slices of organic bread,
  briefly toasted
2 tablespoons butter, plus
  extra to butter the bread
4 slices of aged Cheddar or
  another aged cheese

JALAPEÑO & SWEET PEPPER GRILLED SANDWICH

Combine the jalapeños with the cilantro, garlic, goat cheese, grated aged cheese, and sweet pepper and stir into a spreadable paste.

Butter the bread. Turn the slices over so the butter is on the bottom. Cover 2 slices with the cheese mixture, top with a slice of Cheddar or aged cheese and press the other slices of bread, butter side up, on top.

Melt the butter in a skillet. Over medium heat, cook the sandwiches on both sides until golden brown, pressing them with a spatula so the sandwiches and the topping stick together nicely. Cover the pan with a lid so that the cheese gets hot enough to melt more easily.

PREPARE: 10 MINUTES
MAKES 2 LARGE GRILLED
SANDWICHES

4 slices of sourdough bread
2 tablespoons butter
4 tablespoons (60 ml) apricot
  jam (for home made jam,
  see page 43), or another
  kind, like rhubarb, plum, or
  blackberry jam
7 ounces (200 g) fresh
  goat cheese
4 sprigs of thyme, just the
  leaves
freshly ground black pepper

GRILLED GOAT CHEESE SANDWICH WITH APRICOT & THYME

Butter all of the sourdough slices. Turn the bread slices over so that the butter is on the bottom side. Spread 2 slices of bread with a thick layer of apricot jam. Divide the goat cheese on top and sprinkle generously with thyme leaves and season with black pepper.

Put the other slices on top (with the buttered side facing up!) and press them slightly.

Place the sandwiches in a hot skillet over medium heat. If you want, you can weigh them down with a plate upon which you can place a can of tomatoes or something heavy like that. Cook the sandwiches until they are golden brown, then turn them over and fry the other side until crispy.

BAKED BREAKFAST

BRUSCHETTA WITH FAVA BEANS & RICOTTA

PREPARE: ABOUT 20 MINUTES MAKES 8 PIECES FOR A BREAKFAST, LUNCH, OR SNACK

1 pound 1 ounce (500 g) fresh shelled fava beans (shelled weight)

8 medium radishes, thinly sliced

1 tablespoon finely chopped fresh mint leaves

1 tablespoon minced fresh dill

zest and juice of ½ organic lemon

sea salt, preferably Maldon salt flakes or *fleur de sel de Guérande*

freshly ground black pepper

8 crusty slices of white bread

1 clove garlic

a generous 5 tablespoons olive oil

1 scant cup (250 g) ricotta cheese

Blanch the fava beans in boiling water for 2 minutes, drain, and rinse with ice-cold water immediately so they stay nice and green. Using a pointed knife, make a cut in the back of a fava bean and push out the inner bean. Double-shell the rest of the fava beans and coarsely mash them with a fork.

Combine the fava beans with the radish slices, mint, dill, the grated zest and the lemon juice and season with salt and a generous amount of black pepper.

In a dry skillet, toast the bread slices one by one. Also peel and halve the garlic clove. Rub the toasted bread with the cut sides of the garlic. Drizzle each slice of bread with a splash of olive oil (not too sparingly!) and sprinkle with salt flakes.

Spoon fresh ricotta onto the bruschetta and top with the fava bean mixture. Grind some extra pepper on top and serve the bruschetta.

RADISH TARTINE

PREPARE: 5 MINUTES MAKES 4 SANDWICHES FOR BREAKFAST OR LUNCH

Combine 1 bunch thinly sliced (nicely elongated) radishes with 1 tablespoon olive oil, grated zest and juice of ½ organic lemon, and freshly ground black pepper.

Divide 2 sliced avocados over 4 slices of whole-wheat bread and spread out the radishes on top. Sprinkle the tartines with salt flakes.

bruschetta with fava beans and ricotta (and two kinds of radishes!)

PREPARE: ABOUT
20 MINUTES
WAIT: 30 MINUTES
MAKES 6 PIECES FOR
A BREAKFAST, LUNCH,
OR SNACK

for the celeriac remoulade
½ small or ¼ large celeriac
juice from 1 lemon
½ cup (125 g) crème fraîche
1 tablespoon mayonnaise
  (page 129)
1 tablespoon capers
sea salt and freshly ground
  black pepper

for the bruschetta
6 slices of Italian bread
  (e.g., ciabatta)
1 clove garlic
splash of olive oil
salt flakes
1 container of watercress

tool
food processor or coarse grater

BRUSCHETTA WITH CELERIAC REMOULADE

Make the celeriac remoulade: Grate the celeriac in the food processor on the coarse setting. This can of course also be done by hand, but watch out for your knuckles.

Combine the grated celeriac with the lemon juice, crème fraîche, mayonnaise, capers, salt and black pepper. Let stand for 30 minutes so the celery can get softer.

Make the bruschetta: Toast the bread in a dry skillet. Peel and halve the garlic clove. Rub the toasted bread with the cut sides of the garlic. Drizzle the bread with a splash of olive oil and sprinkle with some salt flakes.

Spoon the celeriac remoulade onto the bread and serve the bruschetta sprinkled with some watercress.

FRESH BREAKFAST

Connemara, Ireland

JAM

PREPARE: 15 MINUTES
MAKES 6 TO 8 POTS,
EACH ABOUT 1 CUP
(250 ML)

2¼ pounds (1 kg) berries,
    cleaned and diced if needed
5 cups (1 kg) granulated
    sugar
pinch of salt
squeeze of lemon juice

HIGH PECTIN CONTENT
Red currant
Apple (some are lower acid)
Lemon
Grapefruit
Gooseberry
Quince
Lime
Plum (varies by type)
Orange

MEDIUM PECTIN CONTENT
Apricot
Blueberry
Blackberry
Grape
Raspberry
Mandarin

LOW PECTIN CONTENT
Strawberry
Pineapple
Cherry
Kiwi
Mango (lower acid)
Melon
Nectarine
Pear
Peach
Rhubarb
Fig (lower acid)
Elderberry

The following is the basic procedure to make jam out of stone fruits and berries. To use other fruits, including those that are lower in acid content and may need added acid for safe canning, check the National Center for Home Food Preservation website (https://nchfp.uga.edu) for details.

While stirring, slowly bring the fruit to a boil in a large saucepan. Reduce the heat and cook the fruit for 7 to 10 minutes, until it falls apart and releases its liquid.

Add the sugar and a pinch of salt and cook the jam for about 7 to 8 minutes, until the jam has the desired thickness. Skim the foam that appears on the surface.

Test whether the jam is ready: drip 1 teaspoon of jam onto a cold saucer. Refrigerate for 5 minutes. If the jam has firmed up nicely, it's ready. If it is still too runny, the jam needs to simmer for a few more minutes. I always finish my jam with a squeeze of lemon juice, which improves the flavor balance and adds acidity to improve gelling and safety for lower-acid fruit varieties.

Ladle the hot jam into washed and *sterilized* half-pint jars (see below), screw on the lids, and process in a boiling-water bath for 5 minutes (see the National Center for Home Food Preservation website for detailed instructions). Let the jars cool completely. Check the seals by pressing down in the center of each lid: if you can press it down and it pops back up, the jar hasn't sealed and should be refrigerated right away.

STERILIZING AND SEALING CANNING JARS

Boil empty glass canning jars (even new ones!) for 10 minutes in enough water to cover them in order to sterilize them. Use new flat lids, heated in water but not boiled. Make sure the rings are clean.

Fill and seal the jars (put the flat lids on top and screw on the rings) while they're still hot in order to work as cleanly as possible. The National Center for Home Food Preservation recommends boiling-water-bath processing of the filled canning jars; see the NCHFP website for detailed instructions.

FRESH BREAKFAST

BREAKFAST SYLLABUB WITH LIGHTLY TOASTED GRANOLA

PREPARE: 20 MINUTES
WAIT: PREFERABLY 1 NIGHT
BAKE: 10 MINUTES
SERVES 6 FOR BREAKFAST

for the syllabub mixture
zest and juice of 1 organic
  pink grapefruit
2 organic lemons
piece of mace, crushed (or a
  pinch of grated nutmeg)
1 dried bay leaf, briefly
  rubbed between thumb and
  index finger
1 coffee spoon honey or
  sugar, or to taste

for the granola
heaping ½ cup (50 g)
  rolled oats
2 tablespoons confectioners'
  sugar
1 tablespoon butter
pinch of freshly grated
  nutmeg
pinch of salt
pinch of ground cinnamon

for the syllabub
10 tablespoons (150 ml)
  heavy cream
2½ tablespoons honey or
  granulated sugar
¾ cup plus 1 tablespoon
  (200 g) Greek yogurt

for serving
10½ ounces (300 g) fresh
  summer fruit, cleaned
  and cut into pieces or
  wedges: melon, raspberries,
  peaches, etc.
freshly grated nutmeg

Syllabub is an old-fashioned British dessert, similar to a mousse or very light, soft whipped cream, made with alcohol, but I'll often turn it into a truly delicious breakfast. There's nothing to it, really.

Make the syllabub mixture a day in advance if you can. It's really delicious when the flavors of the spices coalesce overnight. You can put any summer fruit you want in it. A finger-licking binge dessert—uh . . . I mean breakfast!

Make the syllabub mixture: Combine all the ingredients in a bowl, cover, and let stand in the fridge, preferably overnight.

Make the granola: Preheat the oven to 350°F (180°C). Combine all the ingredients for the granola on a parchment paper–lined baking sheet and bake the granola for 8 to 10 minutes, until golden brown and crispy. Stir halfway through. Set aside to cool somewhat.

Make the syllabub: Beat the heavy cream with the honey until almost stiff. Fold it into the yogurt. Strain the syllabub mixture through a sieve and fold it into the whipped cream–yogurt mixture.

Crumble the granola and divide it among six glasses.

Spoon the cream on top, decorate with fresh fruit, grate some nutmeg on top, and serve right away.

**PREPARE: 5 MINUTES
MAKES 4 GLASSES**

1 pound 1 ounce (500 g)
  strawberries, washed and
  hulled, preferably frozen
¾ cup plus 1 tablespoon
  (200 ml) cold, strong
  green tea
1 cup plus 1 tablespoon
  (250 ml) thick yogurt
3 to 4 tablespoons honey
1 tablespoon freshly ground
  cardamom

tool
immersion blender or

STRAWBERRY, YOGURT, GREEN TEA & CARDAMOM SHAKE

Using a blender, puree the strawberries with the green tea until smooth. Stir in the yogurt with a spoon. The shake will quickly become runny if you let the yogurt run in the blender.

Pour into glasses, spoon the honey onto the shakes, and sprinkle

**PREPARE: 5 MINUTES
MAKES 4 GLASSES**

1 pound 1 ounce (500 g)
   peeled and cubed
   watermelon
2 cups plus 1 tablespoon
   (500 ml) cold almond milk
a thumb-size piece of fresh
   ginger, peeled and sliced

tool
immersion blender or
   stand blender

WATERMELON, ALMOND
MILK & GINGER SHAKE

Using a blender, puree all the ingredients into a smooth, frothy drink.

Pour the shake into four glasses.

~ 47 ~

POACHING AN EGG

Bring a large saucepan of water to just under a simmer. You can add a drop of vinegar, this supposedly makes the egg white coagulate faster, but I make do without it and that works fine, too.

Break an egg into a small sieve placed on the countertop (or over a bowl) and let the excess egg white liquid drain off.

The fresher the egg, the tighter the egg white!

Keep the water at just under a slow boil and stir with a spoon to give it a little "whirl." Gently slip the egg in.

Poach the egg for 2 to 3 minutes, then remove it from the pan using a slotted spoon. Keep on a warm plate covered with aluminum foil. If needed, poach another one. Once you've got the hang of it you can try to do two at once.

ÇILBIR WITH PAPRIKA BUTTER, CELERY CARAWAY YOGURT & GRILLED ASPARAGUS

**PREPARE: 45 MINUTES
SERVES 4 TO 6 FOR
BREAKFAST OR LUNCH**

for the paprika butter
4 tablespoons (60 g) butter
½ teaspoon hot paprika
½ teaspoon smoked paprika
sea salt

for the celery caraway yogurt
handful (½ ounce/15 g) of
    celery leaves
1 teaspoon caraway seeds
1 clove garlic, grated
sea salt and freshly ground
    black pepper
generous 1 cup (250 ml)
    Greek yogurt, stirred
    until loose

for the eggs and asparagus
8 eggs
splash of vinegar
1 bunch (about 16 stalks)
    asparagus, the ends peeled
    with a vegetable peeler

on the side
pita bread or slices of toast,
    or carrot fritters (see below)

tool
food processor

These Turkish eggs are so delicious I can just keep eating them. Feel free to replace the celery caraway yogurt with yogurt mixed with fresh mint, or in the winter serve with carrot fritters (below) instead of asparagus. They will be equally tasty.

Make the paprika butter: Melt the butter. Add the hot and smoked paprika and a pinch of salt and stir until you get a beautiful deep orange-red color. Leave the butter on the stove until the foam has subsided. Set aside.

Make the celery caraway yogurt: In a food processor, pulse the celery leaves, caraway seeds, garlic, a pinch of sea salt, and some pepper into a green crumb. Stir into the yogurt in such a way that you can still see swirls. Set the celery caraway yogurt aside.

Make the eggs and asparagus: Poach the eggs in water with the splash of vinegar (see page 49). Continue until you have poached all the eggs. Keep them on a warm plate, covered with aluminum foil.

Meanwhile, heat a grill pan until it starts to smoke. Briefly grill the asparagus stalks, until they have black grill marks and they are al dente. Set aside. Lower the heat under the pan and grill the pitas. They'll burn faster, so keep a close eye.

Warm four plates. Spoon a generous dollop of celery caraway yogurt onto each plate. Add about 4 roasted asparagus stalks and 2 poached eggs. Drizzle with delicious paprika butter and serve with grilled pita bread, some slices of toast, or carrot fritters.

CARROT FRITTERS

In a mixing bowl, combine 4 eggs, 18 ounces (500 g) grated carrots, generous 3 tablespoons chopped fresh cilantro, and 2 tablespoons chickpea flour into a fairly thin mixture. Season with salt and pepper. Heat 2 tablespoons oil in a skillet over medium heat. Use two spoons to form the mixture into small piles in the pan. Fry for about 3 minutes on each side and serve hot.

EGGS FOR BREAKFAST

SWEET OMELET SOUFFLÉ

PREPARE: 15 MINUTES
SERVES 1 (OR 2) FOR
BREAKFAST

2 eggs, separated
2 tablespoons superfine sugar
pinch of salt
1½ teaspoons cornstarch
1 tablespoon (preferably
    salted!) butter

for serving
confectioners' sugar
    (optional)

Whenever we were sick as kids, my mother would cook us a fluffy, cloudlike, sweet omelet. My sister and I thought it was the most delicious thing ever. You should know that in our household we were rarely given any sugar, so a breakfast with sugar was about the most amazing treat we could think of.

So, we often pretended to be sicker than we actually were in the hopes of being treated to this festive dish, served on a bedside tray. The height of luxury!

My mother would sit on our bed while we ate, telling us that her mother also made her this dish whenever she was ill as a child. So, mothers and fathers: know what to do when your child has come down with something. Or, dear children: make your parents read this, and you will recover in a snap. I know from experience. Or wait . . . Better still: learn how to make this omelet soufflé yourself, as I did. Here's the recipe.

Beat the egg yolks along with 1 tablespoon of the sugar until frothy and pale, preferably with an electric mixer.

In another, sparkling-clean bowl, with clean beaters (thoroughly wash them with hot soapy water after beating the yolks; otherwise the egg whites will never coagulate), beat the egg whites with a pinch of salt, the remaining 1 tablespoon sugar, and the cornstarch, until stiff.

Fold the beaten egg whites into the egg yolk mixture—carefully, so that the batter retains as much air as possible.

Heat the butter in a skillet over medium heat, ladle in the egg mixture, and smooth the top with the back of a spoon. Lower the heat, as the mixture will burn quickly. Cook the omelet for about 5 minutes, until the edges start to brown while the top remains frothy. Carefully fold the omelet in half with a spatula.

Slide onto a warmed plate and serve immediately. Dust with confectioners' sugar, if you want.

GREEN SHAKSHUKA

**PREPARE: 15 MINUTES
SERVES 2 TO 4* FOR
BREAKFAST OR LUNCH**

for the shakshuka
3 tablespoons olive oil
2 leeks, cleaned and sliced
 into thin rings
sea salt and freshly ground
 black pepper
10½ ounces (300 g) spinach,
 washed
½ tablespoon cumin seeds
1 teaspoon caraway seeds
2 big handfuls (40 g) of flat-
 leaf parsley, cilantro, and
 mint, the leaves plucked
 and roughly chopped—
 save some for garnish
4 to 6 eggs
1 tablespoon harissa, or to
 taste, and/or a drop of
 home made hot sauce
 (page 141)
⅔ cup (150 ml) thick yogurt

on the side
pita or Lebanese flatbread,
 warmed

*Depending on the number
 of eggs

Heat the olive oil in a large skillet over medium heat. Sauté the leeks, seasoned with a pinch each of salt and pepper, until tender. Add the spinach to the pan in batches, waiting with the next handful until the previous one has wilted a little.

Stir in the cumin, caraway seeds, and the herbs, reserving some for a garnish. Heat everything for a minute and then make 4 to 6 holes in the greens. Break an egg over each hole.

Cover the pan with a lid and cook the shakshuka for 8 to 10 minutes, until the egg white no longer is opaque, but the yolks are still liquid.

Season the eggs with a pinch of sea salt and a twist of the pepper mill. Stir some harissa or home made hot sauce into the yogurt and splash thick blobs over the dish.

Sprinkle with the herbs you saved. Serve with warm pitas or flatbread.

EGGS FOR BREAKFAST

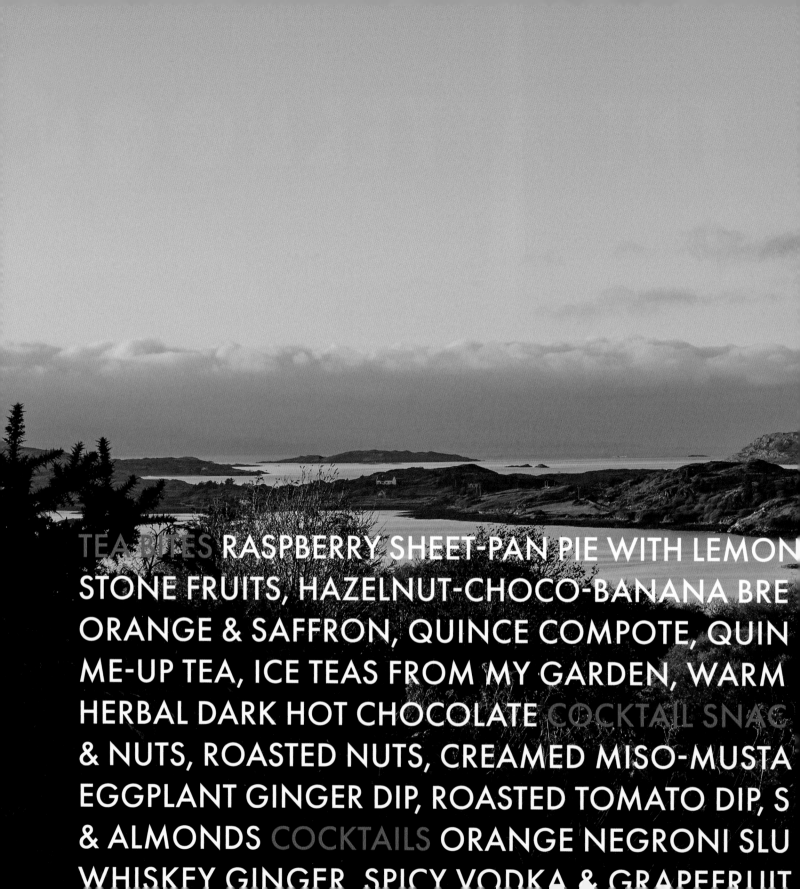

TEA BITES RASPBERRY SHEET-PAN PIE WITH LEMON
STONE FRUITS, HAZELNUT-CHOCO-BANANA BRE
ORANGE & SAFFRON, QUINCE COMPOTE, QUIN
ME-UP TEA, ICE TEAS FROM MY GARDEN, WARM
HERBAL DARK HOT CHOCOLATE COCKTAIL SNAC
& NUTS, ROASTED NUTS, CREAMED MISO-MUSTA
EGGPLANT GINGER DIP, ROASTED TOMATO DIP, S
& ALMONDS COCKTAILS ORANGE NEGRONI SLU
WHISKEY GINGER, SPICY VODKA & GRAPEFRUIT

CREAM, COFFEE ALMOND CRUMBLE CAKE WITH
AD, RICOTTA SEMOLINA CAKE WITH BLOOD
CE PIE NONALCOHOLIC DRINKS SYRUPS, PICK-
WHITE COCOA WITH CARDAMOM, WINTRY
KS APPETIZER WREATH WITH BRIE, DRIED FRUITS
RD BUTTER, WARM OLIVES, OLIVE TAPENADE,
ARDINE NUT TERRINE, SKORDALIA OF WALNUTS
SH, NEGRONI PITCHER, OLD IRISH CURE, THE
TEA

Connemara, Ireland

RASPBERRY SHEET-PAN PIE WITH LEMON CREAM

PREPARE: 10 MINUTES
BAKE: 45 MINUTES
COOL: 2 HOURS
MAKES ABOUT 8 PIECES

for the crust
10½ to 14 ounces (300 to 400 g) frozen puff pastry,* thawed
1 egg, beaten

for the lemon cream
1 (14-ounce/396 g) can sweetened condensed milk
finely grated zest and juice of 2 organic lemons
2 egg yolks, plus the rest of the egg left over from the crust dough, beaten
pinch of salt

for on top
8¾ ounces (250 g) raspberries, but strawberries, blackberries, berries, or other fruit (thin slices of melon or stone fruit, or halved grapes) also work well
confectioners' sugar

*If using Pepperidge Farm or similar, use 1 sheet and cut and attach another ⅓ sheet to one end as you roll it out; if using Dufour or similar, just use 1 full sheet.

Each fall my Irish garden provides me with a bizarre largesse of raspberries. I grow both yellow and red ones. The yellow ones are sweeter. If you can find them on the market, you should definitely give them a try.

Raspberry bushes are a real asset to your garden, should you consider cultivating a fruit bush. They tend to "wander" around quite a bit, by the way: you have to keep trimming, because before you know it, your garden will be brimming with them. But the yield is delicious: picking fresh raspberries first thing in the morning and sticking them, warm from the rising sun, in your mouth is one of the most delicious ways to start the day. I use the rest of my raspberries for making jam (see page 43).

Make the crust: Preheat the oven to 425°F (220°C). Line a baking sheet with parchment paper.

Roll the dough out into a slab of 6 by 10 inches (15 by 25 cm). Place it on the lined baking sheet. Using the back of a knife, score a margin 1 inch (2.5 cm) wide along the edges of the dough to form a frame. Make sure that the knife does not go all the way through the dough. Brush the edge with beaten egg (reserve the remaining egg wash). Prick holes in the dough inside the frame with a fork.

Blind-bake the crust for 15 minutes. Let the pie crust cool on the counter and reduce the oven temperature to 325°F (160°C).

Make the lemon cream: Beat the condensed milk with the finely grated lemon zest, lemon juice, egg yolks, remaining egg wash, and a pinch of salt until smooth.

Use the back of a spoon to lightly press the inside of the crust (i.e., the area inside the frame), as it will have risen a little with pre-baking.

Pour the lemon filling onto the pie crust. Return the pie to the oven and bake for an additional 25 to 30 minutes, until the filling has just set but is not yet browning.

On a rack on the counter, let the sheet-pan pie cool and firm up for an hour or two.

Arrange the raspberries over the lemon cream and dust the top with confectioners' sugar before serving.

TEA BITES

PREPARE: 20 MINUTES
BAKE: 1 HOUR
MAKES 8 SLICES

for the crumb
½ cup (70 g) almonds, finely chopped to a coarse crumb (not flour)
⅓ cup (80 g) firmly packed light brown sugar
1 teaspoon instant espresso powder
2 teaspoons coriander seeds, ground in a mortar
pinch of sea salt

for the cake
14 tablespoons (200 g) butter, at room temperature, plus extra for preparing the pan
¾ cup plus 2 tablespoons (200 g) firmly packed light brown sugar
4 eggs
7 tablespoons (100 ml) sour cream
grated zest of 1 lemon
1½ cups (200 g) all-purpose flour
¾ cup plus 2 tablespoons (100 g) almond flour
2 teaspoons baking powder
pinch of salt
2 teaspoons instant espresso powder
1 tablespoon cocoa powder
4 nectarines, pitted and sliced into wedges; or 8 apricots, cut into halves

finishing touch
confectioners' sugar (optional)

tool
8½- or 9-inch (22 cm) springform pan

COFFEE ALMOND CRUMBLE CAKE WITH STONE FRUITS

Bake this cake in the summer using any kind of stone fruits you can find; two handfuls of pitted fresh cherries make for a very delicious crumble, too. During the winter, I sometimes make this cake with pear wedges, in which case I use about three small pears for this recipe.

First, make the crumb by mixing all the ingredients for it. Set aside.

Make the cake: Preheat the oven to 350°F (180°C). Butter the springform pan with a brush. Line the bottom with parchment paper and butter that as well.

Beat the butter with the brown sugar until light and smooth. Now beat in the eggs one by one and then the sour cream and lemon zest.

Combine the flour, almond flour, baking powder, and salt with a whisk and fold into the egg mixture.

Scoop half of the batter out of the bowl and stir the espresso powder and cocoa powder into the other half.

Alternately ladle some of the light and dark batter into the springform pan, and after each scoop sprinkle some of the crumb on top. Keep some crumb for the top of the cake as well.

Using a knife, cut through the batter to mix the two colors so you get a marbled effect.

Divide the fruit wedges or halves over the top of the cake and sprinkle with the last remaining crumb.

Bake the cake for about 1 hour, or until an inserted skewer comes out clean. Let cool for a few minutes and then remove the side of the springform pan and allow the cake to cool further on a rack. If you like, serve it dusted with some confectioners' sugar.

TEA BITES

Rhea, my neighbor

HAZELNUT-CHOCO-BANANA BREAD

PREPARE: 20 MINUTES
BAKE: 35 TO 45 MINUTES
MAKES 1 CAKE

2 cups (250 g) all-purpose
  flour
¾ teaspoon baking powder
½ teaspoon salt
1 cup (200 g) sugar
3½ tablespoons (50 g) butter,
  at room temperature
2 eggs
10½ ounces (300 g) ripe
  bananas (about 2 large),
  pureed
6½ tablespoons (100 ml) milk
1 teaspoon vanilla extract
scant 1 cup (250 g) hazelnut
  chocolate spread (see below)

tool
1½-quart (1½ L) cake pan

HOME MADE HAZELNUT-CHOCOLATE SPREAD

In a food processor, very finely grind a scant 1 cup (125 g) hazelnuts. This will take a while, factor in at least 5 full minutes.

Add ¼ cup (25 g) cocoa powder, ¾ cup (75 g) sifted confectioners' sugar, 1 teaspoon vanilla extract, and a pinch of salt and pulse until you get a thick brown paste. While pulsing, add 4 to 6 teaspoons hazelnut oil, 1 teaspoon at a time. Be careful that you don't pour in too much, or the spread will become too runny. Keep scraping the paste from the bottom of the mixing bowl and blend until completely smooth.

A tasty and super-easy recipe to use up those last few bananas in the fruit bowl and for delighting any expected (or unexpected) tea guests. Simply slicing one of these cakes always makes me so happy. It's such a sight to behold.

Preheat the oven to 350°F (180°C). Grease the cake pan.

Mix the flour with the baking powder and salt in a bowl.

In another bowl, cream the sugar with the butter into a velvety mixture. Beat in the eggs one at a time, adding the next egg after the previous one has been fully incorporated. Swiftly whisk the mashed bananas, milk, and vanilla extract into the egg mixture. Fold in the flour mixture. Don't stir longer than necessary to mix the batter.

In a saucepan, briefly heat the hazelnut chocolate spread, until it turns slightly more runny. Do not let it boil! Pour the lukewarm hazelnut chocolate spread into a bowl and stir to allow the spread to cool somewhat. Fold one-third of the banana batter into the hazelnut chocolate spread and stir until the batter is an even light brown.

Alternating between the two bowls, ladle the batter into the prepared cake pan. Run a knife through the batter so both colors of batter mix a little, creating a marbled effect.

Bake the cake for 35 to 45 minutes, depending on the depth of the pan. After 30 minutes, insert a skewer or knitting needle into the cake to test if it comes out nice and dry. If not, the cake will have to bake a little longer.

Let the cake cool in the pan for 10 minutes and then invert onto a rack and allow the banana bread to cool further.

TEA BITES

RICOTTA SEMOLINA CAKE WITH BLOOD ORANGE & SAFFRON

PREPARE: 1 HOUR
15 MINUTES
BAKE: 40 MINUTES
MAKES 9 OR 16 SQUARES

3 or 4 blood oranges
zest and juice of 1 organic
  lemon
1 packet saffron or a pinch
  (¼ g)
1⅓ cups plus 1 tablespoon
  (250 g) semolina flour
1 teaspoon baking powder
1 cup (250 g) ricotta cheese
1 tablespoon vanilla extract
1 cup plus 3 tablespoons
  (250 g) packed light
  brown sugar
4 eggs
3 to 4 tablespoons acacia
  honey*

tools
round or square 9-inch
  (23 cm) cake pan
food processor

*For more info about acacia
  honey, see page 12.

Peel 2 oranges, remove seeds if any, and cook the segments in ample boiling water for 1 hour. Drain.

Preheat the oven to 350°F (180°C). Grease the cake pan. Line the bottom with parchment paper cut to size and grease the parchment paper as well. Cut the remaining raw oranges into razor-thin half slices and cover the bottom in a single layer.

Puree the cooked oranges together with the lemon juice and saffron in a food processor to a pulp. Add the semolina and baking powder and continue processing the mixture for a while.

Beat the ricotta with the vanilla extract, light brown sugar, lemon zest, and eggs until light and fluffy. Beat the semolina mixture into the egg-ricotta mixture and pour the batter onto the oranges in the cake pan.

Bake for about 40 minutes, until an inserted skewer comes out clean. Let the cake cool for 5 minutes, then flip it onto a nice plate. Peel the parchment paper from the orange roof. Allow the cake to cool and brush with acacia honey just before serving.

quince pie (page 72)

QUINCE PIE

PREPARE: 20 MINUTES*
WAIT: 30 MINUTES
BAKE: 45 MINUTES
MAKES 1 PIE

for the dough
2⅓ cups (300 g) all-purpose
  flour
⅓ cup (35 g) sifted
  confectioners' sugar
pinch of salt
12 tablespoons (175 g) cold
  butter, cubed
1 egg yolk

for the filling
2 eggs, beaten
1½ half-pint (240 ml) jars
  (or one 1½ cup/350 ml jar)
  quince compote (see recipe
  on the right)

*Assuming the quince
  compote is ready

Making this pie with another fruit puree or compote, like apple or pear, is perfectly fine. Even some freshly picked blackberries thrown in, now that I think of it. If you do use another kind of fruit, be sure to also mix in a handful of fresh breadcrumbs. My quince compote is much firmer and contains less moisture than a regular apple compote. Without the crumbs, the pie crust may not dry properly, resulting in a soggy bottom.

Make the dough: Combine the flour with the confectioners' sugar and salt in a bowl. Swiftly cut in the cold butter until your dough looks like coarse crumbs. Mix in the egg yolk and a drop or two of ice-cold water, and knead until the dough just comes together.

Divide the dough into two parts: one-third and two-thirds of the total amount. Shape each ball into a disk, wrap the dough disks in plastic wrap, and let them rest in the refrigerator for 30 minutes.

Preheat the oven to 350°F (180°C). Grease a deep pie pan.

Roll out the larger dough disk on a flour-dusted counter. Place the dough in the prepared pan and let the edges hang over.

Stir half of the beaten eggs into the quince compote and spoon the compote into the pan.

Now roll out the smaller dough disk on a flour-dusted counter into a lid that will fit comfortably over the pie. Cut holes into the dough sheet; these openings will allow the moisture in the quince to escape, so that the bottom of the pie will cook nicely and not get soggy.

Brush the overhanging edges of the dough in the cake pan with some of the remaining beaten egg and then cover with the dough lid you just rolled out. Using your fingers or with a fork, press the edges together tightly. Trim the edges and use the leftover dough scraps to make decorations. Stick them on the pie with some egg. Once you are done decorating, brush the whole top with beaten egg as well.

Bake the quince pie for 35 to 45 minutes, or until it is nicely golden brown. Let the pie cool completely before cutting it.

QUINCE COMPOTE

PREPARE: 1½ TO 2 HOURS
MAKES SIX HALF-PINT
(240 ML) JARS OR FOUR
1½-CUP (350 ML) JARS

4½ pounds (2 kg) quinces
1¼ cups (300 ml) apple cider
    or juice
1 cup plus 3 tablespoons
    (250 g) packed light
    brown sugar
1 teaspoon ground cinnamon
½ teaspoon ground cloves
pinch of salt

tools
immersion blender
canning jars and flat lids
    with rings

You can find quinces at farmers
markets or well-stocked
grocers in the fall.

This recipe would also work
well with stewed pears or
mashed apples.

This isn't a recipe for quince jelly as you know it. It won't make a firm jelly you can cut, but rather a thick compote or jam—or maybe a sort of quince butter. Anyway, we can spend time fretting over the name, but whatever you call it, it's terribly delicious and a perfect way to use up a pile of quince. If you have a tree (or neighbors with a tree), you're surely aware of how one sometimes simply doesn't know what to do with the abundant quince harvest in the fall. Here is a solution! Once they're canned in spotless jars, they'll keep for months in a cool place. Use this preserve in the pie on the next page; it also tastes great alongside a roast, in yogurt, or on a cheese platter.

Peel the quinces with a vegetable peeler and quarter them. They are hard, so be careful not to cut your fingers.

Cook the quinces in the apple cider for about 45 minutes over low heat in a deep pot—I say "deep" because the mixture will bubble and splash—until they are very soft. Depending on the type and size of your quinces, this will take more or less time: pierce the quarters with a pointed knife to test whether they are cooked.

Using an immersion blender, puree the quinces along with the cider.

Add the light brown sugar, cinnamon, cloves, and a pinch of salt and bring to a boil again, covered, over high heat, then lower the heat, remove the lid, and let the puree cook until reduced by about half. Stir every now and then. It can splash lots, so put the pan on the back burner.

Ladle the hot jam into washed and *sterilized* half-pint jars (see page 43), screw on the lids, and process in a boiling-water bath for 5 minutes (see the National Center for Home Food Preservation website at https://nchfp.edu for detailed instructions). Let the jars cool completely. Check the seals by pressing down in the center of each lid: if you can press it down and it pops back up, the jar hasn't sealed and should be refrigerated right away. The compote will firm up as it cools.

TEA BITES

SYRUPS

Syrup can be made in a heartbeat. And it isn't hard, either. In fact, a basic syrup is just part liquid (sometimes water) and part sugar.

But that's where the creativity comes in.

Because what kind of liquid is it, exactly?

Is it an alcoholic drink, tea, coffee, or a home made extract of flowers, herbs, or spices? You see, now it suddenly becomes an interesting ingredient.

And which type of sugar will you choose?

Regular granulated sugar will bring out the flavor of the liquid ingredient beautifully, because it only adds sweetness. Another choice of sugar, however, can greatly change the flavor. Think about cane sugar, light brown, or even dark brown sugar! A wintry syrup made with dark brown sugar can be so delicious—with full-bodied flavors such as clove, star anise, black pepper—and that, boiled down with pear juice, would be an outstanding combination with some cinnamon ice cream. But it would be just as interesting as a hot drink if you pour in some boiling water and turn it into sweet lemonade tea. Do you feel me? Pretty sweet, no?

Here, however, I'm trying to preserve a little summer in a bottle for use in the fall. Therefore, I opt for light syrups, made with green lemon verbena tea or muscat wine, for example. Or you can do the same with a beautiful dry rosé!

People, the syrup possibilities are endless . . . as are the number of things you can make with it.

Syrup isn't just delicious as lemonade mixed with soda water, in a cocktail, or over ice cream; you can use it to make desserts or breathe life into an older, slightly dry cake, simply by pouring some over it.

All of this and more can be done with surprisingly mouthwatering home made syrups. Thirsty yet?

MAKING SYRUPS

Bring 1 (750 ml) bottle white wine, or 3 cups plus 2 tablespoons of another liquid, such as tea, to a gentle simmer with 2½ cups (500 g) sugar and spices to taste. Boil over low heat for 5 minutes, then turn off the heat, cover, and allow to infuse for an afternoon.

Strain the syrup into another saucepan.

Bring to a boil again and slightly reduce, also thickening it somewhat.

Pour the hot syrup into a squeaky-clean stoppered bottle through a funnel. Put the lid on the bottle. Now let it cool. You can keep the syrup in the refrigerator for several weeks, so make a lot of it right away.

BAY LEAF & THYME WHITE WINE SYRUP
ingredients as above + 6 to 8 bay leaves + 3 sprigs of thyme

LEMON VERBENA & GREEN TEA SYRUP
3 cups plus 2 tablespoons (750 ml) mix of strong verbena and green tea + 2½ cups (500 g) sugar

VERMOUTH ROSÉ GREEN TEA SYRUP
1½ cups (375 ml) red vermouth + 1½ cups (375 ml) dry rosé + 2 cups (400 g) sugar

MUSCAT BASIL SYRUP
1 (750 ml) bottle muscat wine + 2 cups (400 g) sugar + 2 large sprigs basil

MELON LIMONCELLO SYRUP
1 melon (preferably honeydew or Galia), cubed (about 2¼ pounds/1 kg) + 10 tablespoons (150 ml) limoncello + juice of 3 limes + ½ cup (100 g) sugar. Process in a blender until smooth. Strain through a cheesecloth, before reducing to a syrup.

The Long Strand, County Cork

PICK-ME-UP TEA

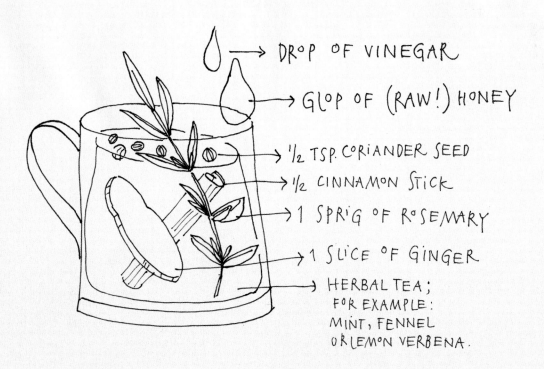

→ DROP OF VINEGAR

→ GLOP OF (RAW!) HONEY

→ ½ TSP. CORIANDER SEED

→ ½ CINNAMON STICK

→ 1 SPRIG OF ROSEMARY

→ 1 SLICE OF GINGER

→ HERBAL TEA; FOR EXAMPLE: MINT, FENNEL OR LEMON VERBENA.

ICE TEAS FROM MY GARDEN

PREPARE: ABOUT 5 MINUTES
COOL: ABOUT 2 HOURS
MAKES 4 GLASSES

PREPARATION

For all tea recipes except the "Tea" of Coconut Water with Blackberries & Lemon Balm: First steep the tea, verbena, or other herbs in boiling hot water in a large jug (or other container) that fits in the fridge.

Let the tea cool to room temperature.

Remove any tea bags (if using) and refrigerate the tea for at least 2 hours, allowing it to completely cool off and the flavors to infuse.

Pour the cold tea through a sieve into another jug or directly into glasses. Serve the tea with ice cubes in the glass—if you want—and leftover fresh herbs or other ingredients from the tea making.

Set aside some extra fresh ingredients to use to garnish each tea for serving!

LEMON VERBENA TEA WITH HONEY & GINGER

1 small bunch (4 to 5 sprigs) fresh or 1 tablespoon dried verbena in a tea infuser
1 quart (1 L) boiling water
1 small organic lemon, thinly sliced
2 inches (5 cm) fresh ginger, shaved into razor-thin slices
2 tablespoons honey, or to taste

PEACH CHAI WITH PURPLE BASIL & THYME

2 chai tea bags
1 quart (1 L) boiling water
1 peach, pitted and sliced
2 sprigs of purple basil (purple looks beautiful)
2 sprigs of lemon thyme (regular thyme also works)

EARL GREY, LIME & ROSE PETAL TEA

2 Earl Grey tea bags
1 quart (1 L) boiling water
½ organic lime, thinly sliced
1 tablespoon dried rose petals (available at specialty tea shops)
raw honey (optional, to taste)

OOLONG, CUCUMBER, MINT & WATERMELON TEA

2 oolong tea bags
1 quart (1 L) boiling water
¼ cucumber, thinly sliced
2 to 3 sprigs mint
7 ounces (200 g) very thinly sliced watermelon

"TEA" OF COCONUT WATER WITH BLACKBERRIES & LEMON BALM

½ organic lemon, thinly sliced
2 sprigs lemon balm
1 quart (1 L) coconut water
handful of blackberries (about 5 ounces/150 g)

Put everything in a large jug or jar that fits in the fridge. Let the lemonade steep for an afternoon before serving. Serve the coconut water with a handful of ice cubes.

wintry herbal dark hot chocolate with marshmallows

WARM WHITE COCOA WITH CARDAMOM

PREPARE: 1 HOUR
MAKES 4 CUPS

scant ½ cup (80 g) coarsely
    chopped white chocolate
4½ cups (1 L) whole milk
1 (14-ounce/396 g) can
    sweetened condensed milk
4 cinnamon sticks
2 teaspoons vanilla extract
4 cardamom pods,
    cracked open
½ teaspoon freshly
    grated nutmeg

topping
marshmallows (page 429) or
    whipped cream

Put all the ingredients except the marshmallows in a heavy pan and
cook for 1 hour over very low heat.

Strain the milk through a sieve that you placed over a jug. Discard
the flavorings and pour the hot white chocolate into four cups.

Serve with marshmallows or whipped cream on top.

WINTRY HERBAL DARK HOT CHOCOLATE

PREPARE: 5 MINUTES
MAKES 1 MUG

½ cup minus 1 tablespoon
    (75 g) finely chopped
    extra-dark chocolate
    (at least 70%)
pinch of cinnamon
pinch of ground ginger
1 tablespoon honey
1 cup plus 1 tablespoon
    (250 ml) hot (but not
    boiling) whole milk

topping
marshmallows (see page 429)

In a large mug, combine the extra-dark chocolate with the cinnamon,
ginger, and honey. Pour in the hot milk. Stir so the chocolate melts.

Let the marshmallows melt while floating on the hot chocolate. You
can also quickly roast them first over the fireplace or grill, or with a
brûlée torch!

NONALCOHOLIC DRINKS

appetizer wreath
with brie, dried fruits
and nuts

warm olives

creamed miso-
mustard butter

APPETIZER WREATH WITH BRIE, DRIED FRUITS & NUTS

PREPARE: 15 MINUTES
BAKE: 20 MINUTES
SERVES 12 AS AN APPETIZER

10½ to 14 ounces (300 to 400 g) frozen puff pastry,* thawed
3 heaping tablespoons chutney, or to taste
7 ounces (200 g) brie cheese, cut into small cubes
about ½ cup (75 g) diced dried fruit (dates, figs, apricots, etc.)
2 tablespoons shelled, roughly chopped pistachios
1 egg, beaten

*If using Pepperidge Farm or similar, use 1 sheet and cut and attach another ⅓ sheet to one end as you roll it out; if using Dufour or similar, just use 1 full sheet.

Preheat the oven to 400°F (200°C). Line a baking sheet with parchment paper.

Roll out the puff pastry and cut out as large a circle as possible—you can use a 10- to 12-inch plate, for example, to get a perfect circle. Place the pastry round on the parchment-lined baking sheet.

Press a soup bowl into the center of the circle, creating another circle. Don't press down all the way, but press lightly just to leave an imprint. With a knife, divide the small inner circle into 8 wedges, cutting just to the inner circle imprint (see the illustration).

Spread the outer rim with chutney, cover with pieces of brie, and sprinkle the brie with the dried fruit and pistachios. Now fold each point from the inner circle outward, over the filling, and pinch it onto the outer edge of the rim. Stick the points to the outer edge using some beaten egg. Brush the entire wreath with beaten egg as well.

Bake the puff pastry wreath for about 20 minutes, until golden brown and puffed. Serve it warm.

ROASTED NUTS

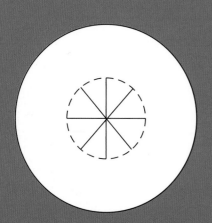

Make your own mix. Roast nuts (whether raw or roasted) and/or seeds spread out on a baking sheet in a preheated oven at 350°F (180°C) for about 12 minutes.

Let them cool for a while. Briefly roasted nuts are wonderfully tasty and always crunchy.

Season your own nut mix with a pinch of sea salt, some freshly ground black pepper, and herbs or spices of your choice. In the mix pictured on the previous page, I use fresh rosemary. But a pinch of paprika powder or cayenne would also work. Some dried oregano, or a pinch of curry powder on salted cashews is also delicious. But I'll leave that to you.

CREAMED MISO-MUSTARD BUTTER

PREPARE: 5 MINUTES
SERVES 4 AS A SIDE DISH
OR APPETIZER

4 to 5 tablespoons (55 to
   70 g) butter, at room
   temperature
1 tablespoon spicy mustard
1 tablespoon white or
   red miso

This butter is heavenly on a piece of baguette with a nice cold beer but also delicious melted on a mashed vegetable dish (see page 217) served with meatballs. Just for example.

Thoroughly beat all the ingredients with a hand mixer until the butter is light and fluffy, it will make the butter taste absolutely terrific. If you want, you can let the butter firm up in the fridge afterward. Do, however, allow it to come to room temperature before serving; otherwise you won't be able to spread it.

WARM OLIVES

One time a restaurant in San Francisco served me warm olives with my aperitif. I had an epiphany right then and there: of course you eat olives WARM! Naturally the oils in olives are much more flavorful warmed up than they are straight from the fridge. This is basically true for everything containing fat. A cheese board is served at room temperature, and an ice-cold terrine is also much less tasty than one that has been sitting on the kitchen counter for a while.

Warm the olives of your choice in a splash of the most delicious olive oil you have on hand. Add some herbs to taste: rosemary, thyme, or fennel seeds, for example. You can also add a lemon twist.

OLIVE TAPENADE

In a blender, grind 1⅓ cups (200 grams) pitted olives (preferably Kalamata) with 1 clove garlic, 2 to 3 salted anchovies, 1 tablespoon capers, a drop of lemon juice, and a few sprigs of parsley to a coarse paste. Add a splash of olive oil and blend until the tapenade has the desired thickness.

COCKTAIL SNACKS

EGGPLANT GINGER DIP

PREPARE: 30 MINUTES
SERVES ABOUT 4 AS AN
APPETIZER OR SAUCE

2 whole eggplants
2 tablespoons olive oil
1 teaspoon fennel seeds
1 teaspoon coriander seeds
1 clove garlic, pressed
pinch of cayenne pepper or
   chile flakes
1 teaspoon ground turmeric
2 inches (5 cm) fresh ginger,
   peeled and grated
sea salt and freshly ground
   black pepper
juice of 1 lemon

tool
mortar and pestle

This is my version of baba ganoush. If you plan on barbecue grilling instead of broiling, place the eggplants on the grate while you're heating the grill. That low heat won't just cook the insides of the eggplants; it will also lend them a nice smoky flavor! Serve the dip with some flatbread or crackers as an appetizer. Or call your dip a "sauce" and serve it with meat (lamb or beef, for instance) or fish.

Preheat the broiler on the highest setting. Place the eggplants on a small baking sheet and place it under the hot broiler. Turn the eggplants over regularly with kitchen tongs. Broil them until they are charred and softened—the cooking time will vary depending on your heat source and the size and shape of the eggplants, so watch them carefully. Of course you can also do this directly over a gas stove burner or on the barbecue grill, because the more direct the fire, the smokier (and tastier!) they become.

Slice the eggplants open lengthwise and scoop out the soft flesh. Let the pulp drain in a colander and cool somewhat.

In a skillet over low heat, heat the olive oil and fry the fennel and the coriander seeds. Also add the garlic, cayenne, turmeric, and ginger. Let everything gently cook over low heat for 5 minutes.

In a mortar, grind the spices from the pan a tad more finely. In a bowl, mash the drained eggplant using a fork. Combine the eggplant with the spice mixture. Season the eggplant ginger dip with salt, black pepper, and lemon juice.

ROASTED TOMATO DIP

PREPARE: 25 MINUTES
SERVES ABOUT 4 AS
AN APPETIZER

25 flavorful tomatoes, sliced
   into wedges
1 large onion, cut into rings
splash of olive oil
sea salt
1 teaspoon ground cumin
1 chipotle in adobo sauce, or
   1 teaspoon smoked paprika
   plus Tabasco sauce to taste
Freshly ground black pepper

Delicious as a dip with some crunchy toasted tortillas, with chicken skewers from the grill, with spicy meatballs, or spread on a grilled sandwich.

Preheat the broiler to 400°F (200°C).

Arrange the tomatoes and onion on a baking sheet. Drizzle with olive oil, sprinkle with salt and cumin, and swiftly toss everything together. Broil the vegetables for 15 minutes, until almost charred.

Place the vegetables in a tall pitcher, add the chipotle or smoked paprika and Tabasco to taste and using an immersion blender, briefly puree the vegetables into a smooth sauce. Season with salt and pepper.

COCKTAIL SNACKS

sardine nut spread

PREPARE: 5 MINUTES
SERVES 4 AS AN APPETIZER

1 can (about 3½ ounces/
  100 g) sardines in oil,
  drained (but reserve the
  oil!), roughly chopped
3 cherry tomatoes
1 clove garlic, pressed
1 bunch (½ ounce/15 g)
  flat-leaf parsley, tough
  stems removed
a few sprigs of chives
3 tablespoons chopped
  walnuts
3 tablespoons chopped
  almonds
2 to 3 tablespoons red
  wine vinegar
sea salt and freshly ground
  black pepper

SARDINE NUT SPREAD

There isn't a single appetizer quicker to whip up than this one.
Double the recipe while you're at it, because there certainly won't be
any leftovers.

Mash all the ingredients with a fork, or puree them in the food
processor into a coarse paste. Add salt and pepper to taste. If the
spread is a little dry, stir in a splash of reserved oil from the can
of sardines.

½ cup (50 g) walnuts, briefly
  toasted in a dry frying pan
heaping ⅓ cup (50 g)
  blanched almonds, also
  briefly roasted
heaping 1 cup (50 g) fresh
  breadcrumbs
2 cloves garlic, minced
about 3 tablespoons red
  wine vinegar
3 to 5 tablespoons (45 to
  75 ml) cold water
about 6½ tablespoons
  (100 ml) olive oil
sea salt and freshly ground
  black pepper
pinch of sumac or a splash
  of lemon

tool
food processor

SKORDALIA OF WALNUTS & ALMONDS

Skordalia is a kind of spreadable puree—this one is made from nuts—
that is delicious on bread or vegetables.

Grind all the nuts into a paste in a food processor.

Add the breadcrumbs, garlic, vinegar, and 3 to 5 tablespoons (45 to
75 ml) of cold water. Continue pulsing into a thick, hummus-like puree.

Pour in the olive oil while pulsing until the sauce is smooth. Season
with salt and pepper and spoon into a bowl. Sprinkle with sumac and
serve with vegetables, more nuts, crackers, and bread for dipping.

for serving
raw vegetables, such as
  chicory leaves, celery,
  cauliflower florets
nuts
crackers
flatbread for tearing

COCKTAIL SNACKS

orange Negroni slush

ORANGE NEGRONI SLUSH

CHILL GLASSES: 30 MINUTES
PREPARE: 5 MINUTES
MAKES 2 GLASSES

1 ounce (30 ml) gin
1 ounce (30 ml) Campari
1 ounce (30 ml) red
 vermouth
3⅓ ounces (100 ml) freshly
 squeezed orange juice
 (from about 1½ oranges)
2 handfuls of crushed ice
a few sprigs of thyme and
 orange slices, for garnish

tool
blender

The Negroni is one of my favorite drinks. You make it by mixing the first three ingredients, after which you usually serve it with one big ice cube and an orange twist. Here you'll find two variations for a warm summer day, somewhat less strong, so you can have another one without immediately falling over.

For this first drink you'll need crushed ice. To make this, take a large pile of ice cubes, dump them on a clean dish towel, carefully tie the ends together, and crush the ice with a rolling pin or another heavy object. That will do the trick.

Chill glasses in the freezer for 30 minutes.

Mix the gin with the Campari, red vermouth, and orange juice in a blender. Add the crushed ice. Blend, starting at the lowest setting and slowly increasing the speed to the highest setting. Add more crushed ice if you want a thicker slush.

Pour the Negroni slush into the pre-chilled glasses and garnish each with a sprig of thyme and a slice of orange.

NEGRONI PITCHER

PREPARE: 5 MINUTES
MAKES 8 TO 10 GLASSES

1 (750 ml) bottle Campari
1 (750 ml) bottle red
 vermouth
1 (750 ml) bottle prosecco,
 properly chilled
3 generous handfuls of
 ice cubes
large strips of organic orange
 zest
1 organic orange, cut into
 wedges
a large sprig of rosemary
 (optional)

When throwing a party, I love to serve a festive version of my favorite cocktail. I replace the gin with a bottle of prosecco, but otherwise I keep the classic proportions of three equal parts. If you don't have a punch bowl, serve the cocktail in a large—truly spotless—glass vase and arrange every drinking glass you have around it. Let your guests serve themselves with a ladle that you hang on the vase.

Pour the Campari, red vermouth, and prosecco into a large, spotless vase (or punch bowl) filled halfway with ice cubes. Add the orange zest and wedges. Briefly stir everything together.

You can also garnish with a sprig of rosemary.

COCKTAILS

old Irish cure

OLD IRISH CURE

PREPARE: 5 MINUTES
MAKES 1 GLASS

handful of ice cubes
a touch more than 1½ ounces
(50 ml) whiskey
½ ounce (15 ml) dark rum
½ ounce (15 ml) lemon juice
1 teaspoon honey
1 teaspoon finely grated
ginger

finishing touches
1 slice fresh ginger
1 slice roasted lemon
(see page 123)

My favorite spirit, besides a good red or white wine, is whiskey. Of course, I like drinking it straight—especially when it's a special vintage, I won't mix it with anything. Occasionally I'll add maybe a drop of water to loosen it up. Apart from that, I don't even add ice. There are a few simple whiskey cocktails, however, that make me very happy. They always include ginger, because you can't go wrong with ginger.

Fill a cocktail shaker with the ice cubes. Add all the ingredients except the slice of ginger and the roasted lemon and thoroughly shake. Strain the cocktail into a chilled glass. Decorate the glass with a slice of ginger and serve with the roasted lemon so you or your guest can add a little squeeze to taste.

THE WHISKEY GINGER

PREPARE: 5 MINUTES
MAKES 1 GLASS

a touch more than 1½ ounces
(50 ml) whiskey
about 6½ ounces (200 ml)
ginger ale (see recipe at
right for home made)
splash of lime
a few ice cubes

Mix all the ingredients in a tall glass.

QUICK GINGER ALE
(recipe from my book Home Sweet Home*)*

Blend 2½ cups (100 g: or more to taste) finely grated ginger, 1 lemon cut into pieces, and ½ cup (100 g) cane sugar or ⅓ cup (100 g) honey in a blender, add 1¼ cups (300 ml) water and blend until the sugar has dissolved and a thick smooth paste has formed.

Strain the pulp through a sieve into a bowl and using the back of a spoon, press out as much liquid as possible. Pour it into a bottle and keep until ready to use.

Fill a glass with ice cubes and a splash of the ginger-lemon juice. Mix with seltzer water to taste.

COCKTAILS

SPICY VODKA & GRAPEFRUIT TEA

PREPARE: 5 MINUTES
WAIT: AT LEAST 1 HOUR
MAKES 4 GLASSES

2 cups plus 1 tablespoon
(500 ml) brewed mint tea
2 cups plus 1 tablespoon
(500 ml) pink or white
grapefruit juice
1¼ cups (300 ml) vodka
4 limes, cut into wedges,
juice squeezed, but add the
wedges to the jug too
1 hot green chile, halved
lengthwise
2 sprigs of mint
a few sprigs of cilantro
2 to 3 handfuls of ice cubes

This cocktail is nice and refreshing. It doesn't contain too much alcohol, so it makes for the perfect spicy welcome drink to kick off a great party. Make it with white grapefruit juice if you prefer your drink slightly more bitter, but always add the chile. It is the punch this light, refreshing cocktail needs.

Leave out the vodka if you want to make a mocktail.

Mix all the ingredients except the ice cubes in a large jug.

Refrigerate for at least 1 hour, allowing the flavors to steep. Before serving, fill the jug with ice cubes.

DINNER TIME

SOUPS MAKING BROTH, VEGETABLE BROTH, CHICKEN BROTH, BEEF BRO
SOUP, CRAWFISH FENNEL SOUP, CREAMY SOUP OF PEARL BARLEY, WHIS
CONGEE WITH CASHEW CREAM & RAYU, CHEESE SOUP WITH PUMPERNI
SOUP WITH AVOCADO **SAUCES/SALSAS/TJAP** MAKING MAYO, MORE
MUSTARD CAVIAR, HOME MADE HOT SAUCE, SESAME RAYU **SALADS** MA
DRESSINGS WITHOUT OIL, RADISH & CAULIFLOWER SALAD WITH BUTTER
SMASHED CUCUMBER, AVOCADO & PEACH SALAD, BROCCOLI STALK SLA
SALAD WITH SARDINES, BEAN SALAD WITH CRUNCHY HALLOUMI CHIPS
FRESH RICOTTA & THYME OIL, DOUBLE-SHELLING FAVA BEANS, FAVA BEA
STEAMED MACKEREL, FRESH PLUM SALAD WITH FENNEL, HERBS & MOZ
FETA, WATERMELON, ORANGE & FETA SALAD WITH TARRAGON, HOME
QUICK PICKLING, NEW POTATO SALAD WITH RADISH & YOGURT WITH PI
VEGETABLE DISHES COCONUT CURRY WITH EGGPLANT, CAULIFLOWER C
GARLIC NAAN, ZUCCHINI & CORN BURGERS, VEGGIE SAUSAGES, BEET B
CAULIFLOWER-CELERIAC CURRY & CARAMELIZED LEEKS, ROASTED CARR
CHARRED BRUSSELS SPROUTS WITH SCORCHED HONEY, BAKED SWEET
MISO, GRILLED AVOCADO WITH SPICY HUMMUS & SESAME YOGURT SA
WITH CHANTERELLES, FRISIAN WÂLD BEAN STEW WITH CHICORY & FETA,
CROUTONS, MAKING FRIES, CHEST HAIR FRIES, POTATOES "CACIO E PEP
WITH PESTO, LEMON PASTA WITH SAMPHIRE, SPAGHETTI WITH SHRIMP,
STEW PAPPARDELLE WITH ROSEMARY & TANGERINE, PASTA WITH BROCC
WHOLE-WHEAT SPAGHETTI WITH CHORIZO TOMATO SAUCE, CURRIED CA
SESAME PEANUT SAUCE, SESAME RAYU & CUCUMBER SALAD, QUICK NO
GNOCCHI WITH WARM CHIVE ALMOND SAUCE, WARM SALAD OF SWEET
RISOTTO, WHEAT BEER RISOTTO WITH COCKLES, ORZOTTO WITH PORCIN
WITH BROWN RICE, CUTTING ORANGE SEGMENTS, ORANGE GRAIN SA
COUSCOUS WITH FRIED ONIONS, SEMOLINA WITH SHRIMP, FAVA BEAN
SHEET-PAN PIE WITH BEETS, BRIE & WALNUTS, DARK MALT FLOUR TOMAT
PIZZA DOUGH, WHOLE-WHEAT PIZZA WITH EGGPLANT & SAUTÉED ONIO
CORN TORTILLAS, FLOUR TORTILLAS, TORTILLAS WITH HOISIN SHRIMP, A

H, FISH STOCK, RED LENTIL SOUP, CREAMY GREEN ASPARAGUS & CASHEW
EY, BLOOD SAUSAGE & STEAMED CELERY LEAVES, GINGER PUMPKIN
KEL BREADCRUMBS, EGGPLANT CREAM SOUP, BROCCOLI SPINACH
AUCES, FAT-FREE SAUCES, TARTAR SAUCE, ROSE HIP KETCHUP, HOISIN,
ING MUSTARD VINAIGRETTE, MORE OIL-BASED SALAD DRESSINGS,
ILK DRESSING, BRUSSEL SPROUTS–APPLE SALAD WITH PARMESAN,
, ENDIVES WITH CAULIFLOWER COUSCOUS, APPLE & MAGOR, CHICKPEA
RED JALAPEÑO DRESSING, BABY SUMMER SQUASH, YELLOW TOMATOES,
SALAD, ASPARAGUS & CUMBER RIBBONS, QUICK GREEN SALAD WITH
A, PEELING STONE FRUITS, PEACH TOMATO SALAD WITH CHORIZO &
ADE STRACCIATELLA, STRACCIATELLA WITH LEEKS & OYSTER MUSHROOMS,
KLED CUCUMBER & HERRING, SPICY STRAWBERRIES WITH FETA CREAM
RRY WITH KIDNEY BEANS, BEET CURRY WITH ALMONDS & YOGURT,
RGERS, BRUSSELS SPROUTS CLAFOUTIS WITH HARISSA & FETA, MASHED
TS & ORANGE GREMOLATA, ROASTED RADISHES WITH SOUR BUTTER SAUCE,
TATOES WITH GRAPES, SPINACH & GOAT CHEESE, BRAISED ESCAROLE WITH
CE, HOISIN EGGPLANTS WITH SPICY PEANUT SAUCE, BAKED CELERIAC
ANZANELLA WITH CHICKPEAS, SWEET-SOUR ENDIVE WITH SALTY
" POTATO CAKES PASTA MAKING PASTA, THE PERFECT MACCHERONI
EEN HERBS & PEPPERS, FETTUCINE WITH SARDINES, RABBIT (OR CHICKEN)
LI, LEMON & MOZZARELLA, SPICY PENNE WITH EGGPLANT & BACON,
LIFLOWER WITH PASTA & SPINACH-CASHEW PESTO, NOODLES WITH
ODLES WITH SRIRACHA SAUCE & SHRIMP, MAKING GNOCCHI, PURPLE POTATO
OTATO GNOCCHI WITH TOMATOES & CASHEW-BASIL PESTO GRAINS GREEN
MUSHROOMS, VANILLA & MAGICAL POACHED EGG, UMAMI BOMB BOWL
D WITH HALLOUMI, SPANAKORIZO: GREEK SPINACH-LEMON RICE, BEET
CHORIZO SHEET-PAN BAKING MAKING SHORT CRUST, WHOLE-WHEAT
GALETTE, BUTTERNUT SQUASH GALETTE WITH BURRATA, MAKING BREAD OR
NS, PIZZAS WITH BROCCOLINI & FAUX TUNA TORTILLAS MAKING TORTILLAS,
GE TOSTADAS WITH PULLED CHICKEN, MANGO & MINT-COCONUT RELISH

SOUP

Galway, Ireland

Owenahincha, West Cork

MAKING BROTH

Broth can be made with anything: vegetables, fowl, bones, any fish or meat—whatever's left over or has to go.

Make a well-balanced combo of flavors because you'll taste them later: fish bones, carrot, fennel, onion, and fennel seed, for instance.

Put in a pan of cold water, simmer gently, without letting it boil and without a lid.

Continue until your house is infused with a lovely broth smell and you are happy with the intensity of the flavor.

Strain the broth through a fine sieve, or, better still, through a sieve lined with a clean cloth. This will result in an even clearer broth.

Seasoning the broth often requires more salt than you might expect. But you can also use soy, Worcestershire sauce, fish sauce—you name it.

USE HOME MADE BROTH IN EVERYTHING FROM SOUP TO SAUCE. STORE IN SMALL BATCHES IN THE FREEZER.

VEGETABLE BROTH

2 onions, unpeeled, halved
4 cloves, one inserted in each
    half onion
1 celeriac, peeled and chopped
1 bunch celery, cut into
    three pieces
2 leeks, coarsely chopped
    and cleaned
3 large carrots, peeled and
    coarsely chopped
6 cloves garlic, unpeeled
3 bay leaves
1 small (10 g) bouquet garni
    flat-leaf parsley, rosemary,
    and thyme
1 tablespoon black
    peppercorns
2 tablespoons coriander seeds
3 or 4 pieces of mace
sea salt and freshly ground
    black pepper

When they are in season, I sometimes put some turnips in my broth. The more vegetables, the better.

Place all the ingredients except the salt and freshly ground black pepper in the biggest stockpot you can find. Pour in at least 5 quarts (5 L) cold water and bring to a boil. Reduce the heat. Let the broth simmer over very low heat for 1 to 2 hours, until it's reduced by about half. In the meantime, carefully skim the foam off the surface with a slotted spoon. Otherwise, the broth will end up cloudy.

Strain the stock or pour it through a colander lined with a clean tea towel. Let it cool to room temperature.

Season the stock some more with salt and pepper.

CHICKEN BROTH

1 whole chicken
2 onions, unpeeled, halved
4 cloves, one inserted in each
    half onion
1 celeriac, peeled and chopped
½ bunch celery, cut into
    three pieces
2 leeks, coarsely chopped
    and cleaned
3 large carrots, peeled and
    coarsely chopped
6 cloves garlic, unpeeled
3 bay leaves
1 small (10 g) bouquet garni
    flat-leaf parsley, rosemary,
    and thyme
1 tablespoon black
    peppercorns
2 tablespoons coriander seeds
3 or 4 pieces of mace
sea salt and freshly ground
    black pepper

Place all the ingredients except the salt and freshly ground black pepper in the biggest stockpot you can find. Pour in at least 5 quarts (5 L) cold water and bring to a boil. Reduce the heat. Let the broth simmer over very low heat for 3 hours, or until it's reduced by about half. Occasionally carefully skim the foam off the surface with a slotted spoon. Otherwise, the broth will end up cloudy.

Strain the stock or pour it through a colander lined with a clean tea towel. Let it cool to room temperature.

Refrigerate. Once it has cooled completely, scoop the solidified fat from the surface and discard. Season the stock some more with salt and pepper.

BEEF BROTH

1 pound (500 g) beef bones (ask your butcher)
2 beef shanks (about 1 pound/500 g total)
2 onions, unpeeled, halved
1 small bunch (10 g) thyme
a few bay leaves
a few cloves garlic, unpeeled
4 to 5 tablespoons (60 to 75 ml) olive oil
1 bunch celery, cut into three pieces
2 leeks, coarsely chopped and cleaned
1 large carrot, peeled and coarsely chopped
1 bunch (½ ounce/15 g) flat-leaf parsley
3 or 4 pieces of mace
1 tablespoon black peppercorns
2 tablespoons coriander seeds
sea salt and freshly ground black pepper
Worcestershire sauce and/or salty soy sauce (optional)

You can substitute deer or wild boar bones for the beef bones and shanks, for a game broth. Or use a mix of bones. Anything goes.

Preheat the oven to 350°F (180°C).

Combine the beef bones, shanks, onions, thyme, bay leaves, and garlic in a roasting pan. Drizzle with the olive oil and toss everything with a spoon. Roast for 30 minutes, until the bones begin to slightly brown.

Spoon everything from the roasting pan into a large stockpot.

Pour in at least 4 quarts (4 L) water and add the remaining ingredients except the salt, freshly ground black pepper, and Worcestershire sauce. Bring to a boil. Reduce the heat and let the stock simmer over very low heat for 3 hours, or until the broth is reduced by about half. Occasionally skim off the foam with a slotted spoon. Otherwise, the broth will end up cloudy.

Strain the stock or pour it through a colander lined with a clean tea towel. Let it cool to room temperature.

Refrigerate. Once it has cooled completely, scoop the solidified fat from the surface and discard. Season the stock some more with salt and pepper. I often add some Worcestershire sauce and sometimes salty soy sauce to lend the stock a deeper, more intense flavor and color.

FISH STOCK

2¼ pounds (1 kg) fish bones and heads (ask the fishmonger)
1 onion, cut into rings
1 carrot, peeled and coarsely chopped
4 stalks celery, cut into three pieces
1 bunch (½ ounce/15 g) flat-leaf parsley
1 small fennel bulb, chopped
1 teaspoon black peppercorns
½ tablespoon coriander seeds
½ tablespoon fennel seeds
2 or 3 pieces of mace
2 bay leaves

Rinse the fish bones under running water. Combine the bones and the rest of the ingredients in a large stockpot and add 2 quarts (2 L) cold water.

Let the stock simmer over low heat for 30 minutes. The stock shouldn't boil, but a few air bubbles occasionally floating to the surface is fine. If the water does get to a boil, the released fish protein emulsifies with the fat in the water and the broth will turn cloudy. Therefore, broth should steep slowly at a temperature below the boiling point. Occasionally skim off the foam from the surface with a slotted spoon. Let the stock cool for 1 hour.

Line a sieve with a clean dish cloth. Place the strainer over a clean pan. Pour the stock through the dish cloth and the sieve and let it drain completely.

Now the stock is ready to be frozen in several small batches.

SOUP

RED LENTIL SOUP

PREPARE: 15 MINUTES
COOK: 30 MINUTES
SERVES 4

1 tablespoon olive oil,
    plus extra
7 ounces (200 g) Spanish-
    style cured chorizo, cut into
    small pieces
1 large onion, chopped
2 carrots, cut into small cubes
1 teaspoon ground cumin
3 cloves garlic, minced
1 teaspoon smoked paprika,
    plus extra
2 teaspoon honey or
    granulated sugar
2 to 3 tablespoons red
    wine vinegar
8¾ ounces (250 g) red lentils
1 (14½-ounce/411 g) can
    whole peeled tomatoes, the
    tomatoes squeezed (see
    page 266)
4½ cups (1 L) vegetable or
    chicken stock
sea salt and freshly ground
    black pepper
8 tablespoons (120 ml)
    yogurt

tool
blender

I have various ways of making this hearty soup. I love the smoky, fatty flavor of chorizo, but I eat so little meat that I sometimes also simply replace it with, say, feta or goat cheese. So just use this recipe as a base. I'll offer further suggestions for toppings below. Pick one from each list for the right balance.

Heat the olive oil in a large pan. Fry the chorizo pieces until crispy. Remove the chorizo slices from the pan with a slotted spoon and set aside on a plate.

Sauté the onion, carrot cubes, and cumin in the same pan for about 10 minutes, until the vegetables are tender. Add the garlic and fry for 1 minute. Add the smoked paprika and honey and deglaze the pan with a splash of red wine vinegar.

Stir in the red lentils and pour the squeezed tomatoes and stock into the pan. Bring to a boil. Reduce the heat and cook the lentil soup, partly covered with a lid, for 30 minutes over low heat. Occasionally check whether the lentils are done, or if necessary, cook them a little longer. Add a splash of water if the soup gets too thick.

Puree the soup with an immersion blender until smoother, but not completely smooth. Some individual lentils should still be visible. Taste the soup and decide whether to add salt and pepper.

Serve the soup in large bowls, each topped with 2 tablespoons yogurt and sprinkled with the fried chorizo. Drizzle the soup with a little olive oil and sprinkle with more paprika.

CRUNCHY

Croutons, baked in butter with anchovies or sea salt
Seeds, popped: like whole buckwheat or pumpkin seeds
Bacon cubes, fried
Nuts, crispy fried (in butter/olive oil), possibly with spices and/or garlic
Tortilla chips, crumbled
Crispy fried onions

CREAMY

Double cream
Crème fraîche
Quark cheese or yogurt, stirred
Cashew cream (see page 119)
Coconut milk
Cheese, any kind of grated or crumbled
Olive oil or pesto (see pages 131 and 133)
Avocado, cubed
Egg, hard-boiled or poached (see page 49)

ZESTY

Fresh herbs, finely chopped
Onion, chopped and briefly pickled in vinegar (see page 191)
Watercress or sprouts
Scallions, cut into rings
Celery, or other raw vegetables, cut into very small cubes
Apple or pear, cut into small cubes
Jalapeño, fresh or preserved (from a jar), finely chopped

SOUP

CREAMY GREEN ASPARAGUS & CASHEW SOUP

SOAK: 1 HOUR
PREPARE: 25 MINUTES
SERVES 3 TO 6

for the soup
1 pound 1 ounce (500 g)
    green asparagus
2 tablespoons olive oil
1 onion, chopped
scant ⅔ cup (75 g) whole raw
    cashews, soaked in a bowl
    of hot water for 1 hour
    and drained
6½ cups (1½ L) vegetable
    stock
a few drops of lemon juice,
    or to taste

for the nutty croutons
3 slices of stale white bread,
    shredded into small pieces
2 anchovies, minced
    (vegans can use salt or
    1 teaspoon miso)
2 tablespoons coarsely
    chopped raw cashews
pinch of chile flakes, to taste
2 tablespoons olive oil
sea salt and freshly ground
    black pepper

tool
stand blender or immersion
    blender

Except for the anchovies, this soup is suitable for people who follow a plant-based diet—just leave out the fish and add a little extra salt or some miso instead.

Make the soup: Clean the asparagus stalks and trim off about 1 inch (2.5 cm) from the ends. Cut 2 inches (5 cm) off the tips and set aside. Cut the middle part of the stalks in half or in thirds.

Heat the olive oil in a stockpot, add the onion, and sauté until translucent. Now add the center pieces of asparagus and cook for a few more minutes, stirring continuously. Stir in the soaked cashews and cook briefly. Pour in the stock, bring the soup to a boil, then reduce the heat and allow to gently cook for 15 minutes.

Make the nutty croutons: Preheat the oven to 325°F (170°C).

Arrange the bread pieces, along with the anchovies, chopped cashews, and some chile flakes on a baking sheet and drizzle with the olive oil. Add salt and pepper to taste. Thoroughly combine everything and place in the middle of the oven. They should be nice and crispy after 7 to 8 minutes, but keep a close eye—sometimes it can go fast. Halfway through the baking time give them a good stir.

In the meantime, puree the soup in the blender until you get a silky-smooth cream soup; if using an immersion blender, take your time (and blend for a long time to get it nice and smooth!)

Add the reserved asparagus tips to the warm creamy soup and cook until al dente. Add a few drops of lemon juice, if you think the soup needs it. Ladle the soup into four preheated plates and sprinkle with the oven-fresh nutty croutons.

You can serve this soup cold as well. Let cool to room temperature and refrigerate to let it *truly* chill (this usually takes up to 2 hours, depending on the size of the pot). Serve ice cold topped with croutons. Pretty dainty!

SOUP

CRAWFISH FENNEL SOUP

PREPARE: ABOUT 2 HOURS
30 MINUTES
SERVES 8 AS A STARTER

about 2¼ pounds (1 kg)
  crawfish
sea salt
1½ tablespoons plus
  7 tablespoons to ⅔ cup
  (100 to 150 g) cold butter
2 tablespoons fennel seeds,
  briefly crushed in a mortar
a few sprigs of rosemary
6 cloves garlic, pressed
2 tablespoons tomato paste
4 shallots, chopped
1 leek, sliced into rings
  and cleaned
2 fennel bulbs, very thinly
  sliced
1 carrot, peeled and cut into
  small pieces
3 bay leaves
¾ cup plus 1 tablespoon
  (200 ml) brandy or cognac
10 tablespoons (150 ml)
  Pernod
2 quarts (2 L) strong
  fish stock (page 109)
cayenne pepper to taste
1 teaspoon paprika
freshly ground black pepper

on the side
fennel seed rouille (page 133)
croutons (see page 187)
  or toast

Of course you can buy the crawfish tails cleaned and precooked, but the shells are like the bones to a broth: THAT'S WHERE THE FLAVOR IS.
    If you find it scary to cook living crustaceans, you can buy them frozen in boxes at the fishmonger and in Asian supermarkets. Then it's just a matter of thawing them.

Cook the crawfish for just a few minutes in boiling salted water in a large stockpot (or use precooked crawfish). Peel them and store the tail meat, covered, in the refrigerator.

Crush the shells and carcasses as finely as possible. The best way to do this is to put them in a sturdy plastic bag and thoroughly smash them with something heavy like a rolling pin.

In a large stockpot, cook the shells in about 1½ tablespoons butter. Add the fennel seeds, rosemary, garlic, and tomato paste. Fry everything for about 3 minutes, then add the shallots, leeks, two-thirds of the sliced fennel, the carrots, and bay leaves.

Stir the vegetables and deglaze everything with the brandy and Pernod. Over high heat, reduce the liquid for a few minutes. Pour in the fish stock and let the soup simmer for 2 hours, the pan half-covered with the lid. Don't let the soup boil, or it will turn bitter.

Strain through a fine sieve. Return the liquid to the pan and bring to a boil again. Add the remaining fennel slices and cook them in the hot soup. Cube the cold butter and beat in the cubes one by one until the bisque (that's what you call this crustacean soup) starts to thicken a little.

Season the soup with cayenne, paprika, salt and, if necessary, some freshly ground pepper. Heat thoroughly and serve the soup in large bowls. Add the crawfish tail meat. Serve with rouille and croutons or toast.

SOUP

CREAMY SOUP OF PEARL BARLEY, WHISKEY, BLOOD SAUSAGE & STEAMED CELERY LEAVES

**PREPARE: 45 MINUTES
SERVES 4 AS A LUNCH OR
STARTER DISH**

2 tablespoons olive oil
1 large onion, chopped
¾ cup (150 g) barley
   (Alkmaar barley or
   pearl barley)*
about 6½ cups (1½ L) hot
   chicken or vegetable stock,
   plus a little extra (optional)
⅔ cup (150 g) butter
3 tablespoons whiskey
sea salt and freshly ground
   black pepper
core of a celery bunch,
   soft ribs and leaves
   roughly chopped
4½ ounces (130 g) blood
   sausage or black pudding,
   skin removed, the sausage
   meat crumbled; or use
   5¼ ounces (150 g) bresaola,
   cut into thin strips
6½ tablespoons (100 ml)
   heavy cream

*See "Particular Ingredients"
on page 12.

Oh, blood sausage, love of my life. If you're not a fan of blood sausage, you can easily replace it with bresaola or crumbled chorizo. A salty cheese such as pecorino or hard goat cheese works as well, if you prefer to keep it vegetarian.

Heat the olive oil in a large stockpot and sauté the onion until translucent. Add the barley and fry it, like you'd do with risotto rice. Deglaze the pan with 1 inch (2.5 cm) of stock, reduce the heat, and simmer, uncovered, in a shallow layer of stock. Add stock every time the barley becomes too dry. Cook the barley al dente, and stop adding stock as soon as the barley is more moist than risotto. The cooked barley should look a tad soupy. This should be after about 30 minutes of cooking and adding stock.

In a saucepan over very low heat, melt the butter and cook until the clear part has turned caramel colored. Strain the butter in a very fine sieve over a bowl and reserve the brown clarified butter solids.

Stir the whiskey and 1 to 2 tablespoons of the clarified butter into the barley soup and, if you want, add salt and a generous amount of black pepper. Remove from the heat.

In a skillet, heat 2 tablespoons of the clarified butter. Add the celery and cook slowly, stirring, over medium heat. Scoop out the celery and keep it warm between two plates.

Turn the heat under the skillet to high, allowing the pan to get properly hot. Add the crumbled blood sausage and fry until crispy.

Ladle the barley soup into four preheated bowls; divide the celery and crumbled blood sausage on top. Drizzle with cream and brown butter, season with black pepper and serve immediately.

If you reheat the soup later, the barley may have absorbed all the stock. In that case, add extra. Or eat the dish like a barley risotto.

SOUP

SOAK: 30 MINUTES
PREPARE: 45 MINUTES
SERVES 4

6½ tablespoons (75 g)
   long-grain white rice
2 tablespoons sunflower oil
about 1 pound 1 ounce
   (500 g) pumpkin, peeled
   and cubed
4½ cups (1 L) chicken stock
4 inches (10 cm) fresh ginger,
   half grated and the other
   half peeled and sliced
   into julienne
1 to 2 tablespoons fish sauce
splash of lime juice
pinch of chile flakes
2 scallions, cut into rings
cashew cream (recipe
   follows)
sesame rayu (page 143)

CASHEW CREAM

1⅔ cups (200 g) whole
   raw cashews
splash of lemon juice
pinch of sea salt

Soak the cashews in
a bowl of cold water
for at least 1 hour, but
preferably overnight.
Drain them and grind in a
blender together with about
¾ cup plus 1 tablespoon
(200 ml) clean, cold water
into a thick cream. Season
with a splash of lemon and a
pinch of sea salt. Refrigerate
and use as you would sour
cream.

GINGER PUMPKIN CONGEE WITH CASHEW CREAM & RAYU

Congee is a hearty rice porridge, or thick rice soup, if you will. And it's so terribly comforting that I wouldn't mind eating it every day. Here, I make it with pumpkin, but every kind of vegetable is delicious, and possible to use. In this recipe too, you can throw in pieces of leftover meat or fish. Go ahead and make it, then dig in and make variations of your own. It's highly addictive. And extra-delicious with a dab of cashew cream, a scoop of sesame rayu (a crunchy Japanese chile oil; see page 143), or the Thai green sauce from page 134. Some leftover pork belly from page 349 or chicken in coconut from page 355 also makes for a perfect topping.

Put the rice in a small bowl and pour in water to cover. Let soak for 30 minutes. Rinse the rice in a fine strainer under running water until the water turns clear. Let drain.

Heat 1 tablespoon of the sunflower oil in a heavy-bottomed stockpot over medium heat. Add the rice and pumpkin cubes and fry for 1 to 2 minutes, stirring continuously. Add the chicken stock, the grated ginger, and a drop of fish sauce to taste and bring to a boil. As soon as the soup is boiling, reduce the heat. With the lid partly on, let the soup simmer very gently for about 45 minutes, until the congee is thick and creamy and the rice is very soft, stirring regularly to avoid burning.

Heat the remaining 1 tablespoon sunflower oil in a skillet. Add the ginger slices and fry them for about 6 minutes, or until golden brown and crispy. Let the ginger drain on a paper towel.

Season the congee with lime juice, chile flakes, and, if desired, some more fish sauce. Divide the soup among four bowls; sprinkle with the scallion rings and ginger. Spoon some cashew cream and rayu on top and serve.

SOUP

PREPARE: 45 MINUTES
SERVES 6

for the cheese soup
2 tablespoons butter
2 onions, finely chopped
1 clove garlic, pressed
2 carrots, diced
2 stalks celery, cut into
 small cubes
4 tablespoons (30 g)
 all-purpose flour
2 cups plus 1 tablespoon
 (500 ml) white wine
2 cups plus 1 tablespoon
 (500 ml) milk
4½ cups (1 L) good-quality
 chicken broth, preferably
 home made (see page 108)
1 pound 5 ounces (600 g)
 aged farmhouse cheese,
 grated
1 generous tablespoon
 Worcestershire sauce, or
 to taste
pinch of cayenne pepper
1 teaspoon paprika
sea salt and freshly ground
 black pepper
a few fresh sage leaves, finely
 chopped

*for the pumpernickel
 breadcrumbs*
2 tablespoons butter
2 slices of pumpernickel
 bread (or Frisian rye bread),
 ground to crumbs in the
 food processor
sea salt and freshly ground
 black pepper

to garnish
4 tablespoons (60 ml)
 sour cream

tool
food processor

CHEESE SOUP WITH PUMPERNICKEL BREADCRUMBS

On page 111, I gave you several options for soup garnishes, including croutons. Aside from wheat bread, these can also be made using other types of bread—pumpernickel, for example.

The bitter notes of rye suit the rich flavor of cheese soup really well. Frisian pumpernickel bread tastes great to begin with, but ground to crumbs and fried in butter, it is even more delicious as a soup topping. By all means, do experiment with the various types of bread you use for making croutons. All those diverse flavors do make a difference. Cooking is pretty exciting, no?

Make the cheese soup: Melt the butter in a large saucepan. Add the onions and garlic and fry for about 5 minutes, until the onions are translucent. Add the carrot and celery cubes and cook the vegetables over low heat for 5 minutes. Stir in the flour, cook for a few more minutes, then deglaze with the white wine. Thoroughly stir until all lumps have dissolved.

Pour in the milk and chicken stock, bring the soup to a boil, and add the aged farmhouse cheese. Keep stirring until the cheese has completely melted.

Season the soup with Worcestershire sauce, cayenne, paprika, and salt and pepper and stir in the chopped sage.

Simmer over low heat for about 30 minutes, stirring occasionally, until the soup has a nice consistency, thinner than cheese fondue.

Make the pumpernickel breadcrumbs: In a skillet, melt the butter and while stirring, add the breadcrumbs and fry for a few minutes, until crispy. Season with salt and pepper. Drain on a paper towel.

Serve the soup in deep bowls, topped with sour cream and sprinkled with the pumpernickel breadcrumbs.

SOUP

EGGPLANT CREAM SOUP

PREPARE: 10 MINUTES
BAKE: 1 HOUR
SERVES 4 AS A STARTER

for the soup
about 2¼ pounds (1 kg)
   eggplants
6 large cloves garlic, whole
1 lemon, quartered
1 teaspoon honey or sugar
1 tablespoon plus
   5 tablespoons (75 ml)
   olive oil
sea salt
2 cups plus 1 tablespoon
   (500 ml) hot water
5 tablespoons (75 ml)
   heavy cream
5 to 6 anchovies
freshly ground black pepper

to garnish
1 bunch (½ ounce/15 g)
   flat-leaf parsley, minced;
   or 1 tablespoon pesto
   (page 131 or 133) per
   bowl, diluted with a drop
   of water
4 tablespoons (60 ml) heavy
   cream; about 7 tablespoons
   (100 ml) thin yogurt
   (as pictured); and/or a
   scoop of whipped and
   lightly salted ricotta cheese
½ cup (75 g) crumbled
   feta cheese
pinch of smoked paprika

tool
food processor or blender

This soup is a sort of base recipe to which I subsequently add every leftover—I call them "fridge daughters"—I happen to have on hand, like that tail end of pesto: just too much to throw away, just too little for an entire dish. The same goes for a scoop of yogurt or mascarpone, a dab of ricotta, the leaves of those final few sprigs of garden herbs. You can throw in some chopped raw vegetables as well. Or a spoonful of leftover cooked lentils or chickpeas . . . Anyway, you get the idea. This soup changes every day. I garnished the pictured bowl with whatever was left in my fridge. I'm curious what your soup will taste like.

Preheat the oven to 350°F (180°C).

Halve the eggplants and place them on a baking sheet, cut sides up, along with the garlic and lemon. Brush the eggplant halves with honey and the 1 tablespoon olive oil and sprinkle with salt. Roast for 1 hour, or until the surfaces of the eggplants are dark brown and the insides are really soft.

Let them cool slightly. Scrape the flesh of the eggplants from their skins (which can be discarded) and spoon the pulp into a food processor or blender. Add the roasted garlic. Scrape the roasted flesh from the lemon peel and add it to the eggplant. Puree everything until completely smooth.

Pour in the hot water, the 5 tablespoons (75 ml) olive oil, and the heavy cream and puree until you have a smooth cream soup. Add the anchovies one at a time and check after each addition whether the taste is good or whether you should add another fish. Season the soup with a generous pinch of black pepper.

This soup can be served immediately lukewarm, or briefly reheated first. Before serving, sprinkle the soup with chopped parsley or a spoonful of pesto, a dollop of whipped cream or a swirl of yogurt or whipped ricotta and/or crumbled feta and a mandatory pinch of smoked paprika.

SOUP

BROCCOLI SPINACH SOUP WITH AVOCADO

PREPARE: 25 MINUTES
SERVES 4 AS A STARTER

1 tablespoon olive oil, plus
  extra for serving
1 onion, chopped
2 cloves garlic, pressed
pinch of chile flakes
6½ cups (1½ L) vegetable
  stock
1 large head of broccoli,
  cubed, including the stem
10½ ounces (300 g) spinach
2 avocados, diced
sea salt and freshly ground
  black pepper
½ cup (20 g) watercress

tool
immersion blender or
  stand blender

The simplest soup in the world—so simple that I wasn't even sure whether I should include it here! But it's one I make often. I regularly use avocado as a thickening, creamy agent; that way I get a smooth, creamy soup without using any cream, and it's so nutritious. I'll often have this for lunch, and afterward I'm good to go for the afternoon. Feel free to add more ingredients as toppings, as described at the bottom of page 111.

Heat the olive oil in a large stockpot over medium heat. Add the onion, garlic, and chile flakes and sauté, stirring, until the onion is soft, and everything starts smelling good.

Pour in the vegetable stock and slowly bring to a boil. Add the broccoli and cook for about 15 minutes, until tender. Stir in the spinach and cook for 2 more minutes.

Add 1 cubed avocado. Puree the soup with an immersion blender or in a stand blender, but not until completely smooth. It's fine if you leave some pieces whole. Season the soup with salt and pepper.

Ladle the soup into four large bowls. Garnish with the rest of the avocado and a sprig of cress, and drizzle with olive oil.

SOUP

the Amsterdam kitchen

SAUCE / SALSA / TJAP

Almost every plate I serve contains sauce. Sauce is the cement of a dish. Without it, you'd just be eating a pile of ingredients. But a sauce holds it all together.

This can be a simple oil with a squeeze of lemon for the balance, or a sophisticated pan sauce based on a fond thickened by way of a *monter au beurre* (a fancy culinary term for binding with cold butter) technique. It all comes down to the same thing: connecting the ingredients on the plate and lending the dish flavor and character.

In salads, sauce is called dressing or vinaigrette; I'll devote a little story to that as well (you can find it, a little further ahead in the book, on page 150).

For every other dish, whether warm or cold, the sauce will have a different name, depending on the origin of the dish, the thickness of the sauce, or the ingredients. A sauce made with ground nuts and herbs, for instance, sometimes including a little cheese, oil, and lemon, is usually called a pesto. If it involves South or Central American ingredients, a pesto suddenly becomes a salsa. When the ingredients are Asian, I call the sauce *tjap*.

Once upon a time I was working at a Chinese restaurant and the *tjap* were the most important things I had to serve. Small ceramic dishes containing hoisin sauce, for instance, the requisite sauce for steamed buns with a savory filling.

The mother of all sauces is the sauce based on egg, oil, and an acid: mayonnaise. It's so incredibly easy to make at home that from now on, you'll be ashamed that you ever drizzled your exquisite "chest hair fries" (see page 241) with yucky industrial mayo.

The possibilities are endless. I've jotted down several variations on the following pages, but feel free to come up with better ones yourself.

MAKING MAYO

MAKES ABOUT 1 CUP (250 ML)

In a bowl, combine 1 egg yolk with pepper, salt, lemon juice, and 1 tsp mustard.

Whisking with a hand mixer, add ¾ c plus 1 tbsp (200 ml) sunflower oil, drop by drop at first.

Once the mayo coalesces, you can start pouring the oil in a thin stream.

Taste well and finish by seasoning the mayonnaise with pepper, salt, a spice or herb, another flavor that you like, or one more squeeze of acid.

SAUCE

MORE SAUCES

SMOKY MAYO

Smoky mayo works well with fish or crustaceans (like the prawns on page 371) or to enhance the flavor of things that are already smoky, like grilled vegetables or fries.

7 tablespoons (100 ml) mayonnaise (page 129)
splash of lemon juice
about 3 tablespoons yogurt
½ teaspoon smoked paprika
1 tablespoon whiskey, preferably peated or smoky, like Laphroaig
sea salt and freshly ground black pepper

Thoroughly combine all the ingredients with a whisk. Taste whether more acid (lemon juice), more freshness (yogurt), or more spice (whiskey) is needed. Add salt and pepper to taste.

MUSTARD THYME MAYONNAISE

I would add this mayo to a ham and cheese toastie, a Reuben sandwich, anything with pork, or roasted root vegetables, like celeriac.

4 tablespoons (60 ml) coarse mustard
2 tablespoons Dijon mustard
7 tablespoons (100 ml) mayonnaise (page 129)
1 teaspoon fresh thyme leaves
sea salt and freshly ground black pepper

Combine all the ingredients, then taste: does it need more acid (coarse mustard), more freshness (thyme), more spice (Dijon mustard)?

Finally, season some more with salt and pepper.

GREEN PEA, CAPER & MINT MAYO

Instead of green peas you can also use another vegetable—a cooked beet with dill or cilantro, or two handfuls of baby spinach with fresh basil leaves. I hope you understand what I'm getting at: experiment!

¾ cups (100 g) shelled peas (fresh or frozen)
sea salt
2 tablespoons capers, plus 1 tablespoon extra
2 tablespoons chopped fresh mint leaves
1 clove garlic, coarsely chopped
freshly ground black pepper
2 egg yolks
2 teaspoons sharp (Dijon) mustard
juice of 1 lemon
¾ cup plus 1 tablespoon (200 ml) canola oil or sunflower oil

tool
food processor or blender

Cook the peas in salted water for 4 to 5 minutes. Drain the peas and rinse with cold water.

In a food processor or blender, puree the green peas along with the 2 tablespoons capers, the mint, garlic, and, if you want, a pinch of salt (capers and mustard are salty already, so add carefully) and black pepper.

Add the egg yolks, mustard, and lemon juice and puree once more. With the food processor still running, pour in the oil in a thin stream until it starts to properly coalesce and thicken. At the end, add a drop of ice water. This will stabilize the mayo.

MUSHROOM MAYO

This one is so simple and yet so magnificent. Serve it with grilled asparagus—white or green, it doesn't matter. You simply *have* to make this.

3½ ounces (100 g) mushrooms, cleaned
juice of ½ lemon
4½ tablespoons (70 ml) mayonnaise (page 129)
freshly ground black pepper

tool
blender

Puree the mushrooms with the lemon juice in a blender to a smooth pulp. Add the mayonnaise and pulse the blender a few times until everything is combined well. Season the sauce with pepper.

CILANTRO AIOLI

1 clove garlic
1 egg yolk
sea salt
handful (½ ounce/15 g) of fresh cilantro leaves
grated zest and juice of 1 organic lime, or more
  juice to taste
about ¾ cup plus 1 tablespoon (200 ml) light
  olive oil
sea salt and freshly ground black pepper

tool
mortar and pestle, food processor, or blender

In a mortar or a small food processor or blender puree the garlic with the egg yolk, a pinch of sea salt, the cilantro, lime zest, and lime juice to a smooth sauce. While whisking or blending, add the olive oil in a very thin stream, until a thick mayonnaise forms.

If you want, add more lime juice, salt, and pepper. Store the cilantro aioli in the fridge.

MISO PESTO

This pesto has a strong, distinct flavor. That's how it should be; when you mix the pesto with pasta, the taste will mellow. See the recipe on page 254 for the pasta.

3 large bunches (each about ¾ ounce/20 g) basil
3 cloves garlic
2 brimming tablespoons white miso paste,
  or to taste
juice of ½ to 1 lemon
¼ cup (60 ml) olive oil, plus extra

tool
blender or food processor

Puree all the ingredients except the olive oil in a blender or food processor until smooth. Continue running the blender or food processor and slowly pour in the oil then add enough water to achieve a consistency that makes you happy.

Taste whether you are happy with the flavor balance. If you taste too little acid: add another squeeze of lemon. If you taste too much acid: add another drop of oil.

CASHEW-ARUGULA PESTO

scant ⅔ cup (75 g) whole cashews, briefly toasted
  in a dry skillet
1½ tablespoons white wine vinegar
1 bunch (½ ounce/15 g) flat-leaf parsley
4 ounces (115 g) arugula
about ¼ cup (60 ml) olive oil
sea salt and freshly ground black pepper

tool
blender or food processor

Puree the cashews, white wine vinegar, parsley, arugula, olive oil, and maybe a splash of water in a blender or food processor into a fine pesto. Season with salt and pepper.

SAUCE

the Irish garden, West Cork

ALMOND GARDEN HERB PESTO

1 bunch (½ ounce/15 g) basil
1 bunch (½ ounce/15 g) flat-leaf parsley
1 clove garlic, minced
⅓ cup (35 g) slivered almonds, briefly toasted in
  a dry skillet
about ⅔ cup (65 g) grated Parmesan cheese
zest of 1 organic lemon
about ¼ cup (60 ml) light olive oil
sea salt and freshly ground black pepper

tool
food processor

Puree the basil, parsley, garlic, almonds, Parmesan,
and half of the grated lemon zest in a food
processor into a smooth sauce.

While continuing to run the food processor, pour
in the olive oil in a thin stream until you get a
nice runny pesto. Season with salt and pepper
(and more of the zest, if needed).

MELON SALSA WITH TARRAGON

This is delicious on tacos (like those on page 373)
or to garnish a soup, or on a halved avocado as
an appetizer.

½ small, ripe cantaloupe, finely diced
1 red onion, chopped
juice of 2 limes
2 to 3 tablespoons finely chopped tarragon
1 jalapeño or other green chile, seeds and
  membrane removed, very finely chopped
a few drops of good-quality olive oil
pinch of sea salt

Stir together the cantaloupe, red onion, lime juice,
tarragon, and green chile. Refrigerate for 1 hour,
allowing the flavors to absorb. Fold in the olive oil
and salt.

FENNEL SEED ROUILLE

Serve with toasted or fried bread or croutons, and
crawfish and fennel soup (page 114).

1 red bell pepper (or one jarred roasted pepper,
  if you like)
2 to 3 cloves garlic
1 to 2 slices of white bread, crusts removed, cut
  into pieces
1 egg yolk
1 tablespoon Dijon mustard
juice of 1 lemon
1½ teaspoons fennel seeds, crushed in a mortar
sea salt and freshly ground black pepper
about 6½ tablespoons (100 ml) olive oil
pinch of cayenne pepper

tool
food processor

If using a fresh red bell pepper, preheat the oven
to 450°F (230°C). Roast the bell pepper for about
25 minutes, until the outside is blackened. Place
the pepper in a small heatproof bowl, place a plate
on top, and let the pepper cool. Remove the skin
and seeds.

In a food processor, puree the roasted bell pepper,
garlic, white bread, egg yolk, Dijon mustard,
lemon juice, fennel seeds, and sea salt and freshly
ground black pepper to a smooth sauce.

With the food processor running, pour in the
olive oil and blend until a thick sauce forms.
Season the fennel seed rouille with cayenne
pepper.

SAUCE

FAT-FREE SAUCES

All of these sauces can be stored in the fridge. Provided they're properly covered, they keep for at least a couple of days.

THAI GREEN SAUCE

1 tablespoon long-grain white rice
2 to 6 dried whole chiles, to taste
1 scallion, chopped
2 tablespoons chopped fresh mint leaves
2 tablespoons chopped fresh cilantro leaves
2 teaspoons sugar
3 tablespoons fish sauce
grated zest and juice of 1 organic lime

tool
mortar or small chopper

In a dry skillet over medium heat, fry the rice for 1 minute, or until light brown. In a mortar or a mini chopper, grind the rice along with the chiles to a coarse powder.

Add the scallion, mint, cilantro, sugar, fish sauce, and lime zest and juice and grind or chop briefly until the sugar has dissolved, but the sauce still has a coarse texture.

JALAPEÑO SALSA

5 to 6 fresh jalapeños, seeds and membranes removed, coarsely chopped
3 shallots, peeled and halved
2 to 3 tomatillos, or 1 to 2 yellow tomatoes, cut into wedges
4 cloves garlic
grated zest of 1 organic lime, juice of 1½ limes

1 coffee spoon sea salt
1 bunch (½ to ¾ ounce/15 to 20 g) cilantro

tool
blender or food processor

Puree all the ingredients in a blender or food processor until smooth. With the blender or food processor running, slowly pour water into the salsa until it has the desired consistency.

GREEN GODDESS

This is either a thick dressing, or a thin sauce. If you use it as a sauce—over the Veggie Sausages (page 209), for example—then opt for a thicker yogurt. If you instead prefer it thinner, for use as a dressing, then use a runnier yogurt or thin it out by adding a drop of water at the end.

1 scallion, chopped
2 to 3 anchovies, to taste
1 bunch (½ ounce/15 g) flat-leaf parsley
½ bunch (¼ ounce/7 g) chives
3 to 4 sprigs tarragon, stems removed
juice of 1 lemon
5 to 6 tablespoons (75 to 90 ml) yogurt or sour cream
sea salt and freshly ground black pepper

tool
blender or food processor

Puree the scallion, anchovies, parsley, chives, tarragon, and half of the lemon juice in a blender or food processor until smooth. Stop from time to time and use a spatula to scrape down any sauce from the sides.

Gently stir in the yogurt by hand. Blending or beating too fast will render the yogurt thin.

Check if the flavor is good. Does the sauce need more lemon juice, salt, or pepper?

Aran Islands

tartar sauce

hoisin

TARTAR SAUCE

PREPARE: 10 MINUTES
MAKES ENOUGH FOR
4 SERVINGS OF FRIES

1¼ cups (300 ml)
  mayonnaise (page 129)
scant 1 cup (100 g) drained
  capers, chopped
1 cup (150 g) finely
  chopped pickles
½ shallot, finely chopped
2 tablespoons chopped dill
2 tablespoons finely chopped
  chives
3 tablespoons finely chopped
  flat-leaf parsley
juice of ½ lemon

I use this mayonnaise-like sauce with everything. It is traditionally eaten with fried fish (such as the home made fish sticks on page 369), but I also use it as dip for my French fries or the "green fingers" on page 209. So yummy.

In a bowl, combine all of the ingredients, except for the lemon juice. Taste the sauce and add the lemon juice a splash at a time; you may not need all of it.

ROSE HIP KETCHUP

PREPARE: 1 HOUR
45 MINUTES
MAKES 3 TO 4 HALF-PINT
(250 ML) JARS

2¼ pounds (1 kg) rose hips,
  large ones halved
1 small clove garlic, finely
  chopped
2 large onions, finely chopped
3¼ pounds (1½ kg)
  tomatoes, cut into wedges
6½ tablespoons (100 ml)
  distilled white vinegar
¼ cup (60 g) firmly packed
  dark brown sugar
2 teaspoons grated fresh
  ginger
2 teaspoons paprika
1 clove
2 teaspoons freshly grated
  nutmeg
sea salt and freshly ground
  black pepper

tools
canning jars and flat lids
  with rings
blender

Pick rose hips that are nicely plump and somewhat soft. They should give a little when you squeeze them with your fingers—that's when you know they're sweet and ripe.

In a large pot, bring 1 cup (240 ml) water to a boil and add the rose hips, garlic, and onion. Cover with a lid and cook everything for 25 minutes over medium-high heat, or until the rose hips are tender. Add extra water if the liquid is evaporating too quickly.

Scoop the rose hips in batches into a strainer placed over a bowl and press them through with the back of a spoon. This is a bit of a chore but absolutely necessary in order to separate as much of the pulp from the seeds and skins as possible. If it's too difficult, stir in a splash of water. Return the rose hip pulp to the pan and add the tomatoes, vinegar, dark brown sugar, ginger, paprika, clove, and nutmeg. Bring the sauce to a boil and let simmer for about 1 hour over low heat, stirring occasionally to prevent burning. If needed, add water.

Sterilize canning jars as described on page 43 and keep them hot.

Puree the ketchup with an immersion blender, until smooth. Season with salt and pepper. Pour the hot ketchup into the hot sterilized jars and let cool completely, then put the lids and rings on. It will keep for months in the refrigerator, as long as you don't stick any dirty spoons in it.

HOISIN

PREPARE: 5 MINUTES
MAKES 10 TABLESPOONS
(150 ML) SAUCE

3 cloves garlic, grated
　(½ teaspoon)
½ teaspoon Chinese five-
　spice powder
3 tablespoons sunflower oil
4½ tablespoons (75 g)
　brown rice miso
3½ tablespoons liquid honey,
　or more if needed
3 tablespoons rice vinegar,
　or more if needed

Nowadays you can find five-spice powder in most supermarkets. If not, you should be able to buy it at an Asian supermarket, just like miso and rice vinegar.

Play around a little with the proportions and ingredients. I use a dark miso, made from brown rice, but a red miso would also work fine. Add more or less honey to taste and do the same with the vinegar: one makes a sour sauce, the other a sweeter one. This is how I make it. Hoisin is delicious with roasted meat, but also it's great as a seasoning for grilled or roasted vegetables, like the eggplant on page 229, for instance.

In a small saucepan over medium heat, fry the garlic and the five-spice powder in the sunflower oil for 30 seconds. Add the miso and honey and keep stirring until a sauce begins to form.

Add the rice vinegar to taste.

Stored in the fridge in a sealed container, the sauce will keep for weeks. Just like miso, really.

MUSTARD CAVIAR

PREPARE: 35 MINUTES
COOL: AT LEAST 1 HOUR

1½ teaspoons (100 ml) rice
　vinegar, or another vinegar,
　to taste
⅔ cup (100 g) mustard seeds
2 to 3 tablespoons granulated
　sugar
sea salt

Mustard caviar looks like white caviar but is in fact a very coarse mustard. It's terribly delicious because the seeds will gently pop in your mouth, and they have a light crunch to them. Scrumptious. The caviar goes well with everything from fish (see page 393) to cheese, and instantly turns any dish you serve it with into something quite chic.

Bring the vinegar and 6½ tablespoons (100 ml) water to a boil along with the mustard seeds. Add the sugar and salt to taste. Reduce the heat and simmer over very low heat for at least 30 minutes, stirring occasionally, until the seeds expand and the sauce is tasty. If the liquid evaporates too quickly, the heat is too high. In that case, reduce the heat and add a splash of vinegar and water.

Let the mustard caviar cool completely and store in a clean jar or container in the fridge. Refrigerated, it will keep for months. Use the mustard caviar as you would use coarse mustard.

SAUCE

HOME MADE HOT SAUCE

PREPARE: 20 MINUTES
MAKES 1 LARGE BOTTLE
(ALMOST 3 CUPS/700 ML)

20 fresh hot chiles of your
    choice: Lombok, jalapeño,
    habanero, or a mixture
scant 1½ cups (350 ml) light
    vinegar, but play around
    with it: each vinegar will
    have a different effect on
    the final result
½ teaspoon sea salt
3 cloves garlic, roughly
    chopped

tool
blender

I know: shelves in the supermarket or delicatessen are brimming with
hot sauces. And admittedly, there are some really tasty sauces among
them, but there are really yucky ones as well: too sweet, too sour, or
not spicy enough. You can find the solution below: MAKE YOUR OWN
SAUCE. Because, like to all home made goods, this rule applies: if you
make it yourself, you can cater to your own taste. You're making it for
yourself, after all, while a factory or small-batch producer aims its
wares at the largest possible consumer audience. Besides, making your
own condiments is fun: you get to see what goes into a bottle, and you
know what? Hot sauce is surprisingly easy to make from scratch.

Wearing food prep gloves, wash the chiles. Chile peppers contain
spicy oils, and if you get those on your fingers or under your
fingernails and you rub your eyes later, you'll be very unhappy. Trim
the tops off the chiles and halve them lengthwise.

Pour the vinegar into a saucepan, add the chiles, salt, and garlic.
Bring everything to a boil and reduce the heat. Simmer until the
chiles are soft, about 10 minutes.

Pour the chile mixture into your blender and process until
completely smooth. Store the hot sauce in the fridge in a clean bottle
or jar. The flavors will intensify somewhat after a few days.

If you have more patience, you can strain the sauce through a
cheesecloth-lined sieve. This will yield a more Tabasco-like sauce
that will keep even longer: refrigerated in a clean jar, at least for a
month or two.

SAUCE

SESAME RAYU

**PREPARE: 25 MINUTES
MAKES 1 JAR (ABOUT
300 ML)**

3½ tablespoons (50 ml) plus
6½ tablespoons (100 ml)
sunflower oil
6 cloves garlic, finely
chopped
5 tablespoons (75 ml)
sesame oil
3 slices of fresh ginger
1 bunch scallions (4 to 5),
white part only, very
finely chopped
1 dried hot chile, crumbled
2 tablespoons gochujang
2 heaping tablespoons
gochugaru, or to taste
1 tablespoon light soy sauce
6 tablespoons (55 g) roasted
sesame seeds

tool
canning jar and flat lid
with ring

GOCHUJANG

This Korean chile paste is
made from red peppers,
sticky rice, and fermented
soybeans. Contrary to what the
description suggests, it is—due
to the addition of rice—less hot
than, for example, sriracha.

GOCHUGARU

The basic seasoning for
kimchi: finely ground chile
flakes with just a bit of heat.
You can use it as a substitute
for other mild chile powders.

This crunchy Japanese chile oil is delicious in combination with a variety
of recipes, from noodles (page 273) to rice dishes (page 299), from
soups (page 119) to tacos and wraps (page 334)—or any dish that
could do with a little crunch and spice.

Sterilize a canning jar as described on page 43.

In a saucepan, heat the 3½ tablespoons (50 ml) sunflower oil, add the
garlic, and slowly fry it over very low heat until it browns nicely. Pour
the oil through a sieve placed over a bowl to strain out the garlic
(save the garlic), and return the garlic oil to the pan.

Pour the sesame oil and the remaining 6½ tablespoons (100 ml)
sunflower oil into the garlic oil in the saucepan. Add the ginger,
scallions, and crumbled dried chile. Sauté over low heat until the
scallions are evenly browned and caramelized.

Remove from the heat. Add the gochujang, gochugaru, soy sauce,
sesame seeds, and the reserved fried garlic and stir with a whisk,
thoroughly combining everything. Pour the oil mixture into the
sterilized canning jar, put the lid and ring on, and keep the sesame
rayu in the refrigerator. Provided you use a clean, dry spoon
whenever you scoop out any oil, this rayu keeps for at least a month.
That is, if you haven't finished it by then . . .

SAUCE

VEGETABLES & FRUITS

Farmers' market, Nieuwmarkt, Amsterdam

my kitchen in West Cork, Ireland

SALADS

my vegetable garden in Amsterdam

SALAD DRESSING

Salad dressings are made of an acid and a fat. When you whisk them, they come together (the official term is *emulsify*) and thus form a dressing for your salad.

Naturally, the amount of acid and fat (oil) you use is to taste, but there is a proportion that pretty much always works, 1:3. Meaning one part acid to three parts oil. The level of acidity of the sour ingredient also determines how much oil you should use in order to get a good balance.

The acidic ingredient you use can be any flavor: lemon juice, all kinds of vinegars, sour dairy, or fruit or vegetable juices.

The same goes for the fat: sunflower or grapeseed oil, olive oil, clarified butter, but also puréed avocado, for instance. It's up to you.

You can add all sorts of flavorings. I prefer to use mustard: it helps emulsify the vinaigrette and, due to its salty zest, it's basically a salt and pepper seasoning in one.

Anything goes, though: a finely chopped onion, a dab of mayonnaise or sour cream or yogurt, chopped green herbs, a drop of honey or soy sauce. You're the chef.

Always first dissolve the flavorings (including the salt!) in the acid component before you add the oil in a thin stream. And remember: choose the best ingredients you can afford, for that which doesn't have any flavor cannot be flavored.

So let's begin by making the base for a classic mustard vinaigrette. After that, you'll be able to make *any* dressing. By. Heart.

MAKING MUSTARD VINAIGRETTE

Pour 6½ tbsp (100 ml) white wine vinegar into a bowl. Add 1 to 2 tsp sharp mustard (to taste) and a pinch of salt.

Measure out three times as much oil (choose one with a neutral flavor, such as sunflower oil). So in this case 1¼ c (300 ml).

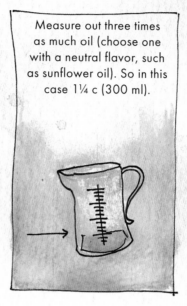

While whisking, pour in the oil in a very thin stream: this way the vinaigrette will emulsify nicely without curdling.

Season with salt and pepper. You can generally be a bit more indulgent than you think: once mixed with the lettuce, the flavor will soften.

Is the dressing too thick?

Finish by stirring in a few drops of ice-cold water until you get the desired thickness.

SALADS

~ 151 ~

MORE OIL-BASED SALAD DRESSINGS

NUT VINAIGRETTE

In this dressing you can replace part of a neutral-flavored oil with a more flavored one. Nut oils naturally have a distinct taste. Using only nut oil will result in an overpowering dressing. Therefore always mix it with a neutral-flavored oil, more or less neutral depending on the type of nut oil. In this recipe, one-third of the oil is nut oil. Make sure to taste it yourself. After all, you are chef and guest at the same time!

3½ tablespoons (50 ml) hazelnut or walnut oil
6½ tablespoons (100 ml) light-colored vegetable oil, such as sunflower or canola oil
3½ tablespoons (50 ml) white wine vinegar
sea salt and freshly ground black pepper

Whisk the oils into the white wine vinegar in a thin stream, then season with salt and pepper.

BUTTERMILK DRESSING

Instead of oil you can use mayonnaise in a dressing. You use oil and egg yolks to make mayo, after all (see page 129). Adjust the dressing's consistency by using more or less buttermilk (or thin yogurt or sour cream).

1 tablespoon cider vinegar
3 tablespoons sour cream or yogurt
3 tablespoons mayonnaise (see page 129 for home made)
⅓ cup (75 ml) buttermilk
1 small shallot, chopped
a few sprigs of chives, finely chopped
1 clove garlic, grated
sea salt and freshly ground black pepper

Whisk all the ingredients together to make a smooth dressing.

CAESAR SALAD DRESSING

In this dressing the oil has been replaced with mayonnaise and cheese. Use a blender or an immersion blender to puree the dressing until smooth. I use anchovies instead of salt. Of course you can adjust any of the amounts to taste.

¾ cup (75 g) grated Parmesan cheese
1 tablespoon white wine vinegar
½ cup (120 ml) mayonnaise (see page 129 for home made)
1 tablespoon spicy mustard
2 anchovies
freshly ground black pepper
1 small clove garlic, pressed

tool
blender or immersion blender

In a blender or with an immersion blender, combine all of the ingredients for the dressing into a creamy sauce. Add a few drops of ice-cold water if the dressing is too thick.

HONEY LEMON DRESSING

Although extra-virgin olive oil is delicious, it's less suited for use in a dressing because of its dominant flavor. Most of the time I find it too bitter, so I'll instead use a lightly colored, almost flavorless olive oil. Or I'll use grapeseed oil, which is mild as well and allows the flavors of the honey and lemon to come to the fore. That's what matters most, after all.

1 heaping tablespoon honey
juice of 1 lemon
grated zest of ½ organic lemon
1 tablespoon light mayonnaise
6½ tablespoons (100 ml) mild olive oil or grapeseed oil
sea salt and freshly ground black pepper

Dissolve the honey in the lemon juice, then stir in the lemon zest and mayonnaise. Whisk in the olive oil in a thin stream until the dressing has the desired thickness. Season with salt and pepper.

TARRAGON MUSTARD DRESSING

You can take the base of this dressing in any direction you like. Replace the tarragon with another herb. Use coarse or yellow mustard; replace the white wine vinegar with red wine vinegar or another kind. These changes will have a big flavor impact.

1 teaspoon mustard
zest of 1 small preserved lemon (optional!)
5 to 6 sprigs tarragon
3 to 4 tablespoons white wine vinegar
1 clove garlic, grated
about 6½ tablespoons (100 ml) light oil

tool
blender or immersion blender

Combine all the ingredients except the oil in a blender or with an immersion blender, then add the oil in a thin stream while continuing to blend.

ROMESCO DRESSING

generous ½ cup (75 g) blanched almonds
4 tablespoons (60 ml) mild olive oil
½ teaspoon smoked paprika
3 roasted sweet peppers, from a jar
½ teaspoon ground cumin
2 tablespoons red wine vinegar, plus extra
½ clove garlic
1 teaspoon harissa, plus extra
sea salt

tool
blender

In a skillet, toast the almonds in 1 tablespoon of the olive oil until they start to become fragrant. Sprinkle with the paprika and cook for 1 more minute. Let cool somewhat. Let the peppers drain and add them to a blender with the remaining 3 tablespoons oil and all the other ingredients. Puree everything to a smooth sauce. Puree longer than you think is necessary. Let stand for 15 minutes. The sauce will thicken slightly. Thin it out to the desired consistency with a splash of water. Season with some extra salt, more vinegar, or harissa.

WATERMELON VINAIGRETTE

1⅓ cups (200 g) peeled, seeded, and diced watermelon
3 tablespoons mustard
1 tablespoon ginger syrup or honey
1 to 2 tablespoons apple cider vinegar
3 tablespoons olive oil
sea salt and freshly ground black pepper

tool
blender or immersion blender

Combine the watermelon, mustard, ginger syrup, and vinegar in a blender or with an immersion blender, then add the oil in a thin stream while continuing to blend. Season with salt and pepper.

PERSIMMON DRESSING

If you puree a persimmon, skin and all, make a dressing out of it, and let it stand for a while, it will start to gel—I discovered. The dressing then resembles jam. In that case, add a drop of water and run the blender to liquify the dressing again. Delicious on a salad with cheese, like mozzarella, goat cheese, or feta.

½ to 1 persimmon (if the persimmon is the same size as an orange use ½ persimmon; if the persimmon is the size of a tomato, use a whole one)
juice of 1 lemon, plus extra
1 tablespoon pickled jalapeños (preferably red), or more to taste
⅓ cup (75 ml) olive oil
sea salt and freshly ground black pepper

tool
blender or immersion blender

Using a blender or immersion blender, puree the persimmon, lemon juice, and jalapeños to a smooth paste. With the blender running, pour in the oil in a thin stream. If you wish, you can thin the dressing with a drop of water. Add salt, pepper, and more lemon juice to taste.

DRESSINGS WITHOUT OIL

BÉARNAISE DRESSING

2 egg yolks, as fresh as possible
2 teaspoons Dijon mustard
2 sprigs tarragon, leaves only
juice of ½ small lemon
4 tablespoons (60 ml) yogurt
sea salt and freshly ground black pepper

tool
immersion blender

Using an immersion blender, combine the egg yolks with the Dijon mustard, tarragon, and lemon juice in a tall mixing container into a frothy and smooth dressing. Stir in some yogurt to taste. Sometimes this can be more and sometimes less yogurt than I indicated, for each yogurt has its own flavor and consistency. So you have to give it a taste. As you do, also check whether the dressing needs more salt. Finish the béarnaise with a generous twist of the pepper mill.

YOGURT LEMON DRESSING

½ red onion, chopped
½ lemon (preferably preserved)
2 tablespoons white wine vinegar
1 teaspoon honey
1 clove garlic, grated
1 teaspoon paprika
1 bunch (¾ ounce/20 g) flat-leaf parsley, leaves only, chopped
sea salt and freshly ground black pepper
3 to 4 tablespoons yogurt

tool
blender

Puree all the ingredients except the yogurt in a blender until smooth. Stir in the yogurt by hand; if you use the blender after adding the yogurt, the dressing will end up very thin.

APPLE MUSTARD DRESSING

2 tablespoons apple cider vinegar
1 shallot, chopped
1 heaping tablespoon Dijon mustard
2 teaspoons honey or maple syrup
sea salt and freshly ground black pepper
1 apple, peeled, cored, and cut into wedges
1 bunch (¾ ounce/20 g) flat-leaf parsley
1 bunch (¾ ounce/20 g) chives

tool
blender

Puree all the ingredients in a blender to a smooth paste. Add water until you get a thin dressing.

ITALIAN DRESSING

⅔ cup (100 g) cooked white beans, rinsed and drained
juice of ½ lemon, plus extra
1 large clove garlic, grated
1 teaspoon dried oregano
2 anchovies (optional)
sea salt (if you are not using anchovies) and freshly ground black pepper

tool
blender

Puree all the ingredients in a blender to a smooth paste. Add water until you get a thin dressing. Taste whether it needs more lemon juice.

CASHEW MISO DRESSING

3 to 4 tablespoons cashew cream (see page 119)
1 teaspoon white miso
grated zest and juice of ½ organic lemon
water or juice of your choice, depending on the salad: orange, apple, or tomato juice

Using a small whisk, beat all ingredients to a smooth sauce, adding water or juice to taste until the dressing has the desired consistency.

Galway, Ireland

RADISH & CAULIFLOWER SALAD WITH BUTTERMILK DRESSING

**PREPARE: 10 MINUTES
SERVES 4 FOR LUNCH OR
AS A SIDE DISH**

½ small cauliflower, very
   thinly shaved
1 bunch (7 ounces/200 g)
   radishes, cleaned and thinly
   shaved
1 Granny Smith apple,
   peeled and thinly shaved
a squeeze of lemon juice
sea salt
2 heads little gem lettuce,
   leaves separated
1 small handful
   (½ ounce/15 g) of fresh
   flat-leaf parsley leaves
buttermilk dressing
   (page 152)
1 tablespoon nigella seeds
   or black sesame seeds
   (optional; for more on
   nigella seeds, see page 12)

Toss the cauliflower, radishes, and apple together and immediately drizzle with the lemon juice and a pinch of salt. It's best to let it stand for 30 minutes so the vegetables soften a little, but you can move on right away.

Stir the little gem leaves and the flat-leaf parsley in with the salad, drizzle with the dressing, toss well until all the vegetables are coated with the dressing. Sprinkle the salad with nigella seeds.

THIN SLICING
I shave all my vegetables on a small Japanese mandolin from the Benriner brand. You can find them from other brands, too. They are fairly inexpensive and available in most cookware stores or online.

I find this slicer indispensable; everything looks better and more professional right away: wafer-thin sliced vegetables and fruit taste different from thick hand-cut slices as well.

Put one of these slicers on your wish list and give it a try. You will enjoy it for a lifetime, especially if you never put it in the dishwasher—but you never do that with any of your knives to begin with, do you? The salt in dishwasher detergent blunts your knives, so rinse them under running hot water immediately after use and dry them straightaway. That way they'll last longer.

Don't have a mandolin?
Use the slicing blade in your food processor (although it tends to smash things due to its speed) or carefully cut by hand, which, of course, is always an option.

SALADS

BRUSSELS SPROUTS–APPLE SALAD WITH PARMESAN

PREPARE: 20 MINUTES
SERVES 4 FOR LUNCH OR
AS A SIDE DISH

for the vinaigrette
1 small shallot, chopped
juice of at least ½ lemon
   (reserve the other half for
   the apples below)
1 small clove garlic, grated
1 to 2 tablespoons spicy
   mustard
about ¼ cup (60 ml) light
   olive oil
sea salt and freshly ground
   black pepper

for the salad
7 ounces (200 g) Brussels
   sprouts, cleaned
2 to 3 heads little gem lettuce
1 Pink Lady apple, or
   another slightly sweet red
   apple, unpeeled
squeeze of lemon juice
generous ½ cup (60 g) grated
   Parmesan cheese
generous ⅓ cup (50 g)
   sunflower seeds, briefly
   toasted in a dry skillet

Make the vinaigrette directly in the salad bowl: Combine the shallot with the lemon juice, the garlic, and mustard and, stirring continuously, add the olive oil in a thin stream until the vinaigrette emulsifies. Taste whether the vinaigrette needs more acidity or oil and season with salt and pepper.

Make the salad: Shave* or cut the Brussels sprouts into thin strips and mix directly with the dressing so that the acid and salt can soften the sprouts a bit as well as somewhat shrink them.

Cut the little gem into thin strips and the apple into thin slices. Drizzle lemon juice over the apple to prevent it from discoloring.

Just before serving, toss the lettuce, the Parmesan, and the apple with the Brussels sprouts, so that everything is coated with a thin layer of dressing. Sprinkle with the toasted sunflower seeds at the very last moment to keep them nice and crispy.

*See my musings on slicing on page 157.

SMASHED CUCUMBER, AVOCADO & PEACH SALAD

PREPARE: 15 MINUTES
WAIT: 15 MINUTES
SERVES 4 FOR LUNCH OR
AS A SIDE DISH

for the dressing
½ teaspoon coriander seeds,
   toasted in a dry skillet
½ teaspoon cumin seeds,
   toasted in a dry skillet
pinch of chile flakes
½ clove garlic
sea salt
grated zest and juice of
   1 organic lime
about ¼ cup (60 ml) good
   olive oil
freshly ground black pepper

for the salad
4 Persian cucumbers (about
   5 to 6 inches/12 to 15 cm),
   cut diagonally
3 ripe peaches, cut into
   wedges
1 large avocado, diced
1 bunch (½ ounce/15 g)
   flat-leaf parsley, roughly
   chopped
1 bunch (½ ounce/15 g) mix
   of lots of herbs: cilantro,
   verbena, lemon balm and/or
   mint, roughly chopped
generous ⅓ cup (50 g) hulled
   pumpkin seeds, briefly
   toasted in a dry skillet until
   puffed
1 teaspoon nigella seeds or
   sesame seeds
1 ball of burrata cheese

on the side
bread

This salad turned into my summer hit. I think I'm eating it weekly now; sometimes I use another kind of fruit: melon works, or other stone fruits such as nectarines, apricots, or plums in the fall.

Smashing the cucumbers isn't without purpose: when cucumbers are smashed (or bruised) instead of cut, the dressing won't slide off but be absorbed into each crack of the vegetable. Today supermarkets offer a wide variety of cucumbers; Persian cucumbers which are slightly sturdier than regular ones, are best suited for this dish. But don't worry, when they're unavailable, I just as easily use regular ones. It's really easy to grow these small cucumbers on a balcony, by the way. My plants regularly give baby cucumbers all throughout the summer. So cheerful.

Make the dressing: In a mortar, grind the spices along with the garlic and some salt. Stir in the lime zest and juice and pour in the olive oil in a thin stream, whisking, until the dressing emulsifies nicely. Taste: Does it need more salt, acid, or oil? Adjust to your taste if necessary.

Use the pestle of the mortar or something heavy—such as a rolling pin or the blade of a heavy knife—to slightly bruise the cucumber pieces, so they will absorb more dressing and it will slide off less easily. Combine the bruised cucumber pieces, peach wedges, avocado cubes, and fresh herbs with nearly all of the dressing. Let stand for a while to let the flavors infuse.

Serve the salad sprinkled with crunchy pumpkin seeds and nigella seeds and a large ball of burrata on the side. If you have a drop of dressing left, you can drizzle the burrata with it. Serve with bread.

This dressing requires a mortar. The flavors will really mix much better. Buy one if you don't have one.

~ 161 ~

BROCCOLI STALK SLAW

PREPARE: 15 MINUTES
WAIT: PREFERABLY
30 MINUTES
SERVES 4 AS A SIDE DISH

for the salad
2 to 3 stalks broccoli, the
    small florets removed and
    saved for something else
1 Granny Smith apple,
    peeled and cored
a few drops of lemon juice
1 bunch (¾ ounce/20 g)
    cilantro, finely chopped
grated zest of 1 organic
    lemon
1½ teaspoons black mustard
    seeds or black sesame seeds,
    briefly toasted in a dry
    skillet until they pop

for the dressing
3 tablespoons mayonnaise
    (see page 129)
juice of 1 lemon
1 tablespoon spicy mustard
sea salt and freshly ground
    black pepper

Reduce waste; use up everything! This also means: eating the stalks. As long as they're thinly sliced, broccoli stalks make for a delicious salad ingredient. Think coleslaw 2.0. Use the broccoli florets in a different recipe—the Pasta with Broccoli, Lemon & Mozzarella on page 263. for instance.

Peel the broccoli stalks, using a vegetable peeler. Cut the stalks into matchsticks or razor-thin strips, using a slicer or a food processor. Do the same with the apple. In a bowl, combine the broccoli with the apple and sprinkle with a few drops of lemon juice to prevent discoloration.

Beat the mayonnaise, lemon juice, and mustard into a thick dressing. Season with salt and pepper and, if needed, thin with a splash of water. Drizzle the dressing onto the salad. Let the slaw stand for about 30 minutes, allowing the broccoli to shrink and soften somewhat, which will make it tastier.

Mix in the cilantro into the slaw, sprinkle with grated lemon zest, mustard seeds or sesame seeds, and serve.

You can also make this dish with a cauliflower stalk!
*
The same goes for any root vegetable, by the way, from kohlrabi to raw beets: yummy.

SALADS

ENDIVES WITH CAULIFLOWER COUSCOUS, APPLE & MAGOR

PREPARE: 20 MINUTES
SERVES 4 AS A SIDE DISH,
OR 8 AS AN APPETIZER

¼ cauliflower, cut into florets
1 green apple, such as
    Granny Smith, peeled,
    cored, and cut into
    matchsticks
juice of 1 lemon
⅓ cup (75 ml) olive oil
1 clove garlic, crushed
1 cup (100 g) walnuts,
    roasted and roughly
    chopped
1 large bunch (1 ounce/25 g)
    flat-leaf parsley, roughly
    chopped
sea salt and freshly ground
    black pepper
3 heads endive, leaves
    separated
2½ ounces (70 g) magor
    cheese (or gormas, which
    is the same cheese with
    another name)
1 tablespoon pink
    peppercorns, crumbled
    (optional)

This is a delicious light appetizer, but it's also perfectly suited to being served as a salad—alongside roasted chicken or sausage, for example. You could even turn it into a dinner salad by spooning in chickpeas or those small dark du Puy lentils. The possibilities are endless. Magor is a delicious combination of creamy mascarpone and blue gorgonzola. If you can't find it, try another creamy blue cheese, fresh goat cheese, or crumbled feta.

Over a bowl, grate the cauliflower to crumbs the size of couscous. Add the apple matchsticks. Sprinkle with some of the lemon juice to prevent discoloration.

Heat the olive oil along with the crushed garlic over low heat. Let the oil simmer for 5 minutes. Scoop out the garlic clove, let cool somewhat, and press over a bowl. Set aside.

In a bowl, toss the walnuts and the flat-leaf parsley with the cauliflower couscous. Whisk the rest of the lemon juice and the crushed garlic in with the garlic oil. Season the dressing with salt and pepper. Drizzle the salad with it and let stand for 10 minutes to allow the flavors to infuse.

Fill each of the endive leaves with a spoonful of salad and crumble the magor on top. Sprinkle the endive boats with the pink peppercorns and serve immediately.

SALADS

CHICKPEA SALAD WITH SARDINES

for the salad

2 cans (about 3½ ounces/
    100 g each) sardines in oil,
    drained and cleaned (leave
    them whole)
1 can (14 ounces/400 g)
    chickpeas, drained and
    rinsed (dried chickpeas
    soaked and then cooked
    and drained is even better)
½ cucumber, cut into small
    cubes
heaping 1 cup (175 g)
    crumbled feta cheese
3 tablespoons Taggiasca
    olives, pitted (see below)
1 small handful (½ ounce/
    15 g) fresh mint leaves,
    roughly chopped
1 large handful (¾ ounce/
    20 g) baby spinach
1 bunch (½ ounce/15 g)
    chives, finely chopped

for the dressing

grated zest and juice of
    1 organic lemon
½ teaspoon ground cumin
1½ teaspoons smoked paprika
¼ teaspoon cayenne pepper,
    or to taste
sea salt
3 to 4 tablespoons olive oil
1 small red onion, cut into
    wafer-thin rings

finishing touch

3 tablespoons olive oil
1 handful of panko or fresh
    breadcrumbs
sea salt and freshly ground
    black pepper

This is my summer "go-to" salad. Sometimes I'll soak and cook a whole bag of chickpeas to keep in the fridge in a container so I can simply scoop out what I need for making this salad each day. Then I'll have it for lunch until I run out, with a new can's worth of sardines on top each time. Without the fish works fine too, though. Addictive nonetheless.

Carefully place the sardines on a paper towel. You can remove the bones by halving the sardines first. I never do that.

Make the dressing: In a bowl, mix the lemon zest with the lemon juice, ground cumin, smoked paprika, cayenne, and salt. Whisk in the olive oil until the dressing has emulsified. Stir in the onion and let stand for 10 minutes, allowing the onion to soften.

Make the salad: Add the chickpeas, cucumber cubes, feta, olives, mint leaves, baby spinach, and chives to the dressing. Toss the salad well.

In a skillet, heat the olive oil and fry the panko until brown and crispy. Season the crumbs with salt and black pepper.

Divide the salad between two plates if you are serving it as a lunch or main course and between four plates if the salad is an appetizer or side dish. Arrange the sardines on top and sprinkle each plate with the fried crumbs.

TAGGIASCA OLIVES

Yes, of course you can also use tasty black olives. But these little sun-ripened olives from Liguria are my preference.

They have a very subtle taste, almost sweet, slightly nutty, and they lack the bitterness you associate with green olives.

They can be found in the Italian section at most supermarkets, in jars of olive oil, always pitted.

BEAN SALAD WITH CRUNCHY HALLOUMI CHIPS & RED JALAPEÑO DRESSING

PREPARE: 25 MINUTES
SERVES 2 AS A LUNCH,
OR 4 AS A SIDE DISH

sea salt
1¾ cups (200 g) freshly
  shelled or frozen fava beans
1⅓ cups (200 g) freshly
  shelled or frozen peas
1 cup (100 g) diagonally
  sugar snap peas
1¾ cups (200 g) diagonally
  cut haricots verts or green
  beans
scant 1 cup (200 g) riso or
  orzo (rice-shaped pasta)
2 tablespoons olive oil
8 ounces (225 g) halloumi
  cheese, very thinly sliced
6 sprigs mint, leaves only
1 tablespoon grated organic
  lemon zest
freshly ground black pepper

for the jalapeño dressing
1 tablespoon pickled
  jalapeños (preferably red),
  or more to taste
juice of 1 lemon
sea salt
⅓ cup (75 ml) olive oil

tool
blender or immersion
  blender

Because it has been sliced razor thin and fried to a crisp, the halloumi in this salad resembles salty chips. And that's exactly what this salad needs. Tasty!

In a large saucepan, bring water to a boil, add salt, and blanch each of the different beans separately for a few minutes, until al dente. Scoop them out of the cooking water with a small sieve. Rinse them with cold water in a colander to stop the cooking process. If desired, shell the fava beans a second time (see page 174). Transfer to a large bowl.

If necessary, add some more water to the pan. Bring to a boil again and then cook the pasta according to directions on package. Drain in the colander. Rinse the pasta with cold water as well. Add to the peas and beans in the bowl.

Heat the olive oil in a large skillet over high heat and fry the halloumi slices for 2 minutes on either side, or until crisp and browned. Set aside.

Spoon the mint leaves and the finely grated lemon zest into the salad and season with salt and pepper.

Make the dressing: Puree the jalapeños and lemon juice using a blender or immersion blender until smooth. Season with salt. With the blender still running, pour in the olive oil in a thin stream until the dressing thickens. Drizzle the salad with the dressing, sprinkle with the halloumi chips, and serve immediately.

SALADS

BABY SUMMER SQUASH, YELLOW TOMATOES, FRESH RICOTTA & THYME OIL

PREPARE: ABOUT
30 MINUTES
SERVES 4 AS A STARTER
OR SIDE DISH

1 bunch (¾ ounce/20 g) thyme, thoroughly washed and dried

6½ tablespoons (100 ml) olive oil (preferably a young, grassy one—often referred to as novello)

1 teaspoon grated organic lemon zest

splash of lemon juice

sea salt and freshly ground black pepper

1 pound 1 ounce (500 g) zucchini and summer squash, as small as possible, in different colors: yellow and green

1 pound 1 ounce (500 g) yellow tomatoes, thinly sliced

pinch of chile flakes

pinch of salt flakes, preferably Maldon or fleur de sel

1 cup (250 g) fresh ricotta cheese (or baked ricotta; see below)

for decoration

I used bronze fennel and marigold petals from my polytunnel (see page 188), but I'm sure you'll be able to also find some beautiful garnish in your garden or patio planter.

This recipe is great for the abundance of zucchini every summer. Visit a farmers' market in the summer and you'll find crates brimming with beautiful small baby summer squash that you can eat raw.

Secretly, the point of this recipe is that it's an excuse to eat delicious fresh ricotta. Not the kind you buy from the supermarket in one of those plastic containers but one you've schlepped all the way to the real artisanal cheesemonger to buy. Once you've had a taste of that heavenly ricotta you'll never want to eat industrial cheese again.

Ricotta is Italian for "re-cooked": when mozzarella is made, the fresh milk is separated from the whey and curds. The curds are made into mozzarella and the whey is cooked once more to make ricotta. So although ricotta contains much less fat, it does have that full-bodied flavor that makes mozzarella so alluring.

Crush the thyme in a mortar or on a cutting board using the dull side of a knife. Pour the olive oil into a saucepan, add the thyme sprigs, and heat the oil slightly—not too hot, or the thyme will scorch. Remove from the heat and let the oil steep, covered, for 20 minutes. Remove the sprigs—loose leaves may stay behind in the oil. Season the thyme oil with grated lemon zest, a few drops of lemon juice, and salt and pepper.

Slice the squash very thinly or use a mandolin slicer (see page 157). Drizzle with half of the thyme oil. Arrange the squash on a nice platter and sprinkle the tomatoes, chile flakes, and salt flakes on top.

Place the fresh ricotta in the center, drizzle with thyme oil, and sprinkle the salad with fresh greens from the windowsill or garden.

DON'T HAVE ANY FRESH RICOTTA? MAKE BAKED RICOTTA

5 tablespoons (75 ml) olive oil
2 cloves garlic, sliced
1 teaspoon grated organic lemon zest
1 red chile, seeded and finely chopped
1 teaspoon fresh thyme leaves
pinch of sea salt
1 cup (250 g) supermarket ricotta

Preheat the oven to 400°F (200°C).

Mix the olive oil with all ingredients except the ricotta. Plop the ricotta from its container into an oven dish, sprinkle with the herb oil, and bake for 30 minutes, or until golden and puffed.

fava bean salad, asparagus & cumber ribbons

DOUBLE-SHELLING FAVA BEANS

VERY YOUNG FAVA BEANS CAN BE EATEN RAW. THE ITALIANS LIKE EATING THEM THAT WAY WITH SOME CHEESE.

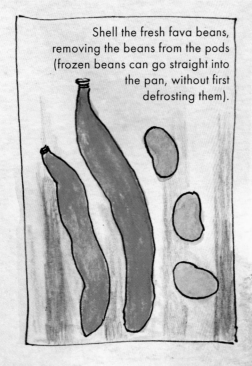

Shell the fresh fava beans, removing the beans from the pods (frozen beans can go straight into the pan, without first defrosting them).

Note: 2¼ lb (1 kg) fava bean pods yields 2 to 2⅓ c (300 to 350 g) shelled beans.

Cook the fava beans in a pan with ample water, adding no salt, for salt will make the beans' skin tough—they say (in case you don't intend to double-shell them).

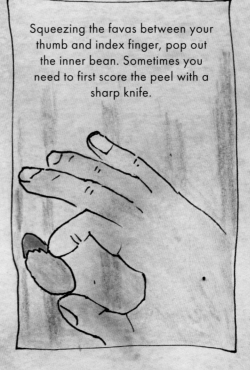

Squeezing the favas between your thumb and index finger, pop out the inner bean. Sometimes you need to first score the peel with a sharp knife.

FAVA BEAN SALAD, ASPARAGUS & CUMBER RIBBONS

PREPARE: 30 MINUTES
SERVES 4 AS A LUNCH OR SIDE DISH

1 cucumber
sea salt
buttermilk dressing (see page 152)
1 bundle (about 16 stalks) asparagus, woody ends snapped off
1⅔ cups (250 g) shelled fava beans
1 bunch (½ ounce/15 g) mint, just the leaves
½ bunch (¼ ounce/8 g) dill, coarsely chopped
thinly peeled zest of 1 organic lemon, sliced into strips

Use a vegetable peeler to shave the cucumber into long ribbons. Place the ribbons in a strainer placed over a bowl and sprinkle them with salt. Let drain for 30 minutes (while you make the dressing).

Double-shell the fava beans; it isn't a must, but you can do it in no time and your guests will be so grateful to you. By the way, see page 174 for more information about double-shelling fava beans.

In a salad bowl, combine the fava beans with the asparagus, mint, dill, and lemon zest strips. Gently squeeze the cucumber to remove excess water and arrange the cucumber ribbons in the bowl. Serve the salad drizzled with the dressing.

QUICK GREEN SALAD WITH STEAMED MACKEREL

PREPARE: 10 MINUTES
SERVES 4 AS A LUNCH OR SIDE DISH

buttermilk or honey lemon dressing (see page 152)
10½ ounces (300 g) arugula
2 heads little gem lettuce, cut into strips
2 Granny Smith apples, with peel, cored
grated zest and juice of ½ organic lemon
2 steamed mackerels
3 to 4 tablespoons garden cress or other microgreens

Make the dressing.

Combine the arugula with the little gem. Cut the apples into thin matchsticks. Sprinkle the apple with lemon juice to prevent discoloration.

Pull the meat from the mackerels and shred it coarsely. Add it to the salad and toss everything together.

Drizzle the salad with the dressing, sprinkle with cress and lemon zest, and serve straightaway in four deep plates.

SALADS

pot over fire in the Irish garden

Galway, Ireland

FRESH PLUM SALAD WITH FENNEL, HERBS & MOZZA

PREPARE: 15 MINUTES
SERVES 4 AS A SIDE DISH,
OR 2 FOR LUNCH

for the vinaigrette
¼ cup (60 ml) light olive oil
2 tablespoons red wine
    vinegar
1 tablespoon mustard
    vinaigrette (see page 151)
but the watermelon
    vinaigrette on page 153
    isn't a bad choice either

for the salad
10½ ounces (300 g) red
    plums, halved and pitted
1 fennel bulb, thinly sliced*
7 ounces (200 g) baby lettuce
    leaves, or the heart of
    1 frisée lettuce, leaves torn
2 balls buffalo mozzarella,
    shredded
handful (½ ounce/15 g) of
    fresh basil leaves, torn
handful (½ ounce/15 g) of
    other fresh herbs (I like to
    pick, in the garden, yarrow,
    arugula, and fennel tops,
    but this combination is not
    a must)
pinch of salt flakes (for
    example Maldon) and
    freshly ground black
    pepper

to serve
crunchy bread

I make this recipe with plums here, but any type of stone fruit is delicious. Cherries in the summer, or nectarines—no wait: even tasty cantaloupe wedges wouldn't be out of place here. Go for it.

In a bowl, combine all the ingredients for the vinaigrette. Add the plums and allow the flavors to infuse for 10 minutes.

In a large bowl, combine the fennel with the lettuce leaves. Add the vinaigrette and marinated plums and the buffalo mozzarella and toss.

Sprinkle the salad with the basil leaves, other fresh herbs, and salt flakes and pepper. Serve the salad with crunchy bread.

*See page 157 for why I love using a mandolin to slice vegetables like this.

> ### EDIBLE FLOWERS FROM THE WINDOWSILL
>
> Every fresh herb plant you buy will—if you take good care of it—at some point grow and produce beautiful flowers. The flowers are edible and they are perfect for using in a dish like this one! Think of herbs like mint, basil, arugula, chives, or thyme.

SALADS

PEELING STONE FRUITS

For peaches, nectarines, tomatoes, or even grapes (anything with a skin) score a cross mark on the top and bottom with a sharp knife.

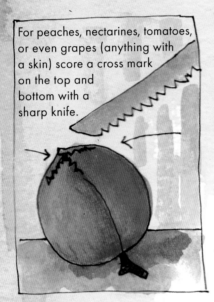

Bring a large pan of water to a boil.

Plop in the fruits and blanch for 30 seconds.

Immediately scoop the fruits out and slide them into a bowl of ice-cold water (preferably with some ice cubes). Now you can easily rub off the peels.

peach tomato salad with chorizo & feta

PEACH TOMATO SALAD WITH CHORIZO & FETA

PREPARE: 15 MINUTES
SERVES 4 AS A LUNCH OR
SIDE DISH

1 pound 10 ounces (750 g)
   ripe peaches (about 4)
1 pound 10 ounces (750 g)
   ripe tomatoes (about 4), or
   2 handfuls cherry tomatoes
3 tablespoons olive oil
1 cured chorizo sausage
   (8 ounces/250 g), cut into
   thin slices
sea salt and freshly ground
   black pepper
1 bunch (½ ounce/15 g)
   cilantro, leaves only
1 bunch (½ ounce/15 g)
   mint, leaves only
⅔ cup (100 g) crumbled feta
   cheese
a few drops of good balsamic
   vinegar

Peel the peaches using the method on page 180. Cut them into wedges. Place the wedges in a large bowl.

Cut the tomatoes into wedges of the same size, then add them to the bowl.

Pour the olive oil over the peaches and tomatoes. Fold the chorizo into the salad and season with salt and pepper. Just before serving, sprinkle with cilantro, mint, and feta. Drizzle the salad with a splash of balsamic vinegar and serve.

WATERMELON, ORANGE & FETA SALAD WITH TARRAGON

PREPARE: 15 MINUTES
SERVES 4 AS A LUNCH OR
SIDE DISH

about 1 pound 1 ounce
   (500 g) watermelon,
   preferably seedless, peeled
   and cut into slices
1 large orange, cut into
   segments (see page 303)
1 small red onion, thinly
   sliced
½ cup (75 g) crumbled feta
   cheese
1 bunch (¾ ounce/20 g)
   flat-leaf parsley, leaves only
2 tablespoons finely chopped
   fresh tarragon
2 tablespoons olive oil
sea salt and freshly ground
   black pepper

Arrange the ingredients on a large, shallow dish. Start with the watermelon, and place the orange wedges on top. Garnish with the red onion rings and the crumbled feta and sprinkle with parsley and tarragon.

Drizzle the salad with a delicious olive oil and season with salt and pepper.

SALADS

HOME MADE STRACCIATELLA

Stracciatella is Italian for, let's say, "tiny shred." A dish with the same name can refer to a clear soup containing pieces of egg and Parmesan, ice-cream with chocolate bits in it, or—in this case—insanely fresh cheese, without shape or rind but made from the most delicious fresh cream and with very finely chopped shreds of curd.

To make it even more clear: you are familiar with mozzarella, and perhaps you also know burrata, a kind of "bag" made of mozzarella cheese with a super-creamy mozzarella-like filling. A seductive soft cheese that, seasoned with only a drop of peppery olive oil and a pinch of black pepper, you can serve alongside just a few leaves of lettuce.

If you are someone who buys this burrata just for its filling you are probably, like me, a lover of stracciatella. In the Netherlands it's pretty difficult to find, because it really needs to be served fresh and cheesemongers don't want to have it in stock for too long. Often they are able to order it for you. I decided to imitate it at home using a store-bought ball of burrata. Naturally: actual fresh stracciatella is even better, but I got away with faking it this time.

PREPARE: 7 MINUTES | MAKES ABOUT 10½ OUNCES (300 G)

1 ball burrata (8 ounces/250 g), 2 tablespoons buttermilk, 3 to 4 tablespoons heavy cream, pinch of sea salt

Very finely chop the burrata. Stir it into the buttermilk and add just enough cream so the cheese won't run off a plate but remains in place like a dab of thin yogurt. Season with a pinch of salt.

SALADS

STRACCIATELLA WITH LEEKS & OYSTER MUSHROOMS

PREPARE: 45 MINUTES
BAKE: 45 MINUTES
SERVES 4 AS A STARTER OR
SIDE DISH

2 leeks
4 tablespoons (60 ml) olive
   oil + about 6½ tablespoons
   (100 ml)
sea salt and freshly ground
   black pepper
splash of lemon juice
canola or other neutral oil
5¼ ounces (150 g) oyster
   mushrooms, the larger ones
   shredded
9 ounces (250 g) stracciatella
   cheese (see page 185)
handful of croutons
2 tablespoons garden cress

tool
blender

MAKING CROUTONS

stale (sourdough) bread
olive oil
sea salt and freshly ground
   black pepper

Preheat the oven to 350°F
(180°C). Tear the bread into
very small pieces. Tearing the
pieces gives them more texture
than cutting them, and thus
they'll become crispier.
   Spread them out on a
parchment paper–lined
baking sheet. Drizzle with
olive oil and sprinkle with salt
and pepper. Thoroughly mix
everything. Bake for about
12 minutes, depending on the
size of the croutons.

If you can't buy or order fresh *stracciatella di buffalo* at your cheesemonger, you can also make it yourself (see page 185).

Preheat the oven to 400°F (200°C).

Cut the leeks in half lengthwise, thoroughly wash out the sand, and trim the dark green part and the root end. Keep the greens.

Cut the white parts of each leek into 3 equal pieces and place them on a parchment paper–lined baking sheet. Drizzle with the 4 tablespoons (60 ml) olive oil and sprinkle with salt and pepper. Cover the baking sheet with aluminum foil and slide it into the oven.

Bake the leeks for 30 minutes. Remove the aluminum foil and bake the leeks for another 15 minutes, or until they are golden brown on the outside and soft on the inside.

Puree 1¾ ounces (50 g) of the washed leek greens in the blender to a smooth paste. Add a splash of lemon juice and a pinch of salt. While the machine continues to run, pour about 6½ tablespoons (100 ml) olive oil into the leeks in a thin stream until a smooth green pulp forms. Let the machine run for a while; it won't take any effort, because it does the job for you. The smoother the better.

Pour the pulp into a tea sieve that you've placed over a pitcher or bowl and strain the bright green oil while moving on with the preparation.

Pour a drop of regular olive oil into a skillet and fry the oyster mushrooms until golden brown and crispy on the edges. Sprinkle with salt and pepper.

Pour the stracciatella onto a large plate. Arrange the roasted leeks and then the fried oyster mushrooms on top. Sprinkle with croutons and cress, drizzle with the green oil, and serve.

SALADS

my completely grown-out polytunnel, which, like a greenhouse, extends our growing season in Ireland

Our garden, Ireland

QUICK PICKLING

RICE VINEGAR
10 TBSP (150 ML)

1½ TBSP GRANULATED SUGAR

2 TBSP SALT

300 GRAM SLICED VEG

In a bowl, stir the sugar and salt into the vinegar until the sugar and salt have dissolved.

Add the vegetables and let them marinate for 10 to 15 minutes. It works even better if you briefly massage everything with clean hands.

IN THIS PICKLING LIQUID, VEGETABLES WILL KEEP FOR A DAY OR THREE IN THE FRIDGE.

NEW POTATO SALAD WITH RADISH & YOGURT WITH PICKLED CUCUMBER & HERRING

PREPARE: 25 MINUTES
SERVES 4 AS A MAIN
COURSE

sea salt
1 pound 1 ounce (500 g)
  purple potatoes or new
  potatoes, cut into pieces
10½ ounces (300 g) pickled
  radishes and cucumber
  (see page 191), thinly sliced
splash of vinegar
2 bunches scallions, sliced
  into thin rings
1 large bunch (1 ounce/25 g)
  cilantro or flat-leaf parsley,
  leaves only
10 tablespoons (150 ml)
  yogurt
freshly ground black pepper
2 tablespoons nigella seeds*
  or black sesame seeds
2 pots (1¾ pounds/800 g)
  pickled herring fillets,
  drained

*See explanation on page 12.

"Pickling" might sound like a lot of work, but what if I teach you a hassle-free method to quick pickle? Then you may want to give it a try. Pickled vegetables are delicious, after all: who doesn't like the occasional kosher dill pickle or a pickled onion? Quick pickling doesn't require any tricky canning procedures or boiling or sterilizing jars. None. It's not about preserving vegetables for months—a few more days in the fridge is already a big plus. Refrigerated vegetables will last longer when you leave them in a sour liquid.

The coolest part is that you can adjust the recipe to your own taste completely: each vinegar has a different flavor and therefore an immediate effect on your pickled goods. Add herbs or spices to pull your pickles in the direction of your main dish. Think yellow—turmeric!—atjar that goes with an Indonesian stew, or sour cucumber slices with caraway on a fried fish.

Basically you can use any hard vegetable—carrots, for example—or cucumber, or a blanched green bean. Make sure the vegetables aren't too thick; if needed, slice them. You should be able to quickly pickle them and that won't really work if you plop a bunch of whole winter carrots in a bowl of vinegar. For this recipe I will use all kinds of radishes, which are particularly pickle friendly: instantly ready, really, for the happiest salad you ever saw.

In a pan with ample boiling salted water, cook the potatoes until al dente, about 18 minutes. Drain them and crush them slightly with a pestle to help them absorb the dressing.

Combine the potatoes with the pickled radish and cucumber, adding a splash of vinegar. Add the scallions and cilantro or flat-leaf parsley.

Spoon the yogurt into the salad. Taste if it needs more salt and pepper. Sprinkle the salad with nigella or sesame seeds.

Divide the salad among four plates. Place the pickled herring on top of the salads and serve immediately.

SALADS

SPICY STRAWBERRIES WITH FETA CREAM

PREPARE: 10 MINUTES
WAIT: PREFERABLY 6 HOURS
OR LONGER, TO LET THE OIL
STEEP
SERVES 4 AS A STARTER

3 tablespoons olive oil
1 teaspoon chile flakes
½ cup (75 g) crumbled
    feta cheese
⅓ cup (75 ml) Greek yogurt
9 ounces (250 g)
    strawberries, quartered,
    large ones in even smaller
    wedges
1 tablespoon sesame seeds,
    briefly toasted in a dry
    skillet
10 fresh mint leaves,
    shredded

tool
food processor

Our village in Ireland, a wee little hamlet surrounded by farmland, cows, and the sea, is home to a surprisingly fine restaurant. Completely unexpected. It's called Pilgrim's and is always packed—and rightly so.

Once I had this particular little dish there. It has been on my mind ever since and I hope I can replicate it here. It's important to use the most delicious, sweet strawberries, so right in the middle of the summer season. The famous Wexford strawberry (a nearby county) would be perfect, for example.

Mix the olive oil with the chile flakes and let stand for as long as possible, so the oil can absorb the spicy flavor.

Chop the feta in a small chopper until smooth. Pulse in the yogurt. Do not pulse for too long, or the yogurt will get too thin.

Pour the chile oil over the strawberries and sprinkle with sesame seeds and mint leaves. Serve the spicy strawberries with a generous dollop of the fresh creamy feta on the side. Tasty, right?

SALADS

VINE
TOMATOES
£2.80
KG

vegetable stall at Borough Market, London

VEGETABLE DISHES

BIO (IT)
FINOCCHI
€1,80 KG

the vegetable stall at a Bologna street market

Isa and Dara make coconut curry

coconut curry with eggplant and naan

COCONUT CURRY WITH EGGPLANT

PREPARE: 35 MINUTES
SERVES 4 AS A MAIN
COURSE

for the curry paste
1 to 3 red chiles (to taste),
  seeded if you'd like less heat
  and chopped
6 cloves garlic, finely chopped
2 inches (5 cm) fresh ginger,
  peeled and minced
2 stalks lemongrass, tough
  outer leaves removed, inner
  leaves chopped
2 tablespoons ground turmeric
1 teaspoon paprika

for the coconut curry
2 to 3 tablespoons sunflower
  oil, plus extra
2 to 3 eggplants (about 1⅓
  pounds/600 g), quartered
  lengthwise, and sliced on
  the bias into long pieces
6 shallots, finely chopped
1 tablespoon ginger syrup,
  honey, or sugar
1 tablespoon Thai fish sauce
  or light, salty soy sauce
1 can (13½ ounces/400 ml)
  coconut milk
1⅔ cups (400 ml) vegetable
  broth
scant ¾ cup (100 g) whole
  blanched almonds
sea salt and freshly ground
  black pepper
1 bunch (½ ounce/15 g)
  cilantro or flat-leaf parsley,
  leaves only coarsely
  chopped

for serving
naan (optional; see page 205)

tool
mortar or food processor

Curries are so convenient and super fast. These can be made vegan and are secretly even more delicious the next day. So perfect for making them a day in advance, or on a weekday. I'll give you a few curry recipes at once so you can mix it up all you want.

Make the curry paste: In a mortar or food processor, grind the chiles, garlic, ginger, lemongrass, turmeric, and paprika into a paste. If the consistency is too thick, add a splash of water.

Make the coconut curry: Heat the sunflower oil in a pan and fry the eggplant slices until they are lightly browned on both sides. Add more oil if necessary.

Remove the eggplant from the pan and sauté the shallots in the same pan until soft. Add a splash of ginger syrup and the freshly ground curry paste. Cook the shallots with the curry paste over medium heat while stirring. Put the fried eggplants back in.

Pour the fish sauce, coconut milk, and vegetable broth in with the eggplant. Bring the liquid to a boil and reduce the heat. Simmer the sauce over low heat for another 15 minutes, until the eggplant is tender but not falling apart.

In the meantime, roast the almonds in a drop of oil in a skillet until golden brown.

Finally, taste whether the curry needs some extra salt and pepper. Spoon the almonds into the curry. Serve the curry, sprinkled with cilantro leaves, in bowls.

Delicious with some naan.

CAULIFLOWER CURRY WITH KIDNEY BEANS

**PREPARE: 20 MINUTES
SERVES 4 AS A MAIN
COURSE**

1⅔ cups (300 g) basmati rice
2 tablespoons olive oil
2 onions, chopped
3 tablespoons korma paste
   (I use Patak's brand)
1 can (14½ ounces/411 g)
   peeled tomatoes, squeezed
   by hand (see page 266)
1 cup (250 ml) vegetable
   broth
½ cauliflower (about 1 pound
   1 ounce/500 g), cut into
   florets
1 can (14 ounces/400 g)
   kidney beans, rinsed and
   drained
7 ounces (200 g) spinach
1 small can (about 8 ounces/
   250 ml) coconut milk
sea salt and freshly ground
   black pepper
1 bunch (½ ounce/15 g)
   cilantro, finely chopped,
   saving some sprigs for
   garnish
about 6½ tablespoons
   (100 ml) low-fat yogurt
1 cup (100 g) grated coconut

It's even faster to use curry paste from a jar instead of making it from scratch. Sometimes this can be the solution to whipping up a quick meal. With all of the fresh vegetables going into this curry, you're still eating super healthy!

Steam or cook the basmati rice, following the directions on the package.

Meanwhile, heat the olive oil in a large heavy pan over medium heat. Add the chopped onions and sauté for 5 minutes, stirring, until soft. Stir in the korma paste and fry for 2 minutes, stirring. Stir in the tomatoes and vegetable broth and slowly bring the broth to a boil. Reduce the heat and let the curry simmer for 5 minutes. Add the cauliflower florets and let the curry simmer for another 5 minutes.

Stir the kidney beans and spinach into the curry, add the coconut milk, and let simmer for 3 minutes, allowing it to thicken slightly. Season the cauliflower curry with salt and pepper and remove the pan from the heat.

Stir in the chopped cilantro. Spoon the rice into wide bowls, ladle the cauliflower curry on top, and garnish each bowl with yogurt, grated coconut, and a sprig of cilantro.

VEGETABLE DISHES

BEET CURRY WITH ALMONDS & YOGURT

PREPARE: ABOUT 45 MINUTES
SERVES 4 AS A MAIN COURSE

2 tablespoons sunflower oil
2 onions, chopped
2 teaspoons yellow mustard seeds
1 tablespoon madras curry paste
2¼ pounds (1 kg) beets (peeled weight), cut into ⅜-inch (1 cm) cubes
1 green chile, halved lengthwise
1 can (14½ ounces/411 g) peeled whole tomatoes, hand crushed (see page 266)
4 tablespoons (60 ml) Greek yogurt
4 tablespoons (25 g) sliced almonds, briefly toasted in a dry skillet
1 bunch (½ ounce/15 g) chives, finely chopped

In a large pan, heat the sunflower oil, add the chopped onions, and sauté until translucent. Add the mustard seeds and curry paste and cook for a few minutes.

Add the beet cubes and stir well. Add the chile and crushed tomatoes and deglaze with 2 cans of water. Cover the pan and simmer the curry over low heat for 30 minutes, stirring occasionally, until the beets are tender.

Remove the lid from the pan, turn the heat to high, and cook to reduce the sauce until thick. Remove the pan from the heat and stir the yogurt into the curry. Sprinkle with almonds and chives and serve.

Zandvoort, the Netherlands

GARLIC NAAN

PREPARE: 20 MINUTES
RISE: 1 HOUR
BAKE: 6 TO 8 MINUTES
MAKES 8 SMALL NAANS

3½ cups (450 g) all-purpose
 flour
1 teaspoon instant yeast
1 teaspoon granulated sugar
generous ½ cup (125 ml)
 lukewarm water
1 teaspoon sea salt
generous ½ cup (125 ml)
 yogurt
1 egg, beaten
generous ⅓ cup (80 g) ghee
 or butter
2 cloves garlic, minced
2 teaspoons nigella seeds (see
 page 12; optional)

tool
pizza stone (see below)

In a large bowl, mix the flour with the yeast and sugar.

In a jug, whisk the water with the salt, yogurt, and egg. Make an indentation at the center of the flour mixture. While stirring, pour in the water and yogurt mixture, in splashes, and knead until a smooth dough forms.

Place the dough on a flour-dusted countertop and knead for another 10 minutes, until a nice elastic and non-sticky dough forms. Return the dough to the bowl, cover, and let rise for 1 hour.

Knead the dough again. Add half of the ghee and knead for another 5 minutes, or until the ghee is well incorporated into the dough.

Place a pizza stone in the oven and preheat the oven to 400°F (200°C).

Melt the rest of the ghee in a skillet and fry the garlic over low heat until slightly discolored. Remove the pan from the heat and set aside.

Divide the dough into 8 equal portions. Roll out each portion into a teardrop-shaped thin slab of 6 by 8 inches (15 by 20 cm). Brush the dough with some water and sprinkle with nigella seeds.

Bake the naan one by one on the hot stone in the oven for 6 to 8 minutes, until the bread is golden brown and puffed. As soon as they come out of the oven, brush the naan with the ghee-garlic mixture and serve with, for example, the beet curry on page 204.

A pizza stone increases the heat in the oven (you simulate a brick oven, which can easily reach over 900°F/500°C), but also gives bread placed directly on top an instant heat boost. The moisture evaporates immediately, resulting in a nice and crispy crust.

NO PIZZA STONE?
I don't have one either; I have a small stack of double-baked floor tiles that were left over from our renovation, and they work perfectly. Stacked, they also fit my kitchen drawer better than a large stone.

ZUCCHINI & CORN BURGERS

PREPARE: 35 MINUTES
WAIT: 30 MINUTES
MAKES 10 BURGERS

1 zucchini, scrubbed
1 teaspoon + a pinch of sea
  salt
2 cups (300 g) corn kernels,
  from 2 cobs (see below)
3 egg whites
3 tablespoons cornstarch
freshly ground black pepper
½ teaspoon paprika
1 bunch (½ ounce/15 g)
  chives, chopped
1 bunch (½ ounce/15 g)
  cilantro, very finely
  chopped
5 tablespoons (75 ml)
  olive oil
home made hot sauce
  (page 141)

Fresh corn kernels, sliced
off the cob raw, lends these
burgers a nice crunchy
texture. If corn is out of
season or you think this step
too much hassle, you can use
canned corn kernels.

Using a coarse grater, grate the zucchini over a colander. Add the 1 teaspoon salt, let the zucchini drain, and then rinse it. Spoon the grated zucchini into the center of a clean kitchen towel and pull the ends of the cloth together. Wring the cloth as tightly as possible; do this over the sink. Wring out as much water as possible from the zucchini. Combine the grated zucchini with the corn kernels.

In a clean bowl, beat the egg whites with a pinch of salt until stiff. Set aside.

Stir the cornstarch, pepper, paprika, chives, and cilantro into the zucchini-corn mixture. Gently fold the egg-white foam into the vegetables.

In a skillet, heat a layer of olive oil over medium heat.

Using 2 tablespoons, drop dollops of the mixture into the hot oil. Press them out slightly with the back of a spoon to flatten the patties. (If you have baking rings, grease the insides and place them in the hot skillet. Fill them with a small layer of vegetable batter and smooth the top with the back of a spoon. That way they'll look even more professional!)

Cook the burgers for about 3 minutes on each side, or until they turn golden brown. Let the burgers drain on some paper towel and continue frying new ones, adding more oil as needed, until the mixture is finished.

Serve the zucchini-corn burgers as you would a meat burger, on a sandwich or with dinner. Top with homemade hot sauce.

VEGETABLE DISHES

VEGGIE SAUSAGES

PREPARE: 20 MINUTES
SET (OPTIONAL): AT LEAST
1 HOUR
BAKE: 8 MINUTES
MAKES 12 FINGERS

3 to 4 tablespoons olive oil
2 onions, chopped
10½ ounces (300 g) spinach
handful of fresh herbs of
    choice, depending on the
    season
5 to 6 slices stale white bread,
    ground into breadcrumbs
    (or about 150 g panko or
    breadcrumbs)
pinch of freshly ground
    nutmeg
5¼ ounces (150 g) aged hard
    cheese, grated
about 1 egg, beaten
sea salt and freshly ground
    black pepper
3 tablespoons all-purpose
    flour

on the side
green goddess (see page 134)
    or tartar sauce (see page
    138)

tool
food processor

Whether you have a green thumb or not, from now on you can at least make green fingers. You don't have to roll this mixture into fingers (or sausages), by the way. You can also shape it into patties and serve them as veggie burgers, just like the beet burgers on page 210.

They are very "snackable." Serve them as an appetizer or as a meat substitute (ugh, I hate that term) along with a few delicious vegetable dishes from this chapter.

In a skillet, heat 1 tablespoon of the olive oil, add the onions, and sauté for about 10 minutes, until very soft; let them cool slightly.

Finely chop the spinach in a food processor. Add the cooled onions, the herbs, breadcrumbs, nutmeg, and cheese and pulse a few times until just combined. Add the beaten egg, just a little at a time (you may not need all of the egg), until the mixture is cohesive. Season the green finger mixture with salt and pepper.

It is advisable to let the mixture set in the refrigerator for at least 1 hour. That way the breadcrumbs can absorb the moisture from the vegetables and you will have firmer fingers later. But if you don't have time for that, you can move on to the next step.

Divide the dough into 12 equal portions and, with wet, clean hands, shape the dough into firm, tight sausages. Sprinkle flour on a plate, dredge your green fingers through one by one, and tap off the excess flour. Keep the green fingers wrapped between sheets of parchment paper in the fridge or freezer until use or fry them immediately.

In a skillet, heat the remaining 2 to 3 tablespoons oil. Add the fingers and fry for 8 to 10 minutes, turning occasionally, until completely cooked. Let the green fingers drain on paper towels, then serve warm.

BEET BURGERS

for the burgers

1 can (14 ounces/400 g)
   chickpeas, rinsed and
   drained

1 teaspoon ground cumin

9 ounces (250 g) beets, peeled
   and grated (you might want
   to wear gloves to prevent
   getting red hands)

1 green chile, seeded (if you
   want less heat) and minced

1 small bunch (¼ ounce/10 g)
   flat-leaf parsley, finely
   chopped

generous 1 cup (50 g) fresh
   breadcrumbs (or slightly
   more) made from stale bread,
   or panko or breadcrumbs

1 egg

sea salt and freshly ground
   black pepper

2 tablespoons olive oil

on the side

7 ounces (200 g) halloumi
   cheese, sliced

4 or 8 hamburger buns,
   preferably tasty brioche rolls

½ cup (120 ml) sour cream

3½ ounces (100 g) arugula

tool
food processor

My editor and I had a small disagreement over this burger. She didn't think halloumi was a good choice as a topping, and would always choose feta or a hard goat cheese and roast this on top of the burger under the broiler. Definitely an option!

I think the greasy, salty meatiness of the baked halloumi slices works really well here. It yields a "whoop" to cut your teeth on before biting into the burger. In any case, you're a grown-up, choose whatever cheese you want. It's all delicious.

Make the burgers: Coarsely mash the chickpeas using a fork or food processor on the pulse setting. Stir in the ground cumin. Add the beets, green chile, flat-leaf parsley, breadcrumbs, egg, and salt and pepper to taste. Knead into a burger mixture that is no longer sticky. If it still is, add some more breadcrumbs.

Shape the beet mixture into 8 burger patties. Keep them covered in the fridge until use, or leave them refrigerated for at least 1 hour.

In a skillet, heat the olive oil and fry the burgers for about 5 minutes on each side, until completely cooked through. Let them drain on paper towels.

Prepare the sides: Fry the halloumi in the same hot skillet until golden brown on both sides, and set aside on paper towels. Slice open the hamburger buns and fry them face down in the hot skillet for half a minute. Keep a close eye, as bread burns quickly.

Spread sour cream on the buns; top with a beet burger, halloumi, possibly a second burger if you are hungry, and a bunch of arugula; and cover with the top half of the bun.

somewhere on the English coast

BRUSSELS SPROUTS CLAFOUTIS WITH HARISSA & FETA

PREPARE: 15 MINUTES
BAKE: 25 MINUTES
SERVES 4 AS A DINNER
MAIN COURSE, OR 6 AS A
LUNCH

3½ tablespoons (50 g)
   melted butter or olive oil,
   plus extra for greasing and
   sautéing
1 cup (250 ml) milk
3 eggs
½ cup plus 1 tablespoon
   (75 g) all-purpose flour
1 tablespoon harissa, or to
   taste
sea salt and freshly ground
   black pepper
10½ ounces (300 g) Brussels
   sprouts, cleaned and halved
⅓ cup (75 ml) white wine or
   stock
generous ⅓ cup (60 g)
   crumbled feta cheese
4 tablespoons (35 g) hulled
   pumpkin seeds, toasted in a
   dry skillet until puffed
pinch of paprika

on the side
1 cup (250 ml) Greek yogurt
½ tablespoon sumac

tool
9-inch (22 cm) springform
   pan

Such a savory clafoutis makes for a fabulous way to use up leftovers. I'm a big Brussels sprouts fan, but you can replace them with absolutely any vegetable. Make sure they are precooked. At the end of this recipe I give a few more ideas.

Grease the springform pan with butter. Line the pan with a sheet of parchment paper that sticks out high above the pan, to avoid leakage, and grease the paper as well.

Whisk the milk, eggs, flour, melted butter, harissa, and salt and pepper to taste to make a batter. Set the batter aside, to let it rest while you carry out the next step. This way, the clafoutis will be nicer and smooth after baking.

Preheat the oven to 350°F (180°C).

Melt some butter in a large skillet over medium heat and add the Brussels sprouts. Sauté until browned. Douse with the white wine or stock, and cook to reduce the liquid somewhat. Cook the sprouts over low heat until tender, about 10 minutes. Season with salt and pepper.

Whisk the batter briefly. Pour the batter into the parchment paper–lined pan, and arrange the Brussels sprouts in the pan. Sprinkle with the feta and pumpkin seeds. Dust the top with a pinch paprika.

Slide the clafoutis into the oven and bake for about 25 minutes, until it has risen nicely.

I serve my clafoutis in wedges, with a dollop of thick yogurt and sprinkled with sumac.

SPINACH & SWEET POTATO

Replace only the Brussels sprouts in the recipe. Boil 1 unpeeled sweet potato until tender, then peel and dice. Sauté the spinach in a wok, with 1 clove minced garlic. Continue as described above.

ZUCCHINI & GREEK YOGURT

Replace the Brussels sprouts in the recipe with a big zucchini chopped or sliced, briefly sautéed in olive oil. Replace the feta with Greek yogurt—or *hangop*, as it's called in Dutch—a pinch of salt, and some minced garlic.

CURRIED CAULIFLOWER-CELERIAC MASH & CARAMELIZED LEEKS

**PREPARE: 50 MINUTES
SERVES 4 AS A MAIN
COURSE**

sea salt
½ celeriac, peeled and cubed
2 bay leaves
1 head of cauliflower, cut into
  florets
1½ tablespoons butter
2 thick leeks, cut into thin
  rings and washed well
1 clove garlic, minced
1 tablespoon hot curry
  powder
freshly ground black pepper
1 tablespoon nigella seeds
  (optional; see page 12)
1 tablespoon coriander seeds

on the side (optional)
creamed miso-mustard
  butter (see page 89)
miso rice meatballs (page
  351)

tool
food processor or a coarse
  grater

In a large pan of salted water, bring the celeriac cubes to a boil. Add the bay leaves. After 30 minutes, add half of the cauliflower florets and cook the vegetables for another 15 minutes, until the celeriac is tender and the cauliflower is al dente. Using a slotted spoon, remove the vegetables and bay leaves from the pan and let them cool down in a colander.

Grind the other half of the cauliflower to coarse crumbs; I use a food processor with a grater blade for this, that way you get a nicely rice-grain-like crumb. You can use a hand grater as well. Blanch the cauliflower crumbs for 1 minute in the cooking water of the celeriac and cauliflower. Drain in a sieve.

In a sauté pan, melt the butter, then add the leek rings and sauté them over high heat until the leeks are almost brown. Add the garlic and curry powder and cook for another minute. Season with salt and pepper.

Toast the nigella seeds, if using, and coriander seeds in a dry skillet until fragrant, then coarsely grind them in a mortar.

Coarsely mash the celeriac with the cauliflower; it doesn't have to be smooth. Stir in the cauliflower crumbs and the seasoned leeks (save some nice leek rings as garnish). Stir half of the crushed seeds through the mash. Season with salt and pepper and garnish with the reserved leek rings and the remaining nigella and coriander seeds and serve.

Lovely with some whipped miso-mustard butter on top and, if you eat meat, with miso rice balls on the side.

VEGETABLE DISHES

~ 217 ~

ROASTED CARROTS & ORANGE GREMOLATA

PREPARE: 7 MINUTES
BAKE: 45 MINUTES
SERVES 4 AS A STARTER

for the carrots
1 bunch of carrots, without
   green tops (about 1 pound
   1 ounce/500 g)
3 tablespoons olive oil
pinch of sea salt and freshly
   ground black pepper
3 tablespoons red wine
   vinegar

for the orange gremolata
1 bunch (½ ounce/15 g)
   flat-leaf parsley, finely
   chopped
grated zest of 1 organic
   orange
1 clove garlic, grated
sea salt and freshly ground
   black pepper

When I put a baking sheet of roasted vegetables straight from the oven on the table, dinner guests will dig in before I even get the chance to serve it officially. Why is that? What makes every dish taste better when eaten directly off the tray? The same is true for salad: just much more delicious if you eat it with your hands, straight out of the bowl.

Preheat the oven to 400°F (200°C).

Spread the carrots on a large baking sheet, drizzle with the olive oil, and sprinkle with salt and pepper. Roast the carrots for 35 to 45 minutes, depending on their size. Drizzle with the red wine vinegar.

For the gremolata, combine the flat-leaf parsley with the grated orange zest and the garlic. Season with salt and pepper. Sprinkle the roasted carrots with the gremolata and serve.

ROASTED RADISHES WITH SOUR BUTTER SAUCE

PREPARE: 10 MINUTES
BAKE: 20 MINUTES
SERVES 4 AS A SIDE DISH

2 bunches (about 14 ounces/
   400 g) radishes
2 tablespoons olive oil
pinch of salt flakes (Maldon)
   and freshly ground black
   pepper
4 tablespoons (55 g) butter
2 tablespoons white wine
   vinegar

Preheat the oven to 400°F (200°C).

Trim the leaves and tail from the radishes. Wash and halve them. Arrange them on a baking sheet, drizzle with the olive oil, and toss to coat. Sprinkle with salt flakes and pepper. Thoroughly toss everything once more.

Roast for about 20 minutes, until just cooked. Turn them over midway through the cooking time.

Meanwhile, in a small saucepan over low heat, melt the butter. Heat the butter until it starts to brown. This will take about 5 minutes. Remove from the heat, stir in the white wine vinegar, and pour the sauce over the roasted radishes on the baking sheet.

Delicious with roast chicken—for example, the one on page 355.

CHARRED BRUSSELS SPROUTS WITH SCORCHED HONEY

PREPARE: 10 MINUTES
BAKE: 25 MINUTES
SERVES 4 AS A SIDE DISH

for the Brussels sprouts
1 pound 1 ounce (500 g)
   Brussels sprouts, cleaned
   and halved
3 tablespoons olive oil
sea salt and freshly ground
   black pepper
3 scallions, diagonally sliced
   into thin rings
1 teaspoon grated organic
   lemon zest

for the honey dressing
5 tablespoons (75 ml) honey
3 tablespoons red wine
   vinegar
3 tablespoons butter
pinch of chile flakes
   (optional)
sea salt

Preheat the oven to 425°F (225°C).

On a baking sheet, toss the Brussels sprouts with the olive oil and salt and pepper and spread in a single layer. Roast for 20 to 25 minutes, until beautifully browned, almost charred here and there.

Make the honey dressing: In a small saucepan over medium heat, bring the honey to a boil. Reduce the heat and cook the honey for about 4 minutes, until it has a nice dark color, but isn't burned.

Remove from the heat and stir in the red wine vinegar and chile flakes. Beware of scalding splashes. Return the pan to the heat and stir in the butter until melted. Season the sweet dressing with salt.

Slip the Brussels sprouts into a large bowl and pour the hot dressing over it. Thoroughly toss and stir in the scallions and lemon zest. Serve warm.

VEGETABLE DISHES

BAKED SWEET POTATOES WITH GRAPES, SPINACH & GOAT CHEESE

PREPARE: 20 MINUTES
BAKE: 1 HOUR
FINISH: 10 MINUTES
SERVES 4 AS A SIDE DISH

4 equal-size sweet potatoes,
  washed
10½ ounces (300 g) spinach
2 tablespoons olive oil
grated zest and juice of
  ½ organic lemon
1 teaspoon paprika
pinch of ground cinnamon
sea salt and freshly ground
  black pepper
generous 1 cup (125 g)
  crumbled fresh goat cheese
2 handfuls of purple seedless
  grapes, halved

In the fall it's really
delicious to make this recipe
with small pumpkins.

We eat this as a main course—with a green salad—even though I categorized this as a side dish.

A perfect little dish that allows you to not eat meat and still be able to put something exciting on the table. Even my husband, Oof, who isn't necessarily a sweet potato fan, easily wolfed down two servings of this. Anything with melted cheese from the oven is appreciated by (almost) anyone. Who's the next sweet potato convert?

Preheat the oven to 400°F (200°C).

Place the sweet potatoes on a small parchment paper–lined baking sheet and roast for about 1 hour. The time depends on the size of the sweet potatoes. If you can pierce the sweet potatoes effortlessly with a knife, they are done. Keep the oven on.

Cut the sweet potatoes in half lengthwise and scrape out most of the roasted potato with a spoon, leaving a shell of about ¼ inch inside the skins.

Sauté the spinach in the olive oil, sprinkle with the lemon juice, and transfer to a colander to squeeze out as much moisture as possible. Finely chop the spinach.

Combine the chopped spinach with the sweet potato flesh and add the grated lemon zest, paprika, cinnamon, and salt and pepper to taste. Fill the hollowed-out sweet potato halves with the spinach mixture and return them to the baking sheet. Sprinkle the tops of the sweet potatoes with goat cheese and grape halves.

Slide the sweet potatoes back into the oven for another 10 minutes, so that they warm up through and through and the cheese forms a brown crust. Serve the sweet potatoes seasoned with a generous sprinkling of freshly ground pepper.

VEGETABLE DISHES

BRAISED ESCAROLE WITH MISO

PREPARE: 20 MINUTES
SERVES 4 AS A SIDE DISH

3 tablespoons olive oil
1 shallot, chopped
2 cloves garlic, sliced
1 red chile, seeds and
    membrane removed if you'd
    like less heat, minced
2 tablespoons red miso*
1 head of escarole, halved
    lengthwise, carefully
    washed

*See page 12.

You could also use a pointed white cabbage for this, but you'll need to braise it longer: factor in about 8 minutes more. Small heads of little gem lettuce also work, but in that case you want to shorten the cooking time to 5 minutes.

In a large skillet, heat the olive oil and sauté the shallot, garlic, miso, and chile until the shallot is tender.

Add one escarole half with any adhering water, placing it in the pan cut side down. Cover with the lid and slightly reduce the heat. Braise the endive for 8 to 10 minutes. Give the pan a shake from time to time.

Test the escarole for tenderness, if you can easily cut through the firmest part of the escarole head with a sharp knife, it is done. If necessary, braise the escarole for a few more minutes. Remove from the pan with tongs and keep it warm under a lid or deep plate.

Similarly, fry the second half in the miso-chile mixture remaining in the pan. Serve warm, cutting each piece in half to serve four.

Delicious with the beef stew with ginger and star anise on page 353, or with the lemon chicken with coconut on page 355.

VEGETABLE DISHES

GRILLED AVOCADO WITH SPICY HUMMUS & SESAME YOGURT SAUCE

PREPARE: 25 MINUTES
SERVES 4 AS A STARTER
OR SIDE DISH

for the hummus
1 can (14 ounces/400 g)
   chickpeas, rinsed and
   drained
2 to 3 tablespoons white
   tahini (see page 13)
juice of 1 lemon, plus extra if
   needed
pinch of chile powder, or to
   taste
a few sprigs of cilantro,
   chopped
2 tablespoons harissa

for the sesame yogurt sauce
¾ cup plus 1 tablespoon
   (200 ml) yogurt
1 to 2 tablespoons white
   tahini
salt and freshly ground black
   pepper

for the grilled avocados
4 firm but ripe avocados
1 tablespoon olive oil
1 lemon

tools
food processor or blender
grill pan or barbecue grill

Grilling avocados makes them richer in flavor, softer, and creamier. A delicious starter if you are planning on a night of barbecue grilling, but it can also be part of a table filled with smaller dishes. I like eating that way: a little bit of everything.

Make the hummus: In a food processor or blender, process the chickpeas with the tahini, lemon juice, and chile powder until smooth. It may take some time to get the perfect smooth hummus. Taste to see if the proportions are correct; sometimes you may need more lemon juice. Pulse for a good while until you have a frothy and light hummus. If necessary, thin it slightly with a splash of water to make it nice and airy. Finally, stir some chopped cilantro and harissa with the hummus, making a swirl of the harissa. Cover and set aside.

Make the sesame yogurt sauce: Stir the tahini into the yogurt and grind some salt and pepper on top. Set the tahini yogurt aside.

Make the grilled avocados: Heat a griddle on the stovetop until the air above it visibly vibrates, or light a charcoal grill and wait for the coals to wear a white coat.

Halve each avocado, remove the stone, and brush the flesh with a splash of olive oil. Place the avocados cut side down on the hot griddle or on the grill grate over the charcoal. Do not move them around; leave them for at least 3 minutes, until they start to release from the griddle or grill grate by themselves.

Cut the lemon in half and place it, cut side down, next to the avocados on the grill. That way the lemons can also roast a bit, more juice will escape, and the caramelized fruit sugars will be extra tasty.

Spoon some hummus into the cavities of the avocados and drizzle with a splash of tahini yogurt. Serve with the grilled lemon for squeezing on top.

VEGETABLE DISHES

HOISIN EGGPLANTS WITH SPICY PEANUT SAUCE

PREPARE: 45 MINUTES
SERVES 2 AS A MAIN
COURSE, OR 4 AS A
SIDE DISH

for the eggplants
2 eggplants
3 tablespoons olive oil
6½ tablespoons (100 ml)
   hoisin sauce, home
   made (see page 139) or
   store-bought

for the peanut sauce
6 tablespoons (100 g)
   unsweetened crunchy
   peanut butter
1 tablespoon dark soy sauce
grated zest and juice of
   1 organic lime
2 teaspoons sambal oelek or
   harissa, or to taste
1 clove garlic, grated

for garnish
4 tablespoons (40 g) salted
   peanuts, chopped
2 scallions, sliced into
   thin rings

These are delicious with fried rice or plain white rice and the quick pickled vegetables on page 191. The braised escarole with miso on page 225 also makes for a tasty combination.

Make the eggplants: Preheat the oven to 325°F (170°C).

Halve the eggplants lengthwise and score the flesh crosswise, being careful not to cut through the skin.

Brush the cut edges of the eggplant halves with olive oil.

Place the eggplants on a parchment paper–lined baking sheet and bake for 20 to 25 minutes, until light brown, but not yet done. Brush the cut sides of the eggplants with a nice lick of hoisin sauce after 15 minutes. Repeat this after 5 to 7 minutes. If you want, repeat a third time a few minutes later. Cook the eggplants until they are tender through and through, have a nice deep brown color, and are fleshy and sticky.

Meanwhile, make the peanut sauce: In a saucepan, heat the peanut butter, adding a splash of water, the dark soy sauce, grated lime zest and juice, sambal, and grated garlic. Simmer until you get a creamy sauce. It will thicken quickly, so add water until the sauce has the desired consistency.

Spoon the peanut sauce onto the eggplants and sprinkle with the peanuts and scallion. Serve the hoisin eggplants immediately.

Jaap

FRISIAN WÂLD BEAN STEW WITH ESCAROLE & FETA

SOAK: 1 NIGHT
PREPARE: ABOUT 1 HOUR
SERVES 4 AS A MAIN
COURSE

3 tablespoons (90 ml) olive
   oil, plus extra
4 cloves garlic, chopped
4 anchovies in oil
1 onion, chopped
1 small fennel bulb, cut into
   small cubes
sea salt and freshly ground
   black pepper
grated zest and juice of
   1 organic lemon
1 tablespoon rosemary
   needles, finely chopped
pinch of chile flakes, or to
   taste
2 bay leaves
14 ounces (400 g) dried
   Frisian *wâld beans* (or white
   beans), soaked overnight
   and drained
4 sprigs basil, roughly
   chopped, plus extra leaves
1 head of escarole, washed,
   leaves roughly shredded
1⅓ cups (200 g) crumbled
   feta cheese

SOAKING BEANS QUICKLY?

Yes, that's possible!
   Put them in a wide pan
and pour in enough water for
the beans to be submerged
by 1 inch (2.5 cm). Bring to
a boil and turn off the heat.
Let the beans cool. Drain and
continue as indicated in the
recipe.

So, I could give you my regular spiel here, about how you can always wake me up for a bowl of beans, but I won't.

What I *do* want to tell you, though, is that in my basement pantry I have a hidden treasure chest filled with all kinds of beans. There is such an enormous variety: local, exotic, small, large, and in every color and pattern imaginable. They're ridiculously nourishing and easy to store. So I challenge you to soak them yourself and then to slow cook them, like you would a stew. You won't believe your taste buds, and from then on you will—like me—only want to eat home soaked and cooked beans. (Canned beans are faster, but not tastier.) These beans hail from the Frisian woods in the northernmost region of the Netherlands, but if you don't feel like going out of your way to source these, you may use any sturdy bean (cannellini, borlotti) for this recipe. You can, by the way, always shoot my bean purveyor an email to see whether he can ship you some. I'll include his address at the back of this book. That way, the mail carrier will have to do all the schlepping. The only thing you will have to do is prepare them. That's about as easy as I can make it.

In a large, heavy saucepan, heat 3 tablespoons of the olive oil over medium heat. Add the garlic and anchovies and fry for 5 minutes, stirring regularly, until the anchovies have melted and the garlic is slightly fragrant.

Add the onion and fennel cubes and sauté, stirring, until tender. Season the vegetables with salt and pepper. Add the lemon zest, rosemary, and a pinch of chile flakes and cook for a few more minutes.

Add the bay leaves and the drained beans and pour in 8 cups (2 L) water. Bring to a boil, then reduce the heat to keep the stew simmering. Thoroughly salt the water. Partially cover the pan with the lid.

Cook the beans for about 40 minutes and then taste every 5 minutes to see if the beans have the desired consistency. One person prefers a bite, the other likes their beans soft. I'll leave that for you to decide.

Add the basil, then the chicory, and stir until both are just wilted. This will usually be after 3 to 4 minutes. Add lemon juice to taste. Crumble the feta over the stew and drizzle with more olive oil. Serve the Italian stew with some tasty brown bread.

BAKED CELERIAC WITH CHANTERELLES

BAKE: 1 HOUR
PREPARE: 15 MINUTES
SERVES 4 AS A STARTER OR
SMALL PLATE

½ celeriac, peeled
7 tablespoons (100 g) butter
sea salt and freshly ground
   black pepper
about 3 tablespoons fresh
   thyme leaves, finely
   chopped
1 head of garlic
7 ounces (200 g) chanterelles
   (or mixed mushrooms),
   cleaned and shredded to
   equal-size pieces
2 to 3 tablespoons olive oil
2 tablespoons capers, drained
   and pressed dry in a paper
   towel
2 to 3 tablespoons white
   balsamic or cider vinegar

One of the tastiest recipes in the book. I mean it.

Preheat the oven to 400°F (200°C).

Rub the celeriac with half of the butter and sprinkle with salt and pepper and 2 tablespoons of the thyme leaves.

Place two large sheets of aluminum foil crosswise on top of each other and place the celeriac with the garlic bulb on top. Fold the foil tightly over the celeriac and garlic and bake for 1 hour, or until the celeriac is tender. It is done when you can easily pierce it with a small sharp knife.

Let the celeriac cool slightly, then cut it into thin slices. Keep them warm on a plate under foil in the still-warm oven. (Or keep the cooled celeriac slices in the fridge until ready to use and warm them covered in the oven just before serving.)

Press the soft pulp from the cloves of garlic and set aside.

Fry the chanterelles in a splash of olive oil and season with salt and pepper. Ladle the mushrooms from the pan onto a plate. Remove the prettiest chanterelles and let them drain on a paper towel.

In the same pan, fry the capers in the remaining oil until crispy. If the pan is very dry, add a splash of olive oil. Place the capers on the paper towel with the chanterelles.

Puree the remaining mushrooms, along with the rest of the butter and the roasted garlic, to a cream. Season the chanterelle cream with a drop of vinegar. Do not add all the vinegar immediately, but taste while pureeing: Does the cream need more vinegar? More pepper? More salt? Follow your taste.

Spoon the warm chanterelle cream onto a preheated plate. Place the slices of warm celeriac on top. Arrange the fried chanterelles and capers on top. Sprinkle with the remaining tablespoon of thyme leaves, followed by a drizzle of olive oil. Serve right away.

VEGETABLE DISHES

Hughie

sweet-sour endive with salty croutons

VEGETABLE DISHES

**PREPARE: ABOUT
20 MINUTES
SERVES 4 AS A SIDE DISH**

1 loaf of ciabatta (about 10½
  ounces/300 g) or stale bread
olive oil
sea salt and freshly ground
  black pepper
1 pound 1 ounce (500 g)
  cherry tomatoes, halved
2 tablespoons red wine vinegar
pinch of dried oregano
generous ⅔ cup (125 g)
  chickpeas (dry weight),
  soaked and cooked; or
  1 can (14 ounces/400 g),
  rinsed and drained
1 can (14 ounces/400 g)
  artichoke hearts
1 red onion, thinly sliced
1 bunch (½ ounce/15 g)
  basil, large leaves torn
6 anchovies

**PREPARE: 40 MINUTES
SERVES 4 AS A SIDE DISH**

4 to 6 heads of Belgian endive
3½ tablespoons (50 g) butter,
  melted
about ⅓ cup (75 ml) sherry
  or red wine vinegar
sea salt and freshly ground
  black pepper
1 tablespoon packed dark
  brown sugar
2 tablespoons chopped fresh
  flat-leaf parsley

for the croutons
3 slices of stale sourdough
  bread, without crust
3 tablespoons butter
2 anchovies, chopped
freshly ground black pepper

PANZANELLA WITH CHICKPEAS

Traditionally panzanella is a dish meant for using up leftover bread. So by all means, use stale bread leftovers if you have them. Of course, in the absence of stale bread you can also make panzanella using fresh bread that you toasted in the oven until dry.

Preheat the oven to 350°F (180°C).

Using the bread, some olive oil, and salt and pepper, make croutons as described on page 187.

Squeeze the halved cherry tomatoes with your hand over a large bowl and whisk the red wine vinegar and oregano into the tomato juice and seeds. While whisking, pour in ¼ cup (60 ml) olive oil until the dressing has the desired consistency. Season with salt and pepper.

Add the croutons, crushed tomato halves, chickpeas, artichoke hearts, onion rings, and basil leaves and toss well. Let stand, allowing the flavors to blend for at least 10 minutes. Place the anchovies on top and serve.

SWEET-SOUR ENDIVE WITH SALTY CROUTONS

Preheat the oven to 425°F (220°C).

Make the endive: Remove the endive's exterior or damaged leaves, but do not cut too much off the end stump, or the leaves will fall apart. Quarter each head lengthwise. Grease an oven dish with some of the melted butter and place the endives in it. Brush each head with the remaining melted butter and drizzle with the sherry vinegar. Sprinkle the endive with salt, pepper and brown sugar. Roast the endive for about 30 minutes in the hot oven, until tender and browned around the edges.

Meanwhile, make the croutons: Tear the bread into small pieces. In a skillet, melt the butter and stir in the anchovies. As soon as the anchovies have dissolved in the butter, add the bread and fry, stirring continuously, until golden brown. Season with pepper and set aside.

Just before serving, sprinkle the endives with the chopped parsley and the croutons.

MAKING FRIES

Peel the potatoes or scrub them clean. Use about 8 oz (250 g) per person. Cut lengthwise into slices ½ in (12 mm) thick and cut those slices lengthwise into strips of the same width.

Place the potato slices in ice-cold water for several minutes to wash off the starch. This will make them even crispier when done.

Drain and thoroughly dry them in a clean kitchen towel. Otherwise they'll splatter terribly when you fry them.

Pre-fry the fries in oil in batches, a handful at a time, at 320°F (160°C). Don't put all of them in the oil at once because the oil will cool down too fast. Fry for about 6 minutes, stirring or tossing regularly so the inside will cook a little.

Scoop them out of the oil and let rest and drain on paper towels for at least 30 minutes before moving on. Let them cool completely, if you can. You can do this a day in advance.

Heat the oil to 190°C (374°F) and again fry the fries in small batches until golden brown and crispy. This will take 3 to 4 minutes per batch.

Sprinkle with some sea salt and serve hot.

CHEST HAIR FRIES

PREPARE: 25 MINUTES
SERVES 4 AS A SIDE DISH,
OR 8 AS AN APPETIZER

3 large starchy potatoes, such
    as Yukon golds or russets,
    with the skin rubbed off
oil for frying
sea salt flakes and freshly
    ground black pepper

tools
mandolin, food processor,
    or spiralizer
deep fryer, wok, or large
    cast-iron pot

The big advantage of razor-thin fries is that they make portions look more generous than they are so you'll eat less. For this recipe for four I only use three large potatoes, which is a lot less than if I were making thick-cut Belgian fries. These are mouthwatering, by the way, I forgot to mention that.

Cut the potatoes into julienne strips using a mandolin or food processor at the finest setting. Or make the fries my way: turn them into delicate curls with a vegetable spiralizer.

Wash the potato strips in ice-cold water to rinse off the starch. Pat them dry in a clean kitchen towel.

Heat the oil in a deep fryer to 350°F (180°C), or use a generous amount of oil in a wok or large cast-iron pot.

Cook a handful of fries at a time for 2 to 3 minutes, until golden brown.

Drain on paper towels and sprinkle with salt and pepper. Eat them as is, or pick a sauce for them from page 129.

These go well with a pint of beer.

VEGETABLE DISHES

POTATOES "CACIO E PEPE"

VEGETABLE DISHES

**PREPARE: 25 MINUTES
SERVES 4 AS A SIDE DISH**

sea salt

2¼ pounds (1 kg) waxy
potatoes, such as new
potatoes or fingerlings,
peeled and cut into thick
slices

3 tablespoons olive oil

1¼ cups (125 g) finely grated
pecorino cheese (or use
Parmesan)

2 tablespoons ground black
pepper (I use a mortar for
such an amount)

This is a side dish, but secretly I find it so terribly delicious that I'll also eat it as a main dish, with a simple bowl of green salad with mustard vinaigrette (see page 151). Just perfect as is. Don't change a thing. Thank me later.

Cook the potatoes in a large pot of boiling salted water until tender, about 18 minutes.

Drain, saving 1 cup (240 ml) of the cooking water, and return the potatoes back to the warm pan; place on the smallest burner. Add the olive oil, three-quarters of the pecorino, and half of the pepper and toss until the cheese has melted. Pour in as much cooking water as you like until all the potatoes are coated in a creamy sauce. To prevent the potato slices from falling apart, do not over mix. They must remain reasonably intact.

Spoon the potatoes into a heated serving dish, sprinkle with the remaining pecorino and pepper, and serve.

POTATO CAKES

**PREPARE: 30 MINUTES
MAKES 16 TO 20 TO SERVE
AS A SIDE DISH**

1 pound 10 ounces (750 g)
waxy potatoes, peeled,
coarsely grated, and rinsed
in ice-cold water

1 large onion, coarsely grated

1 pound 1 ounce (500 g)
mashed potatoes (or any
leftover mashed vegetables)

2 large eggs, beaten

4 tablespoons (30 g)
all-purpose flour

1 tablespoon fresh thyme

sea salt and freshly ground
black pepper

oil for shallow-frying

Leftover potatoes? Mash the remaining cacio e pepe potatoes and use them in the following simple recipe. These cakes can easily be frozen; stash some for an evening when you don't really have time to cook.

Spoon the grated potato into a clean kitchen towel, fold the corners together, and wring them out until barely any water comes out.

In a bowl, combine the grated potato, onion, mashed potatoes, eggs, flour, thyme, and salt and pepper to taste. Stir everything into a nice batter.

In a skillet, heat a few tablespoons of oil. Using two wet tablespoons—or an ice cream scoop—form the batter into dollops and slide them into the hot oil, four or five at a time, leaving some space in between. Flatten them a bit.

Fry the cakes until golden brown, then turn them so that the other side can also nicely brown. Drain on paper towels and repeat with the remaining batter. Serve warm.

Wheat fields in southern England, on our way to Ireland.

PASTA
& GRAINS

Pasta shop, Bologna

PASTA

MAKING PASTA

Make a dough:
3 c (375 g) pasta flour
(preferably tipo 00)
⅔ c (125 g) semolina or
durum wheat flour
1 tsp sea salt
3 whole eggs plus 5 yolks

I like firm pasta with a bite, so I use a lot of durum wheat and plenty of egg yolks. But Jamie Oliver's basic recipe of 100 g flour to 1 egg also works fine. It results in a softer pasta dough. Try it out sometime.

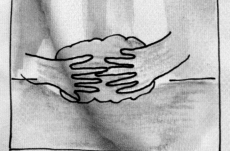

Knead patiently and thoroughly; this is a stiff dough. I have a stand mixer, which is more convenient for this type of task: the dough is pretty hefty, but if you put in a little muscle, it's doable by hand.

Cover and let rest in the fridge for at least 1 hour. This way the flour can fully absorb moisture and the dough will be easier to process later.

In a pasta machine, roll the dough into long sheets, which you can then turn into spaghetti or tagliatelle with the help of the noodle-cutting attachment. Just look at the following pages.

With the pasta machine at its widest setting, roll a piece of well-rested dough through for as long as it takes to become nice and smooth. Then adjust the machine a bit tighter so the dough will get a little thinner each time it passes through the machine. Stop once the desired thickness is achieved.

Always first let freshly cut pasta dry. For this you can also use coat hangers, a broomstick, et cetera.

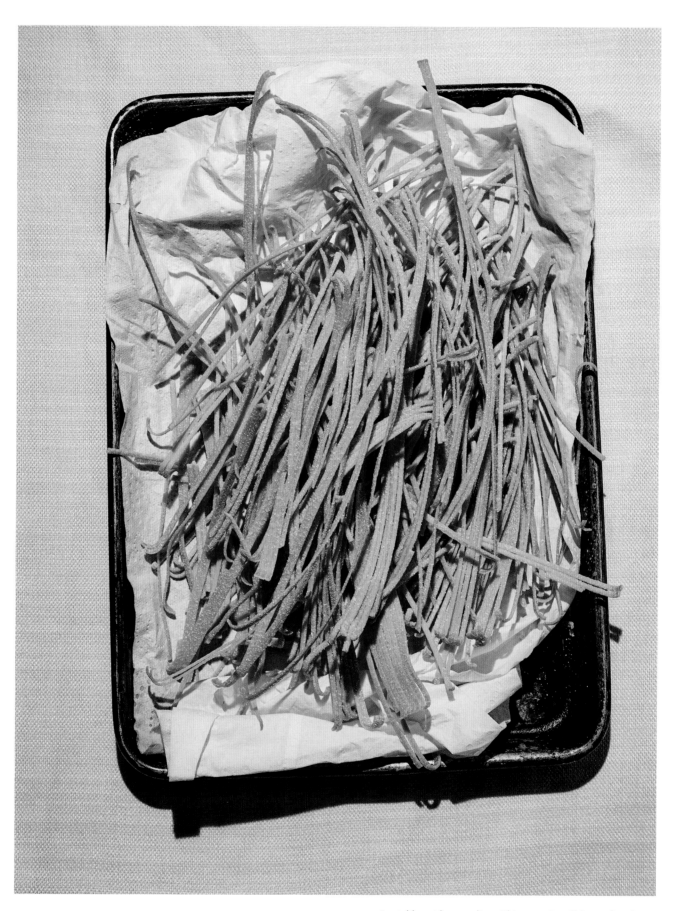

Sprinkle with semolina. This way it will keep for days.

THE PERFECT MACCHERONI WITH PESTO

PREPARE: 15 MINUTES
SERVES 4 AS A MAIN
COURSE

1 heaping tablespoon sea salt
14 ounces (400 g) short pasta
1 serving of miso pesto (see
   page 131), almond garden
   herb pesto (see page 133),
   or cashew-arugula pesto
   (see page 131)

Right now, I will give you a recipe that technically isn't one, but more of a manual for how to make a plate of pasta, with just a few other ingredients, taste great without fail. The secret? The pasta cooking water. You may have known this already, but for those who didn't, I'll lay out my method below. I was taught to cook pasta this way by my Italian friend Maria. It is the only proper way.

Bring a large pot of water to a rolling boil. When it boils, add a generous amount of salt and add the pasta straightaway. The salt will temporarily make the water a lot hotter, something you can see, because it suddenly turns very fizzy. This way the water won't cool down too much the moment you dump in the pasta.

Cook the pasta until it is nearly al dente. Test this yourself, as each pasta has a different cooking time.

Scoop out 2 cups (480 ml) of the pasta water and save it.

Drain the pasta in a colander, and set it aside.

Heat the sauce—this could either be one of the pestos on the right or a few ingredients you gathered together—in a sauté pan. Add the drained pasta and gently stir it to coat. While stirring, add enough pasta water for there to be a thin coating of sauce around all the noodles. The water will be starchy, which ensures that the sauce binds. Therefore you'll need less oil or cream to give the pasta a creamy taste and mouthfeel.

The pasta will keep cooking for a short while and end up having exactly the perfect bite. You drained it right before it was al dente, after all.

Immediately spoon the pasta into preheated bowls and serve.

PASTA

LEMON PASTA WITH SAMPHIRE

**PREPARE: 20 MINUTES
SERVES 4 AS A MAIN
COURSE**

sea salt
1 pound 1 ounce (500 g)
   spaghetti
6 tablespoons (85 g) butter
juice and thinly peeled zest
   of 2 organic lemons, zest
   cut into strips
freshly ground black pepper
5¼ ounces (150 g) samphire
1 cup (100 g) grated
   Parmesan cheese

On this page, as well as the following ones, you'll find various recipes for easy summer pastas that can be made in a snap. For these you use the pasta water for making the sauce: delicious, quick, and light. So you can quickly go back outside to bask in the setting summer sun.

In generously salted water in a large pan, cook the spaghetti until not quite al dente (the pasta will cook further in the sauce!). Drain the spaghetti and save about 1 cup (say, 200 to 250 ml) of the cooking water.

In a heavy-bottomed skillet, melt the butter and add most of the lemon zest and a generous pinch of ground black pepper. Reduce the heat. While stirring, first add the lemon juice, then the spaghetti, samphire, and grated Parmesan cheese. Continue to stir until the cheese has melted. Increase the heat, pour enough of the pasta water into the pan so the liquid binds (the official term is *emulsifies*) and the spaghetti is coated with a thin, creamy layer of sauce. Taste to see if it could use some more salt.

Plate the lemon pasta immediately, and sprinkle with pepper and the remaining lemon zest. Serve with a large salad.

PASTA

SPAGHETTI WITH SHRIMP, GREEN HERBS & PEPPERS

PREPARE: 15 MINUTES
SERVES 4 AS A MAIN
COURSE

sea salt
14 ounces (400 g) spaghetti
2 tablespoons olive oil
2 cloves garlic, finely chopped
1 red chile, seeds and
    membranes removed,
    chopped
3 tablespoons capers, finely
    chopped
14 ounces (400 g) pink
    shrimp, peeled and deveined
about 1¾ ounces (50 g) in
    total of green herbs, such
    as: flat-leaf parsley, chives,
    and minced basil
grated zest and juice of
    1 organic lemon
freshly ground black pepper

In generously salted water in a large pan, cook the spaghetti until al dente, 8 to 10 minutes. Drain, saving 1 cup (240 ml) of the cooking liquid.

In a sauté pan, heat the olive oil. Add the garlic, chile, and capers and fry for a minute or so. Add the shrimp and the chopped green herbs and cook until the shrimp is almost opaque.

Add the spaghetti and season with salt, pepper, and lemon zest and juice. Add enough pasta water to the pan for a cohesive sauce to form.

Spoon onto four warm deep plates immediately and serve.

FETTUCCINE WITH SARDINES

PREPARE: 35 MINUTES
SERVES 4 AS A MAIN
COURSE

2 fennel bulbs, peeled and
    cut into thin strips, fennel
    tops reserved
2 onions, chopped
2 cans (about 3½ ounces/
    100 g each) sardines in oil
3 tablespoons pine nuts,
    lightly toasted in a dry
    skillet
sea salt and freshly ground
    black pepper
14 ounces (400 g) fettuccine,
    linguine, or another pasta
finely grated zest of 1 organic
    lemon

This is a dish I make when I really don't have anything left in my fridge. I even make it when we're out of fennel. In which case I'll just leave out the fennel. Which is nice too. Adding a pepper is fine, but not a must.

In a sauté pan, fry the fennel and onion in the oil from the sardine cans for about 6 minutes, until soft and browned. Stir the vegetables regularly. Add the pine nuts and brown them for a bit. Season with salt and pepper to taste.

Meanwhile, in salted water in a large pan, cook the pasta until not quite al dente. Remove 1 cup (240 ml) of the cooking water from the pan and drain the pasta. Spoon the pasta directly into the sauté pan with the vegetables and pine nuts and, stirring continuously, add pasta water until a sauce forms.

Spoon the sardines into the pasta and vegetables; they will fall apart by themselves.

Divide the pasta among four heated serving bowls. Season with the finely grated lemon zest, sprinkle with the reserved fennel tops, and serve.

fettuccine with sardines

Owenahincha Beach, West Cork

PASTA WITH BROCCOLI, LEMON & MOZZARELLA

PREPARE: ABOUT
12 MINUTES
SERVES 4 AS A MAIN
COURSE

sea salt
14 ounces (400 g) short pasta
    (spelt, whole wheat, or white)
1 pound (500 g) broccoli florets*
3 tablespoons olive oil
2 cloves garlic, finely chopped
3 anchovies in oil, chopped
pinch of chile flakes
2 balls (about 4½ ounces/
    125 grams each) cow's milk
    mozzarella (not buffalo; it
    is too wet for this)
generous ⅔ cup (100 g)
    whole blanched almonds,
    toasted in a dry skillet
grated zest and juice of
    1 organic lemon

In ample boiling salted water, cook the pasta until al dente, adding the broccoli florets 4 minutes before the end of the cooking time. Drain the pasta and broccoli, saving 1 cup (240 ml) of the cooking water.

In a large sauté pan, heat 2 tablespoons of the olive oil and add the garlic, anchovies, and chile flakes. Sauté over medium heat until the anchovies have dissolved. Stir in the pasta and broccoli.

Add a splash of the cooking water to the pan and cook, stirring continuously, until everything just starts to emulsify. Taste to see if more salt is needed (anchovies are salty too!).

Shred or slice the mozzarella into smaller pieces and, right before serving, toss the cheese and crispy almonds with the pasta and broccoli. Season everything with lemon juice and zest. Serve the pasta immediately.

*Use the broccoli stalk for a salad (see page 162).

SPICY PENNE WITH EGGPLANT & BACON

PREPARE: 35 MINUTES
SERVES 4 AS A MAIN
COURSE

2 tablespoons olive oil
1 large eggplant, cut into
    small cubes
5¼ ounces (150 g) smoked
    bacon, cut into cubes
2 cloves garlic, finely chopped
1 red chile, seeded and finely
    chopped
2 cans (14½ ounces/411 g
    each) peeled whole
    tomatoes, hand crushed
    (see page 266)
sea salt and freshly ground
    black pepper
1 pound 1 ounce (500 g)
    penne or another short pasta
about 1¼ cups (125 g) grated
    Parmesan cheese

In a large pan, heat the olive oil. Add the eggplant cubes and fry, stirring, for 8 minutes, or until soft. Add the bacon cubes and fry until browned. Add the garlic and chile, fry briefly, then stir in the hand-crushed tomatoes with any adhering juices.

Bring the sauce to a boil, then reduce the heat. Let simmer for 20 minutes, then taste to see if it needs salt and pepper.

Cook the pasta in ample boiling salted water until al dente, drain, and stir into the sauce immediately. Divide the pasta and the eggplant sauce among four plates. Sprinkle with Parmesan cheese and serve the spicy penne right away.

PASTA

RABBIT (OR CHICKEN) STEW PAPPARDELLE WITH ROSEMARY & TANGERINE

PREPARE: 20 MINUTES
SIMMER: 45 MINUTES TO
1 HOUR
SERVES 4 AS A MAIN
COURSE

about 2 pounds (900 g)
  rabbit legs (chicken or
  turkey legs are fine too)
sea salt and freshly ground
  black pepper
2 tablespoons olive oil
3½ ounces (100 g) smoked
  bacon, cut into cubes
1 red onion, chopped
1 carrot, cut into small cubes
3 cloves garlic, grated
2 sprigs rosemary, needles
  finely chopped
10 tablespoons (150 ml)
  white wine
2 cups (500 ml) chicken
  stock
14 ounces (400 g)
  pappardelle, or another
  pasta variety such as
  tagliatelle
2 tablespoons sharp French
  mustard
grated zest of 2 organic
  tangerines
1 bunch (½ ounce/15 g)
  flat-leaf parsley
pinch of grated Parmesan
  cheese

My neighbor and I share a passion for this rabbit stew pasta. To the point where he texts me pictures each time he has made it. Our supermarket sells frozen rabbit. Perhaps yours does as well. Rabbit meat resembles chicken, but is a bit tougher, which is why it lends itself to stewing. If you can't find rabbit, use chicken and cook the meat for a shorter time. A stew is ready when the meat falls off the bones. It's that easy.

Chop the rabbit legs in half at the knee (that is easier than you think) so that you have eight pieces. Sprinkle with salt and pepper. In a large pan, heat the olive oil. Sear the pieces of meat on all sides and remove them from the pan as soon as they are browned. Keep the rabbit legs warm on a plate, covered with a lid.

In the same pan, fry the smoked bacon cubes, red onion, and carrot, stirring continuously, for 10 minutes over low heat. Add the garlic and rosemary and cook for 1 to 2 minutes. Deglaze with the white wine and add the chicken stock. Bring to a boil, add the rabbit pieces, cover with the lid, and simmer for 45 minutes to 1 hour, until the meat is fully tender and falls off the bones. Remove the rabbit pieces from the pan and pluck the meat from the bones with two forks. Meanwhile, over high heat, reduce the sauce by about half, or until thicker.

In amply salted water, cook the pappardelle until al dente, then drain and rinse with cold water to stop the cooking process. Let drain.

Stir the rabbit meat, mustard, grated tangerine zest, and flat-leaf parsley into the sauce. Stir the pappardelle into the sauce and divide the pasta among four heated deep serving plates. Serve with Parmesan cheese.

Laura, Joris & Omar

the Long Strand, West Cork

CANNED TOMATOES ARE AMAZING.
ESPECIALLY OUT OF SEASON, QUALITY
CANNED TOMATOES ARE A REAL
LIFE SAVER. (SAN MARZANO IS
MY FAVORITE KIND OF TOMATO)
THE CAN WILL SAY "PELATI" OR
"PEELED" TOMATOES.
DON'T BUY DICED TOMATOES!
THEIR FLAVOR IS MUCH LESS
INTENSE, V E RY WATERY.
BLEH.
YOU CAN MAKE YOUR OWN CHUNKS.
NO GREATER PLEASURE THAN
HAND-CRUSHING TOMATOES
OVER A PAN. ♥

WHOLE-WHEAT SPAGHETTI WITH CHORIZO TOMATO SAUCE

**PREPARE: ABOUT 20 MINUTES
SERVES 4 AS A MAIN
COURSE**

for the chorizo tomato sauce
2 tablespoons olive oil
1 onion, chopped
7 ounces (200 g) chorizo
   Iberico, cut into very small
   cubes
2 cloves garlic, pressed
1 sprig rosemary
2 cans (14½ ounces/411 g
   each) whole peeled tomatoes,
   hand crushed (see page 266)
1 tablespoon red wine vinegar
   or balsamic vinegar
sea salt and freshly ground
   black pepper

for the spaghetti
sea salt
14 ounces (400 g) whole-
   wheat spaghetti
10½ ounces (300 g) spinach
½ cup (50 g) grated Parmesan
   cheese

I never tire of spaghetti with tomato sauce. In this recipe I make it deliciously spicy and smoky by adding some chorizo. Super easy and ready in 20 minutes.

Make the chorizo tomato sauce: In a Dutch oven, heat the olive oil. Add the onion and chorizo and sauté until the meat starts to break apart. Add the garlic and the sprig of rosemary, fry for a while, then stir in the crushed tomatoes and a splash of red wine vinegar. Season the sauce with salt and pepper. Reduce the heat, partly cover the pan with the lid, and let simmer for about 15 minutes. Stir now and then.

Make the spaghetti: Cook the whole-wheat spaghetti, following the directions on the package, in ample boiling salted water until al dente. Save 1 cup (240 ml) of the pasta water and drain the spaghetti.

First stir the spinach and then the spaghetti into the sauce, if necessary adding a splash of cooking liquid to loosen up the pasta.

Spoon the sauce-coated pasta into four heated deep serving plates, sprinkle the spaghetti with Parmesan, and serve.

PASTA

CURRIED CAULIFLOWER WITH PASTA & SPINACH-CASHEW PESTO

PREPARE: 50 MINUTES
SERVES 4 AS A MAIN
COURSE

for the curried cauliflower
1 whole head of cauliflower,
  cut into florets, stalk into
  pieces
2 red onions, cut into rings
3 tablespoons olive oil
2 teaspoons curry powder
sea salt and freshly ground
  black pepper

for the pesto
scant ⅔ cup (75 g) cashews,
  briefly toasted in a dry
  skillet
1½ tablespoons white wine
  vinegar
1 bunch (½ ounce/15 g)
  flat-leaf parsley
3½ ounces (100 g) baby
  spinach
about ¼ cup (60 ml) olive oil
sea salt and freshly ground
  black pepper

for the pasta
14 ounces (400 g) radiatori
  or other short, shell-shaped
  pasta

tool
blender or food processor

Instead of cauliflower, you
can also use canned broccoli
florets, green beans, or
canned artichoke hearts.

Instead of Spinach-Cashew
Pesto, you can use a sauce
from pages 131–133.

This is a bit of a basic recipe: I tend to tweak it a lot. Sometimes my crisper drawer may contain green beans instead of a cauliflower, sometimes may I have some other leftover pesto or sauce I can throw in. Curry powder and pasta? I know: nothing traditional about it, but who in your own house will criticize you? Besides, it is really tasty.

Make the curried cauliflower: Preheat the oven to 400°F (200°C).

Combine the cauliflower with the red onion rings, olive oil, and curry powder. Add salt and pepper and mix well until the cauliflower is fully coated with the seasonings.

Spread everything out on a parchment paper–lined baking sheet and roast the cauliflower until just tender—say, 40 minutes.

Make the pesto: In a blender or food processor, puree the cashews, white wine vinegar, parsley, half of the baby spinach, the olive oil, and maybe a splash of water. Season with salt and pepper.

Cook the radiatori according to the package directions until al dente. Drain the pasta, saving 1 cup (240 ml) of the cooking water, stir in the pesto, and carefully fold in the curry cauliflower and the rest of the baby spinach. Finally, stir in a splash of pasta water to make the sauce somewhat smoother. Serve.

NOODLES WITH SESAME PEANUT SAUCE, SESAME RAYU & CUCUMBER SALAD

PREPARE: 15 MINUTES
SERVES 4 AS A MAIN
COURSE

for the noodles
about 14 ounces (400 g) udon
   or other thick noodles
1 bunch (½ ounce/15 g)
   cilantro, coarsely chopped
4 scallions, thinly sliced
2 teaspoons sesame seeds

for the cucumber salad
1 cucumber
3 tablespoons rice vinegar* or
   white wine vinegar
1 tablespoon tahini
1 tablespoon mirin* or honey
½ teaspoon sea salt
½ tablespoon nigella seeds*

for the sesame peanut sauce
3 tablespoons sesame oil
5 cloves garlic, sliced
6 tablespoons (100 g) peanut
   butter, preferably chunky
juice of 3 limes
4 to 5 tablespoons light soy
   sauce
2 tablespoons grated fresh
   ginger
1 tablespoon sambal oelek or
   Tabasco sauce

on the side
sesame rayu (see page 143) or
   another chile oil

*See the information on
page 12.

When I come home late and don't really have any fresh ingredients on hand, I often make noodles with sesame peanut sauce. I nearly always have everything I need for the recipe in stock and even without fresh cilantro it is delicious. Another great advantage is that it really is ready in less than no time. That's so nice!

Oh, and before I forget: these days you can buy all sorts of unsweetened nut butters at organic food stores. Try making this dish with something other than peanut butter: almond butter, for instance, or tahini! Anything is possible.

Cook the noodles according to the package directions. Drain the noodles, rinse them briefly under cold running water, and let them drain.

Meanwhile, make the cucumber salad: Quarter the cucumber lengthwise. Remove the seeds and chop the quarters into cubes. In a bowl, whisk the rice vinegar, tahini, mirin, sea salt, and nigella seeds together and add the cucumber cubes. Set aside to let the flavors steep.

Make the sesame peanut sauce: In a saucepan, heat the sesame oil and sauté the garlic over low heat until nicely browned. Do not do this over high heat, because burnt garlic tastes horrible, while lightly browned garlic is delicious!

Stir in the peanut butter, lime juice, and soy sauce and dilute the sauce with enough water for it to have the consistency of low-fat yogurt. Taste the sauce and decide whether it needs more sour (lime) or more salt (soy), and add the ginger and sambal to taste.

Spoon the noodles into the sauce, taste the sauce again, and dilute if necessary. Serve the noodles in four bowls, sprinkled with cilantro, scallions, and sesame seeds. Top with a heaping spoonful of sesame rayu. Add the cucumber salad.

PASTA

QUICK NOODLES WITH SRIRACHA SAUCE & SHRIMP

**PREPARE: 20 MINUTES
SERVES 4 AS A MAIN
COURSE**

3 tablespoons sesame oil
9 ounces (250 g) shrimp,
  peeled
sea salt and freshly ground
  black pepper
2 to 3 tablespoons sriracha
  sauce (Thai chile sauce)
1 onion, chopped
1 red chile, cut into small
  cubes
1 tablespoon finely grated
  fresh ginger
4 cloves garlic, pressed
2 tablespoons tomato paste
2 cups (500 ml) chicken
  stock
2 tablespoons light soy sauce
1 teaspoon rice vinegar
10½ ounces (300 g) baby
  spinach
about 14 ounces (400 g)
  udon or other thick noodle
  variety
juice of ½ lemon

Some supermarkets sell precooked noodles. We pretty much always keep a stash of those in our pantry for when we want to whip up a quick meal.

Also always in stock in our freezer: a bag of shrimp. I'm just letting you know, because if you have those two items this dish will be ready in a snap.

Heat 1 tablespoon of the sesame oil in a large heavy saucepan over medium heat. Add the shrimp and fry for 1 minute, until just firm and cooked through. Sprinkle with salt and pepper, remove from the pan, and keep them covered until ready to use.

Pour the rest of the oil into the pan and stir-fry the sriracha sauce, onion, and red chile for about 4 minutes, until the onion and chile are soft. Add the ginger and garlic and fry the vegetables for about 1 more minute. Add the tomato paste and fry briefly until it starts to smell sweeter.

Pour in the chicken stock, soy sauce, and rice vinegar, bring the sauce to a boil, and cook to reduce slightly. Stir in the baby spinach and let it wilt slightly while stirring.

Prepare the noodles according to the package directions, cooking them until almost done. Add the not-quite-fully-cooked noodles to the sauce in the pan and fry them while stirring until all the noodles are coated in sauce.

Just before serving, stir in the shrimp and season the sauce with a squeeze of lemon juice. Serve the sriracha noodles in heated bowls.

PASTA

MAKING GNOCCHI

Cook about 1 lb 5 oz (600 g) unpeeled potatoes, but other vegetables such as sweet potato, carrot, or celeriac also work.

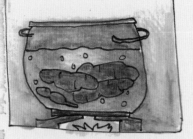

You can also bake potatoes, unpeeled, in the oven at 350°F (180°C), for 1 hour, or until done. As long as they absorb as little water as possible. That's the basic idea.

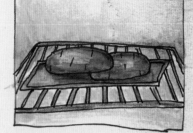

Puree them in a potato ricer. (The skin will stay behind in the ricer.)

You can also use a knife to peel the vegetables before mashing them. Allow as much moisture to evaporate from them as possible.

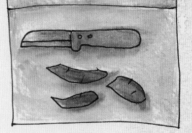

Add 1 egg and about 1⅓ c (180 g) all-purpose flour to the puree. Knead as gently and briefly as possible, adding a tablespoon or so more flour if needed, until the dough is just combined.

Swiftly shape the dough into a sausage. Divide into smaller sausages and cut those into short pieces. Roll them along the back of a fork or a ribbed gnocchi board. Now they're ready to be cooked.

PURPLE POTATO GNOCCHI WITH WARM CHIVE ALMOND SAUCE

PREPARE: 1 HOUR
SERVES 4 AS A MAIN
COURSE, OR 6 AS A
STARTER

for the gnocchi
about 1 pound 5 ounces
    (600 g) Vitelotte or other
    purple potatoes, whole and
    unpeeled
sea salt
1 egg
about 1⅓ cups (180 g) flour
    (preferably tipo 00), plus
    extra
½ teaspoon freshly grated
    nutmeg

for the sauce
1 bunch (½ ounce/15 g)
    chives
generous ⅓ cup (50 g)
    blanched almonds, soaked
    in water for 1 hour
⅓ cup (30 g) grated
    Parmesan cheese
3½ tablespoons (50 g) butter,
    melted and lightly browned
sea salt and freshly ground
    black pepper
squeeze of lemon juice

to finish
3 tablespoons butter
1 handful of lettuce leaves
    (I used red mizuna here)

tool
blender or chopper

PASTA

OTHER TOOLS
It's nice if you have a
potato ricer, but it isn't
mandatory!

Traditionally gnocchi are made from starchy potatoes, but you can also make them from a variety of different root vegetables. Just make sure to let as much water as possible drain or evaporate so the gnocchi will be nice and fluffy. They don't take much time to make: extensive kneading is forbidden, as it will only render the gnocchi tough and rubbery.

Cook the Vitelotte potatoes in generously salted water for about 18 minutes, until done. It should be possible to easily pierce them with a knife. Drain and rinse in a colander under cold running water.

Puree the potatoes and cut in half if necessary to fit skin and all in a ricer. The skin will stay behind. If you do not have a potato ricer, use a sharp knife to peel the potatoes and then mash them.

In a large bowl, combine the potatoes with the egg and as much of the flour as needed to make a non-sticky dough. Season with some nutmeg. Roll the dough into two sausages, then roll it out further into thin sausages; cut them into short pieces about 1 inch (2.5 cm) long. Roll each piece along the back of a fork with your floured thumb to create ridges. This way the sauce will better adhere after cooking. Place the gnocchi slightly apart on a baking sheet, cover with a dish towel, and store in the refrigerator until ready to use.

Make the sauce: In a blender or chopper, mix the chives and the soaked and drained almonds with the cheese, melted butter, and as much water as you need to make a wonderful sauce to your liking—about ½ cup (125 ml). Season the sauce with salt and pepper and lemon juice.

In a large saucepan, cook the gnocchi until al dente in boiling, salted water; they're done when they float to the surface. Drain in a colander and rinse under cold running water.

Finally, heat the 3 tablespoons butter in a skillet. Fry the gnocchi in the hot butter until they have a brown crust on both sides. Add the sauce and serve immediately, topped with a smattering of fine lettuce leaves.

LUKEWARM SALAD OF SWEET POTATO GNOCCHI WITH TOMATOES & CASHEW-BASIL PESTO

PREPARE: ABOUT
20 MINUTES
SERVES 2 AS A MAIN
COURSE, OR 4 AS A
SIDE DISH

for the sweet potato gnocchi
10½ ounces (300 g) sweet
  potatoes
1 egg yolk
¾ cup (100 g) all-purpose
  flour
pinch of sea salt

for the pesto
1 bunch (¾ ounce/20 g) basil
scant ½ cup (50 g) cashews,
  briefly toasted in a dry
  skillet
1 clove garlic, halved
about ½ cup (50 g) grated
  pecorino cheese
juice of ½ lemon
sea salt and freshly ground
  black pepper

to finish
2 tablespoons olive oil
10½ ounces (300 g) small
  tomatoes, all colors, halved
5¼ ounces (150 g) mixed
  lettuces (for example
  mustard leaf, Bull's Blood,
  and mizuna)
juice of ½ lemon
1 bunch (¾ ounce/20 g)
  basil, leaves only

If you can find freshly made gnocchi in your grocery store, by all means use it instead of making them from scratch; you'll need about 14 ounces (400 g) for an easy weekday dish that can be whipped up in a snap. If you make the gnocchi yourself (very fun to do, of course, and so much more delicious), then it will of course take you a little longer. However! The result will also be quite something.

Prepare the gnocchi with the sweet potatoes, egg yolk, flour, and salt according to the recipe on page 279. Bake the sweet potatoes with the skins on. That way the starchy flesh stays nice and dry and you'll need less flour.

In a large pot with ample boiling salted water, cook the gnocchi until al dente, meaning: until they float to the surface (or follow the directions on the package if using store-bought gnocchi). Drain the gnocchi, rinse them briefly under cold running water, and drain in a colander. (This is to stop the cooking process so they don't become too soft.)

Make the pesto: In a small chopper or food processor, puree the basil, cashews, garlic, and pecorino into crumbs. Add the lemon juice and salt and pepper until you think the taste is balanced, then dilute the pesto with enough water—4 to 5 tablespoons (60 to 75 ml)—to form a nice creamy sauce. It should be rather on the thin side, more of a thick dressing than as thick as the pesto you know from Italy. This way it will stick to the vegetables and gnocchi in the salad.

In a skillet, heat the olive oil. Fry the gnocchi, stirring now and then, until golden brown, just like you would fry potatoes.

Spoon them into a bowl and add the halved tomatoes. Add the lettuce leaves at the end so they won't wilt due to the hot gnocchi. Spoon the pesto into the salad. Drizzle with lemon juice and garnish with basil. Serve immediately.

PASTA

Zandvoort, the Netherlands

GRAINS

Owenahincha, West Cork

GREEN RISOTTO

PREPARE: 30 MINUTES
SERVES 4 AS A STARTER OR
SIDE DISH

2 tablespoons olive oil
10½ ounces (300 g) spinach
2 cloves garlic, grated
pinch of freshly grated
    nutmeg
sea salt and freshly ground
    black pepper
1 heaping tablespoon butter,
    or more if needed
1 large onion, chopped
4 stalks celery, very finely
    chopped
2 cups (400 g) arborio rice, or
    some other short-grain rice
10 tablespoons (150 ml) dry
    white wine
about 5 cups (1.2 L)
    vegetable stock, boiling hot
7 ounces (200 g) green beans,
    tops and tails trimmed
1 cup (100 g) grated
    Parmesan cheese
3½ ounces (100 g) soft
    goat cheese
lemon juice

tool
blender

You may think this is a boring recipe, but it's actually one of the better ones in this book. Just make it.

In a wok, heat the olive oil; add the spinach and garlic and stir-fry for a few minutes, until the spinach has wilted. Season the spinach with nutmeg, salt, and pepper. Transfer to a blender and grind to a smooth puree. Set aside.

In a sauté pan or Dutch oven with a large diameter, melt the butter, then add the chopped onion and celery and, while stirring, sauté over medium heat for about 7 minutes, until soft and translucent, but not browned. Add extra butter if needed.

Stir in the arborio rice and, stirring continuously, fry until the grains are translucent. Douse with the white wine. While stirring, allow the wine to evaporate and, one ladleful at a time, stir in the hot vegetable stock. Stir the risotto until all the stock has been absorbed before adding the next ladleful. Continue like this for 16 to 17 minutes: the rice should be almost al dente by now.

Meanwhile, chop the green beans into pieces of barely ⅜ inch (1 cm). Stir into the risotto and cook for 3 minutes. Stir in the pureed spinach, the Parmesan, and goat cheese. Allow the cheese to melt completely.

Cover the pan with a lid, remove from the heat, and let the risotto rest for about 2 minutes. Before serving, season the risotto with a splash of lemon juice, some extra pepper, and some salt if needed, although the cheese and stock may be sufficiently salty already. Serve warm.

GRAINS

WHEAT BEER RISOTTO WITH COCKLES OR CLAMS

PREPARE: 25 MINUTES
SERVES 4 AS A MAIN
COURSE, OR 6 AS A
STARTER

4 tablespoons (55 g) butter
1 pound 1 ounce (500 g)
    cockles (or small clams
    local to your area!)
1 bottle (330 ml) wheat beer
1 shallot, finely chopped
2 cloves garlic, finely
    chopped
1½ cups (300 g) arborio rice,
    or some other short-grain
    rice
grated zest and juice of
    1 organic lemon
about 3¼ cups (800 ml)
    chicken stock, boiling hot
1 bunch (½ ounce/15 g)
    flat-leaf parsley, finely
    chopped
sea salt and freshly ground
    black pepper

Of course, I could also make this risotto with vongole clams, but those have to come all the way from Italy, whereas cockles live right on our doorstep. So not only are these Dutch delicacies locally harvested, they're also several times less expensive. I happen to find cockles just as delicious as vongole, especially in combination with wheat beer and butter. This would also be lovely with littleneck or manila clams. Pure summer on a plate, this dish.

Melt 1 tablespoon of the butter in a wide sauté pan. Spoon in the cockles and add one-third of the wheat beer. Cover with the lid and shake the pan until the cockles are cooked and pop open. Spoon the cockles onto a large plate and let them cool slightly while making the risotto.

Melt 1 tablespoon of the butter in the same pan. It is okay if there is still some moisture inside. Add the shallot and garlic and sauté until the shallot is translucent. Stir in the arborio rice and fry the rice while stirring until the grains are translucent with a white core.

Douse the rice with the rest of the beer and the lemon juice and stir until the moisture has been completely absorbed. Add the chicken stock to the rice, one ladleful at a time, stirring continuously and only adding another ladleful of stock after the previous one has been completely absorbed. This whole process usually takes 20 minutes.

In between stirring the risotto, remove three-quarters of the cockles from the shells. Once the risotto is al dente, stir in the shelled cockles, almost all of the lemon zest, most of the flat-leaf parsley, and the remaining 2 tablespoons butter. Season the risotto with salt and pepper. Put the lid on the pan and remove from the heat so that the butter can melt.

Spoon the risotto into heated deep serving plates and garnish with the reserved unshelled cockles and the rest of the lemon zest and parsley. Serve hot.

GRAINS

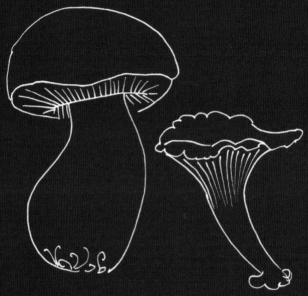

DRY FRESH MUSHROOMS,
THINLY SLICED, IN YOUR OVEN.
IT'S EASIER THAN YOU THINK:
ON THE LOWEST SETTING,
(USUALLY SOMETHING LIKE
125°F/50°C), WITH THE CON-
VECTION FAN TURNED ON
IF YOU HAVE ONE, AND A
WOODEN SPOON TO HOLD THE
DOOR AJAR SO THE MOISTURE
CAN ESCAPE. ARRANGE THEM
ON A WIRE RACK IN A SINGLE
LAYER AND BAKE THEM OVER-
NIGHT, OR UNTIL BONE DRY.
STORE IN AN AIRTIGHT
CONTAINER.

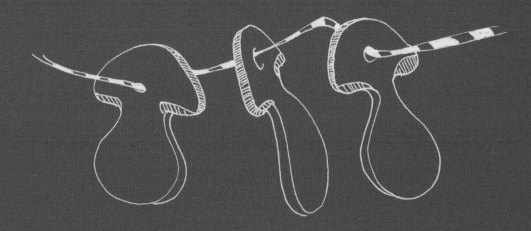

YOU CAN ALSO MAKE A MUSHROOM
GARLAND. DON'T SLICE YOUR
MUSHROOMS TOO THIN. STRING
THEM ON SOME KITCHEN TWINE
USING A BLUNT NEEDLE. HANG
THE GARLANDS IN A WARM, DRY
SPOT IN THE HOUSE. THE WARMER
IT IS, THE FASTER THE MUSHROOMS
WILL DRY. THIS METHOD DOES
TAKE LONGER THAN THE FIRST
BUT: YOU USE LESS ENERGY!
STORE YOUR DRY SHROOMS IN
AN AIRTIGHT CONTAINER.

ORZOTTO WITH PORCINI MUSHROOMS, VANILLA & MAGICAL POACHED EGG

SOAK: 30 MINUTES
PREPARE: 40 MINUTES
SERVES 4 AS A MAIN
COURSE

for the pearl barley risotto
½ ounce (15 g) dried porcini
   mushrooms (see pages 292
   to 295 for home made)
¾ cup plus 1 tablespoon
   (200 ml) lukewarm water
2 tablespoons olive oil
2 shallots
2 cloves garlic
leaves of a few sage sprigs
seeds from 1 vanilla pod, or
   1 teaspoon vanilla extract
1¼ cups (250 g) pearl barley
   (see below)
6½ tablespoons (100 ml) dry
   sherry or white wine
4½ cups (1 L) vegetable
   stock, boiling hot
2⅔ cups (200 g) loosely
   packed sliced kale

for the magical poached egg
4 fresh eggs
splash of vinegar
3 tablespoons sumac

Instead of pearl barley you can also use pot barley, whole spelt, farro, freekeh, or whole-grain bulgur wheat: adjust the cooking times for each grain type. (So taste regularly while cooking.)

Using my home dried porcini from the previous pages, I made such a delicious barley risotto that I had to share it with you. Orzotto is just like risotto but made with pearl barley instead of rice. Pearl barley is hulled and polished barley grains. You can also make this dish with spelt or farro (a type of spelt) in which case it's called "farrotto." If you do, the cooking time will be somewhat longer; keep this in mind and perhaps use a bit more stock.

Make the risotto: Soak the porcini mushrooms in a bowl with the lukewarm water for 30 minutes. Drain the mushrooms, reserving the soaking water. Finely chop the soaked mushrooms and set aside.

Heat the olive oil in a large heavy pan, add the shallots, and sauté until translucent. Stir in the garlic and sage. Reduce the heat to prevent the garlic from burning and cook for about 6 minutes. Add the chopped soaked mushrooms, then stir in the vanilla seeds and pearl barley. Fry everything over low heat until the barley has turned translucent.

Douse with the sherry. Pour in the hot vegetable stock and bring to a boil. Reduce the heat and let the orzotto simmer for about 30 minutes without the lid on. After 15 minutes, pour in the mushroom soaking liquid through a strainer. Stir in the kale and let it simmer for another 15 minutes.

Prepare the eggs: Poach the eggs in water with the vinegar, following my instructions on page 49!

Sprinkle the sumac in a bowl. Pat the poached eggs dry with a paper towel and press one side of each egg into the sumac.

Divide the orzotto and the beautiful red sumac eggs among four heated serving bowls. Serve hot.

GRAINS

UMAMI BOMB BOWL WITH BROWN RICE

SOAK: 10 MINUTES
PREPARE: 30 MINUTES
SERVES 2 OR 3 AS A MAIN
COURSE, OR 4 WITH SMALL
SERVINGS

1¼ ounces (30 g) dried
   mushrooms (see pages 292
   to 295)
4½ cups (1 L) hot vegetable
   or chicken stock
2 eggs (or more: use 1 egg
   per person)
2 heads of baby bok choy
   (or 1 head of full-grown
   bok choy), stems cut into
   ¾-inch (2 cm) pieces,
   leaves left whole
2 tablespoons sesame oil
2 tablespoons red miso
1 large onion, chopped
2¾ inches (7 cm) fresh
   ginger, peeled and grated
3 cloves garlic, finely
   chopped
1 cup (200 g) brown rice
5¼ ounces (150 g) shiitakes,
   dry stems removed
about 5 carrots, peeled and
   sliced diagonally
2 scallions, sliced into rings
2 tablespoons rice vinegar
1 teaspoon black sesame
   seeds, for garnish (optional)

The intense, deep flavor of the broth in this recipe comes from red miso, garlic, ginger, and mushrooms. A savory taste that is also called umami. This recipe will lift the spirits of even the most miserable patient; it is the ultimate pick-me-up.

Brown rice is whole-grain rice with the bran still intact. This makes it the most nutritious of all rice varieties: it's unprocessed and rich in fiber. I adore brown rice for its deliciously nutty flavor, which works really well in this recipe. Feel free to substitute another grain, though. Barley, spelt, oats, whole-wheat bulgur—they all work great. This dish is meant to be a little brothy, and the rice should be cooked not quite dry. The result is delicious and has become a staple on our dinner table. We put in whatever vegetables we happen to have on hand, so we end up with a different umami bomb bowl each time.

Soak the dried mushrooms in the hot stock for 10 minutes. Drain, reserving the stock. Chop the soaked mushrooms. Pour the stock through a strainer into a bowl.

In boiling water in a large saucepan, boil the eggs for 7 minutes. After 6 minutes, add the bok choy to the boiling water and briefly blanch it. Immediately rinse the eggs and bok choy under cold water. As soon as they have somewhat cooled, peel the eggs. Set the eggs and bok choy aside.

Heat the sesame oil in a large pan over medium heat. Stir-fry the miso, onion, and ginger for 6 minutes, or until the onion turns brown and fragrant. Add the garlic and the chopped soaked mushrooms and cook for 2 minutes. Deglaze the pan with the strained stock. Bring to a boil and reduce the heat to keep the stock simmering.

Add the brown rice, bring the stock back to a boil, partly cover with a lid, and cook the rice for 15 to 20 minutes over low heat, until the rice grains are tender. Add the fresh shiitakes and carrot slices 8 minutes before the end of the cooking time. >>>

GRAINS

>> Stir the bok choy and scallions into the rice. Cook everything for 5 minutes. Season the rice with a drop of rice vinegar. Spoon the rice, along with the vegetables and mushrooms, into two wide bowls. Halve the eggs and place them on top. Sprinkle the umami bomb with sesame seeds.

This dish is even more delicious with the sesame rayu on page 143 or the hot sauce on page 141.

OTHER TASTY TOPPINGS

ROASTED PUMPKIN

1 butternut squash, unpeeled, seeds removed, cut into wedges, sprinkled with a splash of olive oil, a pinch of cayenne pepper, sea salt, and ground cumin, roasted for 40 minutes at 400°F (200°C).

CRISPY BROCCOLI

1 head of broccoli or broccolini, cut into florets, roasted like the butternut squash, but for only 25 minutes, or cooked with the bok choy in the recipe.

CHARRED BRUSSELS SPROUTS

See page 221.

SAUTÉED SPINACH

10½ ounces (300 g) spinach and garlic, briefly sautéed in olive oil.

LEFTOVER LEMON CHICKEN

Leftovers from the lemon chicken on page 355.

WARM SESAME CUCUMBER

1 cucumber, unpeeled, thickly sliced, briefly stir-fried in sesame oil with red chile rings.

SPICY PANEER OR HALLOUMI

Fry strips of paneer or halloumi (about 5¼ ounces/150 g) in 2 tablespoons sunflower oil until crispy. After a few minutes, add 1 tablespoon curry paste to the pan and toss the cheese to coat.

SPICY CASHEWS

Fry a handful of cashews in 1 tablespoon butter or ghee, deglaze with a drop of soy sauce, and toss with a pinch of cayenne, paprika, or curry powder. Season with sea salt.

STICKY TOFU

Fry cubes of tofu in a layer of sunflower oil. Drain on paper towels and cook them briefly in some sweet soy sauce, a drop of salty soy, a squirt of hot sauce (page 141), and a dash of sesame seeds.

Lower East Side, New York

CUTTING ORANGE SEGMENTS

Place an orange in front of you on a cutting board, the stem side facing up.

Use a knife to cut downward from the top, removing the orange peel, the white pith, and the thin membrane beneath it.

You should be able to see the flesh.

Holding the orange in your hand—over a bowl to catch the juice—use a sharp knife to cut loose the wedges from in between the membranes.

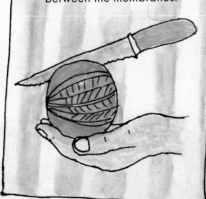

The remaining empty orange hull can be squeezed over the bowl to get that last bit of juice. Now you can use the beautiful clean wedges for whichever recipe you like.

orange grain salad with halloumi

ORANGE GRAIN SALAD WITH HALLOUMI

PREPARE: 15 MINUTES
SERVES 4 AS A SIDE DISH

for the salad
1¼ cups (250 g) dried grain (like pearl barley, bulgur, or whole-wheat couscous)
1 can (14 ounces/400 g) chickpeas, rinsed and drained
1 zucchini, very thinly sliced
3 oranges, cut into segments (see page 303)
3 scallions, thinly sliced
1 bunch (½ ounce/15 g) flat-leaf parsley, coarsely chopped
small handful of fresh mint leaves, coarsely chopped

for the dressing
½ cup (125 ml) olive oil
3 tablespoons lemon juice
2 cloves garlic, minced
2 tablespoons very finely chopped fresh mint

finishing touch
8 ounces (250 g) halloumi cheese
2 tablespoons olive oil
sea salt and freshly ground black pepper

Make the salad: Cook the grain according to the instructions on the package.

In a large bowl, combine the grain with the chickpeas, sliced zucchini, orange wedges, scallions, parsley, and mint.

Mix all the ingredients for the dressing. Stir into the salad.

Prepare the finishing touch: Slice the halloumi and fry in a skillet in the olive oil until nicely browned on both sides. Place the baked halloumi over the salad. Season with salt and pepper and serve right away.

SPANAKORIZO: GREEK SPINACH-LEMON RICE

Wilt 1 pound 5 ounces (600 g) spinach in a skillet with the juice of 1 lemon and a drop of olive oil. Let cool somewhat, chop coarsely, and set aside.

In a pan with a lid, sauté 1 chopped onion in 1 tablespoon olive oil for 6 to 7 minutes, until soft. Add the chopped spinach, 2 teaspoons dried mint, 2 tablespoons finely chopped fresh dill, and 1¼ cups (300 ml) water and bring to a boil.

Add ½ cup (100 g) brown or white rice to the pan, season with salt and pepper, and, once it boils, cover with the lid and simmer for about 20 minutes over very low heat until the rice is cooked.

Stir everything and serve in heated bowls, drizzled with a splash of olive oil and topped with ¾ cup (125 g) crumbled feta cheese and the neatly cut (see page 303) segments of 1 lemon. Season with a smattering of paprika and black pepper.

You can also serve this spinach rice at room temperature as part of an assortment of smaller dishes.

GRAINS

BEET COUSCOUS WITH FRIED ONIONS

**PREPARE: 35 MINUTES
SERVES 2 AS A LUNCH,
OR 4 AS A SIDE DISH**

1 cup (200 g) whole-wheat
   couscous
1 cup (250 ml) hot vegetable
   stock
2 tablespoons olive oil
3 red onions, thinly sliced
1 teaspoon caraway seeds
2 tablespoons balsamic
   vinegar
2 tablespoons lemon juice
2 red beets, precooked, cut
   into ⅜-inch (1 cm) cubes
1 bunch (½ ounce/15 g)
   flat-leaf parsley, chopped
sea salt and freshly ground
   black pepper
4 tablespoons (35 g) mixed
   hulled pumpkin seeds and
   sunflower seeds, toasted
   briefly in a dry skillet

I'm making couscous with the home-cook shortcut, instead of using the traditional steaming method. You steam couscous because it yields a more beautiful, drier, and fluffier grain, but because this salad contains so many different ingredients the effect would be hardly noticeable. So in this case I went with the easier option. Don't let that stop you, by the way: feel free to steam your couscous if you want. Once the onions are in the pan, you'll have plenty of time.

Put the couscous in a large bowl, pour in the hot vegetable stock, and cover with a plate. Let stand for 7 minutes, or until the couscous has absorbed all of the stock and is loose and cooked through. Using a fork, fluff the couscous.

Heat the olive oil in a skillet over medium heat. Add the onion rings and cook for 25 minutes, stirring occasionally, until soft and caramelized. After 20 minutes, add the caraway seeds and fry those as well. Deglaze the pan with the balsamic vinegar and lemon juice. Add the beet cubes and flat-leaf parsley and thoroughly stir everything to warm the beets and combine.

Spoon the vegetables, herbs, and any of their liquid into the couscous. Season with salt and pepper to taste. Sprinkle the salad with the roasted pumpkin and sunflower seeds.

The beet couscous goes well with the lamb chops on page 343 or the "green fingers" (veggie sausages) on page 209. But by itself this salad also makes for a delicious lunch.

SEMOLINA WITH SHRIMP, FAVA BEANS & CHORIZO

PREPARE: 25 MINUTES
SERVES 4 AS A MAIN
COURSE

1 pound 1 ounce (500 g) shelled fresh or frozen fava beans (shelled weight)*

1 fennel bulb, very thinly sliced

2 tablespoons olive oil

3½ ounces (100 g) cured chorizo, very finely chopped

2 shallots or 1 onion, finely chopped

2 cloves garlic, finely chopped

⅓ cup (75 ml) dry white wine

2 cups plus 1 tablespoon (500 ml) vegetable stock

1 sprig of thyme

juice of 1 lemon

splash of Tabasco sauce, to taste

sea salt and freshly ground black pepper

1 pound 1 ounce (500 g) small shrimp, peeled

1 bunch (½ ounce/15 g) flat-leaf parsley, coarsely chopped

for the semolina

sea salt

1 cup plus 2 tablespoons (150 g) semolina (or groats or polenta)

3½ ounces (100 g) crème fraîche

3½ tablespoons (50 g) butter

freshly ground black pepper

*For 1 pound 1 ounce (500 g) shelled fava beans, you'll need 2½ to 4 pounds (1 to 2 kg) unshelled fava beans in their pods. But frozen beans are fine too. That way you can also make this dish in the winter.

I prefer to make this dish with groats (a coarser version of durum wheat sold at organic specialty stores). But if you are unable to find it, you can also use the finer semolina, or polenta. Make sure to adjust how much water you add. Each grain variety or grind requires a different amount of liquid. And each person has their own taste preferences. I like mine nice and soft.

Bring a pot of water to a boil. Cook the fava beans and the fennel for 4 minutes, drain, and rinse with ice-cold water immediately. That way they'll stay nice and green. If you feel like it, you can peel half of the fava beans a second time (see page 174). I usually do.

Heat the olive oil in a large Dutch oven over medium heat. Add the chorizo and fry, stirring, for 4 minutes, or until crispy. Remove the chorizo from the pan and let it drain on a paper towel.

In the same pan in which you fried the chorizo, also sauté the shallots and garlic for a few minutes, until the shallots turn translucent. Deglaze the pan with the white wine, cook to reduce somewhat, then pour in the vegetable stock. Add a sprig of thyme. Bring the liquid to a boil and cook until reduced to two-thirds of the original volume.

While the sauce is reducing, prepare the semolina: Bring 1 quart (1 L) salted water to a boil. Add the semolina, beating with a whisk. Reduce the heat and continue whisking for 5 to 7 minutes, until you get a creamy porridge. Stir in the crème fraîche and butter and season the semolina with salt and pepper.

Season the sauce with lemon juice, Tabasco, and salt and pepper to taste and stir in the fava beans and fennel. Stir in the shrimp and cook for 1 minute, or until the shrimp are cooked through.

Ladle the semolina into four deep plates and spoon the fava bean and shrimp stew on top. Sprinkle with flat-leaf parsley and the chorizo and serve immediately.

GRAINS

SHEET-PAN BAKING

Sheet-pan baking at a bakery in Borough Market, London

MAKING SHORT CRUST

Make dough using whole-wheat or all-purpose flour, salt, cubes of cold butter, a drop of ice water, and sometimes egg.

Weigh everything according to the recipe. Combine in a bowl until the dough resembles coarse crumbs. Ideally with cool, clean hands.

Plop the crumbs on the counter and press them together until the dough becomes cohesive. Don't knead.

Form a flat ball. You may still see specks of butter—that's okay. That will make it delicious! Wrap in foil or parchment paper.

Place the dough ball in the fridge and let rest for 1 hour. Yes, 1 hour.

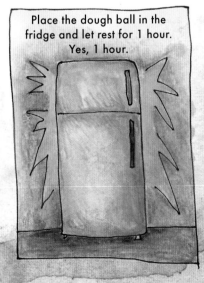

Remove from the fridge and allow to come to room temperature. Roll out on a lightly flour-dusted counter. Turn the dough over constantly, so you get a nice slab.

It's okay if it tears, just press it back together.

PREPARE: 15 MINUTES
WAIT: 30 MINUTES TO
1 HOUR
BAKE: 40 MINUTES

for the crust
¾ cup plus 1 tablespoon
   (100 g) whole-wheat flour
¾ cup plus 1 tablespoon
   (100 g) all-purpose flour
pinch of sea salt
7 tablespoons (100 g) cold
   butter, cubed
1 egg yolk
drop of ice water

for the filling
few sprigs thyme, plus more
   for garnish
1 pound 1 ounce (500 g) red
   beets, precooked, cut into
   wedges
1 red onion, cut into rings
3 tablespoons balsamic
   vinegar
1 tablespoon olive oil
sea salt and freshly ground
   black pepper
7 ounces (200 g) brie cheese,
   cut into small chunks
1 egg, beaten
½ cup (50 g) raw walnuts

WHOLE-WHEAT SHEET-PAN PIE WITH BEETS, BRIE & WALNUTS

YESSS, the sheet pie: so festive, but also a nice fridge-clearing-out recipe. There are so many combinations possible. I added a few more below this recipe. Of course you can use a large sheet of puff pastry, but whole-wheat dough gives it more bite, and I find the flavor more interesting.

Make the dough for the crust: Combine the whole-wheat flour with the all-purpose flour and salt and swiftly rub in the butter until it looks like coarse crumbs. I use a food processor, but you can also do it by hand. Stir in the egg yolk and add as much ice water as needed for the dough to become cohesive. Knead briefly, shape into a rectangular slab, and wrap in plastic wrap. Let the dough rest for 30 minutes to 1 hour in the fridge.

Preheat the oven to 350°F (180°C).

Roll out the dough into a large rectangle on a large sheet of parchment paper placed over a baking sheet. With a dull knife, score a ½-inch (1.5 cm) border all around, but don't cut all the way through. This way you've created a—let's say—picture frame. With a fork, prick holes in the dough inside the edge, to prevent the dough from puffing up in the oven. Prebake the crust for 15 minutes.

Make the filling: Strip the thyme leaves from the stems. Combine the red beets with the onion, balsamic vinegar, olive oil, thyme leaves, and salt and pepper. Arrange the filling over the prebaked crust, inside the frame. Place the brie chunks in between the beet wedges and brush the edges of the crust with beaten egg.

Bake the sheet pie in the oven for 25 minutes. After 15 minutes, sprinkle with the walnuts.

Let the pie cool off somewhat before slicing it. Garnish with some thyme sprigs and serve with a green salad.

LEEK & YAM
Soft precooked and well-drained leeks, coarsely mashed cooked sweet potato, crumbled blue cheese, coarsely chopped hazelnuts.

SPINACH & SAUCE
Cover the crust with hummus or eggplant ginger dip (see page 91), top with sautéed and drained spinach, and sprinkle with crumbled feta or goat cheese.

PORTOBELLO
Portobellos, stems removed, sautéed in olive oil and garlic, sautéed red onion (see pizza on page 325), and cashew-arugula pesto (see page 131).

SHEET-PAN BAKING

DARK MALT FLOUR TOMATO GALETTE

PREPARE: 20 MINUTES
WAIT: 1 HOUR
BAKE: 45 MINUTES
SERVES 2 AS A MAIN
COURSE, OR 4 AS A LUNCH

for the dough
½ cup (60 g) rye or whole-wheat flour
½ cup (65 g) malted barley flour*
1 cup (125 g) all-purpose flour
½ cup (115 g) cold butter, cubed
1 egg
4 tablespoons (60 ml) ice water
½ teaspoon sea salt

on top
1 ball (8 ounces/250 g) mozzarella, from cow's milk (buffalo mozzarella is too wet)
1 pound 1 ounce (500 g) tomatoes in various colors, sliced
1 tablespoon olive oil
a few sprigs of oregano, leaves only
sea salt flakes (for example, Maldon) and freshly ground black pepper

*see page 13 for shopping info

No barley flour?
No problem: use whole rye or wheat flour for a nice nutty flavor.

I have a weak spot for malt flour. In the Netherlands we have to source it directly from the miller, but abroad it's easier to buy. Malt flour is made from germinated cereal grain or barley. Sometimes the germinated grains are roasted. Then you get a *dark* malt flour, which in a natural way gives dough or bread a deep dark color and a mild sweet, almost chocolate-like flavor. Very cool.

Malt flour needs to be combined with another meal or flour, because the enzymes that start the leavening process are burned, making them inactive. So you'd use a handful of malt flour purely for its color and flavor. Your dough or bread will turn wonderfully dark and terribly delicious.

If you've been to the Netherlands you've likely had malt flour, as it's used in Waldkorn bread and other dark breads as a coloring additive so you think it's healthier. This is not true, just so you know. It's not healthier; it's purely a color and flavor enhancer.

If you have a pizza stone or similar (see page 205), put it on a rack in the top third of the oven. Preheat the oven to 425°F (225°C).

Prepare the dough: Combine all the ingredients quickly into a dough that just about comes together. If needed, add a few drops of ice water. Shape the dough into a flat disk, wrap in plastic wrap, and let rest in the fridge for 1 hour.

Roll out the dough until you have an 11- to 12-inch (28 to 30 cm) round. Place on a flour-dusted baking sheet.

Add the toppings: Slice the mozzarella. Arrange on the dough round, leaving a generous margin at the edge uncovered. Cover the cheese with the tomato slices. Drizzle with olive oil, then sprinkle with some of the oregano leaves, salt flakes, and freshly ground black pepper. Fold the edges of the galette over the filling, pleating it rustically.

Bake the galette for 45 minutes. Let cool slightly before serving. Sprinkle with the remaining oregano leaves. Serve with a big salad.

SHEET-PAN BAKING

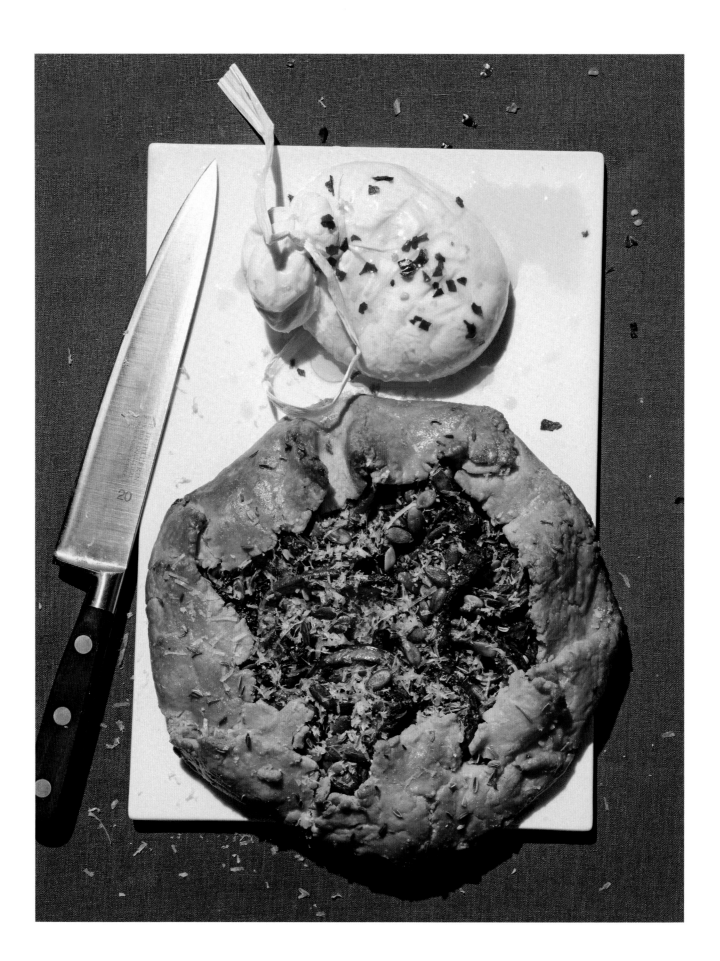

BUTTERNUT SQUASH GALETTE WITH BURRATA

PREPARE: 40 MINUTES
WAIT: 1 HOUR
BAKE: 40 MINUTES
SERVES 2 AS A MAIN COURSE,
OR 4 AS A LUNCH DISH

for the dough
1⅓ cups (175 g) all-purpose
    flour, plus extra
1 tablespoon fennel seeds,
    briefly ground in a mortar
6 tablespoons (90 g) cold
    butter, cubed
1 egg yolk
pinch of sea salt
about 3 tablespoons ice water
1 whole egg, beaten

for the topping
½ butternut squash (about
    1 pound 1 ounce/500 g)
4 tablespoons (60 ml) olive oil,
    plus extra
10½ ounces (300 g) spinach,
    well rinsed, tough stems
    removed
1 cup (100 g) finely grated
    pecorino cheese
2 tablespoons squash seeds,
    roasted
2 balls burrata or mozzarella
    cheese
chile flakes, rubbed between
    your fingers
finely grated zest of ½ organic
    lemon
pinch of fennel seeds

for the rub
1 tablespoon fennel seeds,
    briefly ground in the mortar
1 tablespoon oregano
3 small dried chiles, or
    1 teaspoon chile flakes, or to
    taste
1 teaspoon sea salt

tool
mortar and pestle

Make the dough: In a food processor or by hand, combine all ingredients (save the ice water and the beaten egg) into a cohesive dough, adding a few drops of ice water only if necessary. Don't knead the dough for too long. Press the dough into a flat disk, wrap in plastic wrap, and let rest for 1 hour in the fridge.

Halve the squash half lengthwise; no need to peel. Using a small sharp knife and a spoon, remove the seeds and slice the squash into thin ⅜-inch (1 cm) strips.

Preheat the oven to 400°F (200°C).

Using a mortar, make the rub by grinding all of the ingredients. Arrange the squash slices on a baking sheet and rub with half of the rub. Drizzle the squash slices with some of the olive oil and toss to coat. Roast the squash in the oven for 30 minutes, or until the slices are tender and are about to darken along the edges.

Lower the oven temperature to 350°F (180°C). (If you're finishing the butternut squash galette another time, you can turn off the oven.)

Stir-fry the spinach in 2 tablespoons olive oil over high heat. Let all the liquid evaporate or drain the spinach and press the liquid out of it with the back of a spoon. Combine the spinach with two-thirds of the pecorino.

Roll out the dough on a sheet of parchment paper into a 14-inch (35 cm) round. Place the parchment paper with the dough circle on a large baking sheet. Arrange the spinach and the roasted squash over the dough, leaving a generous margin at the edge uncovered. Sprinkle the vegetables with the rest of the rub, the remaining pecorino, and the squash seeds. Drizzle the top of the galette with 2 tablespoons olive oil. Fold the dough edges somewhat over the vegetables, brush the dough edges with the beaten egg, and bake the galette for 35 to 40 minutes, until browned.

Sprinkle the burrata balls with the chile flakes, grated lemon zest, and fennel seeds, sprinkle with olive oil, and chop it. Serve the butternut squash galette, sliced into wedges, with the burrata.

SHEET-PAN BAKING

MAKING BREAD . . .

Soak 1 sachet (¼ ounce/ 7 g) instant yeast in a small bowl with lukewarm water for 7 minutes.

Combine 1 lb 1 oz (500 g) all-purpose flour (or a combination of all-purpose and whole-wheat flour) with 1 tsp salt. Pour the dissolved yeast and close to 1¼ c (300 ml) lukewarm water in the middle.

Knead into a cohesive dough in the bowl. You may have to add a drop of water, or some flour. Do what feels right.

Transfer the dough to the counter and thoroughly knead for at least 10 minutes. DO IT, or there's no point in making bread.

Return the ball of dough to the bowl. Cover with a clean towel and place the bowl in a warm spot in your house.

Wait 1 hour, or until the dough has doubled in size. (If you're using a combination of all-purpose and whole-wheat flour, your dough won't rise as much.)

...OR PIZZA DOUGH

Press all the air out of the dough with your fist and knead again. Shorter this time. And divide . . .

. . . into two smaller balls if you are making pizza. Cover with a towel and let rise for another 30 minutes . . .

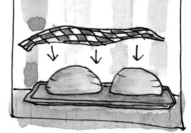

. . . or shape the dough into a loaf that fits into a greased loaf pan and cover with a towel. Let rise for 30 minutes.

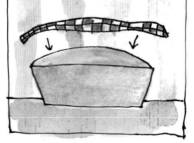

If you're making pizzas: roll out the dough on a flour-dusted counter into the desired thickness.

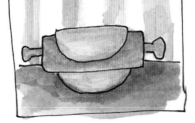

Put toppings of your choice on the pizza (see, for example, page 325) and bake the pizza in a scorching-hot oven at 425°F (225°C) or even hotter, for 8 to 10 minutes.

If you're making bread: bake for 35 to 40 minutes at 350°F (180°C). When you tap on the bottom of the loaf and it sounds hollow, your bread is ready. Otherwise bake for a little while longer.

WHOLE-WHEAT PIZZA WITH EGGPLANT & SAUTÉED ONIONS

**PREPARE: 1 HOUR
15 MINUTES
BAKE: ABOUT 12 MINUTES
MAKES 1 LARGE PIZZA;
SERVES 3 OR 4**

for the dough
1½ cups (200 g) all-purpose
   flour
2¼ cups plus 2 tablespoons
   (300 g) whole-wheat flour
1 sachet (¼ ounce/7 g)
   instant yeast
pinch of salt
1¼ cups (300 ml) lukewarm
   water
semolina (durum wheat
   flour) to sprinkle over the
   baking sheet

on top
2 tablespoons butter
3 large red onions, sliced
sea salt and freshly ground
   black pepper
1 tablespoon caraway seeds,
   or to taste
3 to 4 small eggplants
splash of good-quality
   olive oil
2 balls mozzarella cheese
   from cow's milk
1 teaspoon chile flakes
1 tablespoon dried oregano

*See my spiel about
mandolines on page 157.

Make the dough: Mix all the ingredients and knead for 10 minutes, until the dough is a nice supple ball. Kneading for a long time improves the leavening process, so really knead for 10 minutes on a flour-dusted countertop until the dough is no longer sticky. Place the ball in a bowl, cover the bowl with plastic wrap, and put in a warm spot. Let the dough rise for 1 hour.

Prepare the toppings: Melt the butter in a skillet. Sauté the onion rings for nearly 30 minutes over very low heat until they are entirely red-brown, soft, and sweet. Stir frequently. Add salt, pepper, and caraway seeds to taste. Set the onions aside.

Thinly slice the eggplants, lengthwise, using a mandolin or a large sharp knife.*

Preheat the oven to 400°F (200°C).

Brush one or two baking sheets with olive oil, sprinkle with salt and pepper, and place the eggplant slices on top. Sprinkle the top of the slices with olive oil and salt and pepper. Bake the eggplant slices until just tender, 8 to 10 minutes. Repeat this until all eggplant slices are baked. If you have a griddle, you can bake the slices on the griddle, but it usually takes longer and is more work. I leave it to you.

Grease a large baking sheet and sprinkle with semolina.

Roll out the dough ball into a large oval slab the size of the baking sheet and put the dough on the baking sheet.

Slice the mozzarella and arrange the slices on the dough. Top with the eggplant slices and arrange the sautéed onions over them. Sprinkle the pizza with the chile flakes, oregano, and lots of salt and pepper.

Slide the pizza into the oven and bake for 12 minutes, or until the dough is golden brown and the cheese bubbles. Slice immediately and serve with a salad.

SHEET-PAN BAKING

PIZZAS WITH BROCCOLINI & FAUX TUNA

PREPARE: 15 MINUTES
WAIT: 1 HOUR
PREPARE: 20 MINUTES
BAKE: 13 MINUTES
SERVES 4 AS A MAIN
COURSE

about 1¾ pounds (800 g)
pizza dough (see pages
322–23); ideally make the
dough with flour tipo 00,
which is a softer flour with
a lower gluten content,
making the dough crispier
handful of semolina (durum
wheat flour)

for the faux tuna
1 sheet nori (available in the
Asian foods section)
juice of about ½ lemon
3 to 4 tablespoons white
tahini (see page 13)
2 stalks celery, very finely
chopped
pinch of cayenne pepper
sea salt and freshly ground
black pepper
1 can (14 ounces/400 g)
chickpeas, rinsed and
drained

on top
1 can (14½ ounces/411 g)
peeled tomatoes, hand-
crushed (see page 266)
about 7 ounces (200 g)
broccolini
2 balls (about 4½ ounces/
125 g each) mozzarella
from cow's milk (buffalo
milk is too wet!)
pinch of chile flakes
splash of olive oil

tool
food processor or blender

Admittedly, real tuna does have a different flavor, but there are just too few of them, so it feels funny to spread those tunas over a pizza (or on a toasty). I do have to say, it isn't such a weird idea, faux tuna. Moreover, my skeptical husband, Oof, kept eating it, so mission accomplished. These pizzas were Truly. Really. Delicious. So I'm sharing my recipe with you, so that you can get hooked on faux tuna.

Make the pizza dough according to the recipe. Let the dough rise for 1 hour in a warm spot.

Make the faux tuna: In a food processor or blender, grind all the ingredients, aside from the chickpeas, into a coarse pulp by pulsing a few times. Scoop in the chickpeas and pulse a few more times. It's okay if it's chunky, it shouldn't turn into hummus, if you know what I mean. Taste to see if the faux tuna needs more salt, pepper, or lemon juice. Cover the faux tuna and let stand until the dough is ready, so all the flavors can meld together.

If you have a pizza stone or similar (see page 205), put it on a rack in the top third of the oven. Preheat the oven to 425°F (225°C). Ideally even higher, if your oven is capable. My oven can go as high as 570°F (300°C).

Grease a large baking sheet and sprinkle it with semolina. Divide the dough into two or four portions and roll out each portion into a small pizza. I press the pizza from the center to the edges, and I don't touch the edges so they'll rise nicely during baking.

Top the pizzas: Let the hand-crushed tomatoes drain in a sieve. Brush the pizzas with a thin layer of tomato pulp and arrange the broccolini on top. Crumble the faux tuna over the broccolini. With a coarse grater, grate the mozzarella over the pizzas. Sprinkle the pizzas with a pinch of chile flakes. Drizzle with a splash of olive oil and slide them in the oven. Bake the pizzas for 11 to 13 minutes, or until the edges are nicely golden brown and the mozzarella has melted. Serve with a salad.

~ 326 ~

TORTILLAS

Heir Island, West Cork

MAKING TORTILLAS

Combine an almost equal amount of masa harina with water and salt into a soft and supple dough. Let stand on the counter for 30 minutes.

Roll into balls the size of a golf ball. Press between two sheets of plastic wrap or parchment paper into thin tortillas.

If you don't have a tortilla press, you can roll them out between two sheets of parchment paper with a rolling pin.

Heat a skillet (or the smooth side of a griddle) until very hot, then lower the heat somewhat so the temperature remains stable. Briefly heat the tortillas on both sides, until small dark spots appear.
Keep them covered with a clean dish towel until serving, so they won't dry out.

Paris, 18th arrondissement

whole-wheat tortillas

CORN TORTILLAS

PREPARE: 10 MINUTES
WAIT: 30 MINUTES
MAKES 15

2 cups (250 g) masa harina*
1¼ cups (300 ml) water (a bit
    more—by weight—than
    the flour)
generous pinch of salt

*This is flour made with dried
    corn that's been treated with
    lime (calcium hydroxide);
    it's available in many
    supermarkets and anywhere
    Mexican products are sold.
    NOTE: don't use regular
    cornmeal. If you can't find
    masa harina, make the regular
    flour tortillas below—those are
    very good too.

Make the tortilla dough and shape the tortillas according to the instructions on page 330.

Heat a skillet or the flat side of a griddle until it's very hot and lower the heat, so the temperature remains steady. Briefly heat the tortillas on both sides; they should be just cooked, but still pliable, or they'll become chips. (You could do that too. If you bake or fry tortillas until they are crispy, they are called tostadas.)

Keep the tortillas wrapped in a clean towel until you're ready to eat, so they will remain warm and soft.

FLOUR TORTILLAS

PREPARE: 10 MINUTES
WAIT: 15 MINUTES
MAKES 15

3 cups (400) g all-purpose
    flour, plus generous
    extra (you can also use
    a combination of half
    whole-wheat flour and half
    all-purpose or spelt flour)
1 cup plus 2 tablespoons
    (275 ml) water
1 teaspoon baking powder
pinch of salt
4 tablespoons (60 ml)
    olive oil

Knead all the ingredients into a soft dough that isn't sticky. Divide the dough into 15 small balls and roll them out on a flour-dusted countertop.

Cook them as described above. When you're working ahead, and are rolling out a bunch of tortillas, you'll notice that the tortillas shrink a little after rolling; just roll them again right before cooking. (And don't place uncooked tortillas on top of each other, as they'll stick together.)

TORTILLAS

TORTILLAS WITH HOISIN SHRIMP

PREPARE: 20 MINUTES
SERVES 4 AS A MAIN
COURSE

2 tablespoons sesame oil
1 tablespoon finely grated
   fresh ginger
3 cloves garlic, finely grated
1⅓ cups (150 g) coarsely
   grated or julienned carrot
9 ounces (250 g) shiitakes,
   dry stems removed, large
   ones sliced, smaller ones
   left whole
4 scallions, sliced
1½ cups (100 g) finely
   chopped kale; or ⅓ green
   cabbage, sliced
sea salt and freshly ground
   black pepper
14 ounces (400 g) peeled
   large shrimp (can be
   frozen)
1 tablespoon hoisin sauce
   (see page 139)
8 whole-wheat tortillas (see
   page 333)

Heat a wok or large skillet over medium heat. Pour in 1 tablespoon of the sesame oil and swivel the pan until the entire bottom is coated. Add the finely grated ginger and garlic, sauté for half a minute, and turn up the heat.

Add the carrot julienne and shiitakes, sauté for a few minutes, then add the scallions and kale. Stir-fry the vegetables for a few minutes, until the kale is tender. Season the vegetables with salt and pepper. Scoop the vegetable mix into a large bowl and keep warm under a lid or plate.

Wipe the pan clean with a paper towel and place it back on the stove. Pour the remaining 1 tablespoon sesame oil into the pan and swivel until the entire pan is coated in oil. Briefly fry the shrimp, until they just start to color, stir in the hoisin sauce, and douse with 2 to 3 tablespoons water, thinning the sauce. Combine the stir-fried vegetables with the shrimp.

Reheat the tortillas in a dry skillet and fill them with the vegetables and shrimp. Serve 2 tortillas per person.

LARGE TOSTADAS WITH PULLED CHICKEN, MANGO & MINT-COCONUT RELISH

PREPARE: 1 HOUR
SERVES 4 AS A MAIN COURSE

4 chicken legs
3 tablespoons butter, at room
    temperature
juice of 1 to 2 limes
sea salt and freshly ground
    black pepper
4 cloves garlic, unpeeled
a few sprigs rosemary
1 ripe mango
½ head of radicchio
4 flour tortillas (see page 333)

for the quick pickle
¾ cup plus 1 tablespoon
    (200 ml) white wine vinegar
2 to 3 tablespoons ginger
    syrup or granulated sugar
10 allspice berries
1 tablespoon Szechuan
    peppercorns
3 whole cloves
sea salt
1 cucumber
1 red onion, sliced
1 yellow pepper, cut into
    rings (optional)

for the mint-coconut relish
1 bunch (½ ounce/15 g)
    mint, tough stems removed
juice of 1 lime
1 small chile
3 tablespoons grated coconut
3 to 4 tablespoons coconut
    milk, to taste
1 tablespoon cumin seeds,
    toasted
sea salt

tool
blender or food processor

Preheat the oven to 425°F (225°C).

Place the chicken legs on a baking sheet and brush with butter. Squeeze the lime juice over the chicken and sprinkle with salt and pepper. Arrange the garlic cloves and a few sprigs of rosemary on top. Roast the chicken legs for 15 minutes.

Reduce the oven temperature to 350°F (180°C). Roast the chicken for another 30 minutes and occasionally baste with the juices in the pan, until the legs are tender.

Let the chicken cool a bit and pull the meat off the bones, shredding it. Slice the skin into strips and squeeze the garlic cloves from their peels. Combine the roasted garlic with the pulled chicken.

While the chicken is roasting, make the pickled vegetables: In a saucepan, heat the white wine vinegar, ¾ cup plus 1 tablespoon (200 ml) water, the ginger syrup or sugar, allspice berries, Szechuan peppercorns, and cloves. Taste how much syrup (or sugar) you'd like in it; often 2 tablespoons will suffice, but possibly you have a bigger sweet tooth than I do. Add salt to taste. Pour the vinegar marinade into a bowl.

Quarter the cucumber lengthwise. Remove the seeds and slice the cucumber on the diagonal. Add the cucumber, red onion rings, and yellow pepper to the brine. Let the pickle stand for as long as possible (it's even better after a night in the fridge!).

Make the mint-coconut relish: Put all ingredients in a blender or food processor and process as smooth as you prefer. Season the relish with salt.

Chop the mango into cubes. Tear the radicchio leaves into pieces and sprinkle with the vinegar marinade of the pickled vegetables.

Reheat the tortillas in a dry skillet until the edges are crispy, and top them with the radicchio leaves, pulled chicken, and mango cubes; serve the relish and pickled vegetables separately. As you're eating, tear off pieces of the tortilla and fill them.

TORTILLAS

MEAT &
FOWL

Guinness-braised pork belly (see page 349)

LAMB BUTTERMILK-MARINATED LAMB CHO
TARRAGON WITH WHITE BEANS & RED ON
RED COLESLAW, GUINNESS-BRAISED PORK
FROM THE OVEN BEEF MISO RICE MEATBAL
ANISE CHICKEN ROAST LEMON CHICKEN
CHICKEN EVER WITH SMOKY KETCHUP

view from Knockomagh Wood, West Cork

PS, LEG OF LAMB WITH A CRUST OF
ONS PORK STICKY TAMARIND RIBS WITH
BELLY, HARISSA MEATBALLS WITH RICE
LS, BEEF STEW WITH GINGER & STAR
WITH COCONUT MILK, THE BEST CRISPY

BUTTERMILK-MARINATED LAMB CHOPS

MARINATE: AT LEAST 1 HOUR
PREPARE: 15 MINUTES
SERVES 4 AS A MAIN COURSE

for the marinade
1½ cups (350 ml) buttermilk (see below)
grated zest of 1 organic lemon (save the lemon for dressing the greens below)
2 tablespoons chopped fresh rosemary
4 sprigs of thyme and/or other fresh herbs (such as fennel), finely chopped
1 clove garlic, grated
sea salt and coarsely ground black pepper
8 small lamb chops (half cuts; or 4 double cuts)

on the side
6 ripe vine tomatoes, cut into wedges
handful of fresh flat-leaf parsley leaves
handful of arugula
juice of 1 lemon
1 tablespoon olive oil
sea salt and freshly ground black pepper

All meat will become more tender and succulent after a buttermilk bath: This marinade also works fantastically for chicken. Adjust the amounts to the size of the meat cuts you wish to marinate.

When I'm in Ireland I source my meat from Gaels Lap Farm, a few valleys away. The animals there are living a good life, roaming the mountain pastures, grazing on fresh herbs and West Cork mountain grass all day. The lambs aren't slaughtered after a mere three to four months, as is common practice, but after more than a year, sometimes nearly two. Not only does this grant them longer lives, it also makes the meat taste better. Beautifully dark, and with a deep flavor.

When buying lamb, always ask about its origin. Lamb from the northern Dutch island of Texel, for instance, tastes different from lamb from the southern province of Brabant. And lamb from Colorado will taste different from lamb from New Zealand. This has everything to do with the regional diet of the animal. Just taste it.

I serve a nice meat cut like lamb chops with a simple salad of tomato, parsley, and arugula, which has a nice peppery flavor. Watercress also would work. Simplicity is what matters here.

Make the marinade: In a bowl, combine the buttermilk with the lemon zest, rosemary, thyme and fennel, garlic, and salt and pepper to taste. Submerge the lamb chops in the marinade, covering them completely. Let the meat marinate in the fridge for at least 1 hour (or overnight).

Combine the vine tomatoes with the parsley and arugula, add the lemon juice, olive oil, and salt and pepper to taste, and toss gently.

Heat a grill pan until hot, then reduce the heat to medium-high. Remove the lamb chops from the marinade and pat dry. Grill them on each side for 1 to 2 minutes, until they're medium-rare and have beautiful black grill marks. Serve the lamb chops on a large platter next to the salad. You can also add the roasted carrots with orange gremolata from page 219 to the plate.

LAMB

LEG OF LAMB WITH A CRUST OF TARRAGON WITH WHITE BEANS & RED ONIONS

PREPARE: 1 HOUR
SERVES 6 TO 8 AS A MAIN COURSE

4½-pound (2 kg) leg of lamb on the bone
sea salt and freshly ground black pepper
4 to 5 cloves garlic, finely chopped
2 tablespoons dried tarragon
4 tablespoons (60 ml) olive oil
2 to 3 red onions, cut into neat wedges
a splash of white wine or water
2 cans (14 ounces/400 g each) white or cannellini beans, rinsed and drained (soaked and home-cooked is a hundred times better!)

This is the easiest dish there is. All you have to do is rub the meat with the oil and finish the dish at the end. The oven does all the work!

Preheat the oven to 400°F (200°C).

Rub the leg of lamb with salt and pepper. Combine the garlic with the tarragon and 2 tablespoons of the olive oil and rub the leg of lamb with the mixture.

Place the leg of lamb in a flame-proof roasting pan and roast for about 40 minutes; by then the meat will be rosé or medium-rare. If you use a meat thermometer, the internal temperature should be 140°F (60°C).

Transfer the leg to a cutting board. Let the meat rest covered with aluminum foil for 10 minutes before carving the lamb.

In the meantime, put the roasting pan on the stovetop and add the remaining 2 tablespoons olive oil to the fat in the pan. Add the red onion and fry it until tender, then deglaze with a splash of wine or water and stir to loosen any ingredients stuck to the bottom. Ladle the beans into the onion and gravy and heat everything through and through. Ladle the beans with the gravy into a deep preheated dish and place the leg of lamb on top.

If you feel the urge to add a touch of green, you can make the broccoli slaw from page 162. It can take its time to marinate while the lamb is in the oven.

LAMB

STICKY TAMARIND RIBS WITH RED COLESLAW

PREPARE: 30 MINUTES
MARINATE: 1 TO 6 HOURS
ROAST: 3 HOURS
SERVES 4 AS A MAIN
COURSE

for the tamarind marinade
⅓ cup (100 g) tamarind paste from a jar (not "concentrate")
⅓ cup (100 g) rose hip ketchup (see page 138)
6 tablespoons (90 ml) kecap manis or sweet soy sauce
2 inches (5 cm) fresh ginger, finely grated
3 to 4 cloves black or regular garlic, grated
sea salt and freshly ground black pepper

for the ribs
about 3¾ pounds (1.3 kg) pork spare ribs (1 slab per person)

for the coleslaw
¼ head of red cabbage, sliced into thin strips
2 Elstar apples (Golden Delicious and Jonagold are good substitutes), peeled, cored, and cut into matchsticks
smoky mayonnaise (see page 130), coriander aioli (see page 131), or 6½ tablespoons (100 ml) plain mayonnaise (see page 129)
juice of ½ lemon
6½ tablespoons (100 ml) thick yogurt or sour cream
sea salt and freshly ground black pepper

I always keep one in my fridge: a large jar of almost black tamarind paste. Tamarind is widely used in Asian and Surinam cuisines, but feel free to use it more often. Tamarind (also known as asam) is a hard, suede-brown pod. Inside are sticky, fleshy fruits with a hard seed, which you need to soak in a bowl of water before using so you can remove the seeds. The thick juice, tamarind or asam water, can be used as a sweet-sour flavoring for all sorts of dishes, from stews to lemonade or pie. Lemon or lime has a more perfumed acidity, vinegar is lighter and tangier; tamarind has a full-bodied—spice-like—sour flavor.

I take the easy route and buy my tamarind pre-soaked in a jar in the supermarket, where it's labeled "tamarind paste." Use it to season stews, soups, or marinades for meat, fish, or vegetables. Or use it to make finger-licking-good sticky sauce like this one. Don't use "tamarind concentrate" here, as it's too strong.

Make the marinade: In a bowl, combine all the ingredients. Taste to see if the marinade needs more sweetness (ketchup and sweet soy sauce) or more sourness (tamarind) and season with some salt and pepper if necessary. Place the pork ribs in a large sealable bag or an airtight container that fits in the fridge and drizzle with the marinade. Thoroughly rub the meat with the marinade and close the bag. Allow the meat to marinate in the refrigerator for 1 to 6 hours.

Preheat the oven to 300°F (150°C).

Remove the meat from the marinade (save the marinade!) and place the slabs in a roasting pan. Cover with aluminum foil. Roast in the middle of the oven for 2 hours, turning the slabs over halfway through the cooking time. Remove the aluminum foil, brush the meat with the reserved marinade (put any remaining marinade in a small saucepan), and roast for 30 minutes longer, or until browned.

Meanwhile, make the coleslaw: Combine the red cabbage with the apples. Mix the mayonnaise with the lemon juice and yogurt or sour cream and season with salt and pepper. Thoroughly combine the sauce with the cabbage and apples. Cover the salad bowl with a lid or plate and refrigerate until serving. The red cabbage will become tastier and more tender as it chills.

Cook the remaining marinade over medium-high heat until reduced to a thick sauce. Cut the pork slabs in half, coat with the sauce, and serve with the coleslaw and extra sauce on the side.

PORK

GUINNESS-BRAISED PORK BELLY

PREPARE: 10 MINUTES
BAKE: 4 TO 5 HOURS
SERVES ABOUT 6 AS A
MAIN COURSE; THERE
WON'T BE ANY LEFTOVERS

2¼ pounds (1 kg) pork belly,
    without rind
2 whole cloves
1 tablespoon coriander seeds
1 teaspoon fennel seeds
1 teaspoon caraway seeds
sea salt and freshly ground
    black pepper
2 tablespoons canola or
    peanut oil
1 to 2 cans (about 1 pint/
    500 ml each) Guinness
    or other stout beer (the
    quantity depends on the
    size of the pan)
about 2 cups (500 ml)
    unfiltered apple juice or
    cider
2 large onions, thinly sliced
4 carrots, peeled and sliced
    diagonally

tool
mortar and pestle

HORSERADISH SAUCE

Mix 1 to 2 tablespoons
grated horseradish with
½ cup (125 ml) sour cream.
Season the sauce with
salt, pepper, a few drops
of lemon juice, and some
grated lemon zest.

I like cooking with Guinness or Murphy's. The deep flavor of stout combines well with an autumnal pork roast. My friend Avril Caherberg, who lives two hills down from us in West Cork, keeps her pigs outside in her forest. Their meat is a deep red instead of soft pink, a sign these pigs lived fantastic lives. Such amazing meat deserves to be treated with respect. So find a good pork purveyor and try this recipe.

Preheat the oven to 250°F (120°C). Place the pork belly, fat facing up, on a large cutting board. Score the fat layer diagonally with a sharp chef's knife, spacing the cuts about ⅓ inch (8 mm) apart and being sure not to cut into the meat beneath the fat.

In a mortar, crush the cloves, coriander seeds, fennel seeds, caraway seeds, and salt and pepper. Thoroughly wash your hands and massage half of the spices into the fat layer of the bacon. Turn the meat over and repeat the rubbing with the remaining spices.

In a Dutch oven or a roasting pan, heat the canola or peanut oil over medium heat. Add the meat with the fat layer facing down. If it doesn't comfortably fit in the pot, cut the pork belly in half and fry the two smaller pieces side by side. Cook until nicely browned, then flip and brown the other side. Deglaze the pot with the Guinness. Pour in as much apple juice as you need to fully submerge the meat, or add more beer if needed. Add the onions and carrots. Bring to a boil and place the pot, covered with a lid or with aluminum foil, in the oven. Slowly cook the pork belly for 4 hours. Check the meat every now and then. Although it won't fall apart, it *should* be done. Feel free to let the meat roast for another hour if you don't think it's done yet.

Using two large spatulas, scoop the pork belly from the pan and place it on a parchment paper–lined baking sheet, fat layer facing up. Increase the oven temperature to 425°F (225°C). Return the meat to the oven and roast for about 30 minutes, until the top is crispy.

Meanwhile, strain the cooking liquid from the Dutch oven or roasting pan into a small saucepan. Transfer the vegetables from the strainer back to the roasting pan or a serving dish. Spoon off the fat from the cooking liquid and discard it. Over medium heat, cook the cooking liquid until reduced to a tasty gravy, about 30 minutes.

Place the meat on top of the vegetables and serve with some of the gravy drizzled all around. Serve the remaining gravy in a bowl on the side. Delicious with horseradish sauce (see recipe at left).

PORK

HARISSA MEATBALLS WITH RICE FROM THE OVEN

PREPARE: 15 MINUTES
BAKE: 25 MINUTES
MAKES 8 SMALL BALLS

for the meatballs
9 ounces (250 g) ground
  sirloin
9 ounces (250 g) ground
  pork
⅔ cup (100 g) cooked rice
1 egg
1 shallot, chopped
2 cloves garlic, finely
  chopped
1 tablespoon harissa (or mild
  sambal), or to taste
grated zest of 1 organic
  lemon
sea salt and freshly ground
  black pepper

for the sauce
2 shallots, sliced
a few tablespoons olive oil
1 clove garlic, finely chopped
1 teaspoon ground coriander
2 teaspoons caraway seeds
1 tablespoon harissa (or mild
  sambal badjak), or to taste
1 can (14½ ounces/411 g)
  whole peeled tomatoes,
  hand crushed (see
  page 266)
sea salt
juice of 1 lemon

On this page I'll share with you my favorite way to make use of leftover cooked rice: namely by mixing it into meatballs. You can also use some leftover couscous or bulgur. Use a similar amount of breadcrumbs if you don't have leftover grains at hand. These balls are downright scrumptious, by the way, and you won't believe how ridiculously easy they are to make.

Preheat the oven to 350°F (180°C).

Make the meatballs: Combine all the ingredients for the balls, seasoning the mixture with salt and pepper, and thoroughly knead everything together. This will make the ground meat stickier and easier to shape into balls.

Thoroughly wash your hands and form the meat into small balls the size of a golf ball. Use wet hands (so the meat won't stick as easily).

Make the sauce: Sauté the shallots in the olive oil in a saucepan over medium heat until they are lightly browned. Add the garlic, coriander, caraway, and harissa and fry for 2 to 3 minutes, until the spices become fragrant. Pour in the tomato pulp, bring the sauce to a boil, taste for salt, and stir in the lemon juice.

Place the meatballs spaced somewhat apart in a single layer in a baking dish and pour the sauce on top. Put the dish in the oven for 25 minutes, until the balls are cooked through and the sauce is bubbling.

You can serve the balls along with one of the two grain salads on page 305.

MISO RICE MEATBALLS

**PREPARE: 30 MINUTES
MAKES 16 MEATBALLS TO
SERVE AS AN APPETIZER OR
SIDE DISH**

2 tablespoons uncooked
    basmati rice
1 pound 1 ounce (500 g)
    ground sirloin
3 scallions, finely chopped
2 cloves garlic, finely
    chopped
2 tablespoons fish sauce
2 tablespoons red miso

tool
spice grinder or mortar and
    pestle

Preheat the oven to 400°F (200°C).

In a small skillet, toast the rice over medium heat until light brown. Allow the rice to cool for a while. Grind the rice to a fine powder in a spice grinder or mortar.

Combine all the ingredients, including the rice, in a bowl and divide the mixture into 16 golf ball–sized balls. Roll the minced meat mixture with wet hands to make it less sticky.

Place the miso rice balls on a parchment paper–lined baking sheet and bake for 30 minutes, or until browned. For evenly browned balls, make sure to turn them halfway through the baking time.

The miso rice balls go well with the cauliflower-celeriac-curry mash with caramelized leek, the recipe for which can be found on page 217, where you can see them pictured. Downright delicious with the creamed miso-mustard butter on page 89.

PORK & BEEF

BEEF STEW WITH GINGER & STAR ANISE

PREPARE: 25 MINUTES
STEW: 2 HOURS
30 MINUTES
SERVES 4 TO 6 AS A
MAIN COURSE

3 tablespoons sunflower oil
2¼ pounds (1 kg) beef stew
  meat, in chunks
2 onions, chopped
1 inch (2.5 cm) fresh ginger,
  grated
3 cloves garlic, grated
1 bunch (½ ounce/15 g)
  cilantro, stems and leaves
  separated
4 to 6 cups (1 to 1½ L) beef
  stock
2 teaspoons Chinese
  five-spice powder
6 whole star anise
sea salt and freshly ground
  black pepper
1 can (70 g) tomato paste
3 tablespoons soy sauce, or
  more to taste
3 tablespoons sweet soy
  sauce, or more to taste

This book wouldn't be one of mine had it been lacking a beef stew recipe. Stew—one of the most delicious things you can make with meat—takes time, but little more than that. It even creates its own flavorful sauce. No need to do anything. You assemble the ingredients and time will take care of the rest. I'll use the leftovers for making soup for days afterward. A long time ago, I spent a few years working at a Chinese restaurant. There they called the master stock for the noodle soups (as well as our staff dinner) "thousand-year soup." Each day they threw in any leftovers, added some water, and the soup would continue to steep. So, each day, the soup was a little different. I still think about this whenever I stir some leftover broccoli, spinach, or rice and an extra splash of water, coconut milk, or broth into the leftover stew.

In a Dutch oven, heat the sunflower oil. Add the chunks of beef in batches and brown them on all sides. Remove the pieces of meat from the pan and keep them warm on a plate under a lid.

Meanwhile, in a food processor or by hand, chop the onions, ginger, garlic, and cilantro stems to a coarse paste.

Cook the onion paste in the frying fat in the pot. If the paste is too dry, add a splash of the beef stock. Add the five-spice powder, star anise, and salt and the pepper to taste and cook the spices, stirring. Stir in the tomato paste, cook a little longer, then pour in the salty and sweet soy sauces.

Return the meat to the pot and pour in enough stock to submerge the meat. Bring the stock to a boil. Cover the pot with a lid, turn the heat to its lowest setting, and simmer until the meat is completely done and tender, 2 to 2½ hours.

While simmering, check the stew from time to time. Pour in a splash of stock or water if the meat gets too dry. Serve the stew sprinkled with the cilantro leaves.

Delicious with brown or white rice. Or with fries (see page 238).

BEEF

ROAST LEMON CHICKEN WITH COCONUT MILK

PREPARE: 1 HOUR 30 MINUTES
SERVES 4 AS A MAIN COURSE

1 whole chicken
sea salt and freshly ground black pepper
1 tablespoon paprika
5 tablespoons (75 g) butter
2 tablespoons sesame oil
2 organic lemons
2 cans (14 ounces/400 ml each) coconut milk
1 pound 1 ounce (500 g) new potatoes, larger ones halved
handful of fresh cilantro leaves, plus some for garnish
8 cloves garlic, peeled and roughly chopped
grated zest of 2 organic lemons (use the lemons that go in the chicken for this)
2 to 3 stalks lemongrass, finely chopped
2 inches (5 cm) fresh ginger, grated
2 or 3 cinnamon sticks

Preheat the oven to 350°F (180°C).

Season the chicken with salt, pepper, and paprika.

In a heavy-bottomed, oven-safe pan, heat the butter and sesame oil and sear the chicken all over until golden brown on all sides. Halve the lemons—first grate and reserve the zest—and push them into the cavity of the chicken.

Pour the coconut milk in with the chicken and add the lemon zest and all the remaining ingredients. Rinse the coconut milk cans with a splash of water and add this water as well. Place the uncovered pan in the oven.

Bake the chicken, basting it every 20 minutes with the coconut sauce from the pan and turning the potatoes every now and then, for about 1 hour, until fully done and golden brown.

Allow the chicken to rest for 10 minutes before carving it.

In the meantime, strain the sauce, scoop out the potatoes, and keep them warm in a bowl covered with a lid.

Return the chicken to the pan and serve with the potatoes around it and drizzled with the strained sauce. Sprinkle everything with cilantro.

Serve with green vegetables, such as steamed broccoli or broccolini, and plenty of spinach. Or, do you know what also makes for a delightful combination? The braised escarole on page 225. Or the radishes on page 219.

THE BEST CRISPY CHICKEN EVER WITH SMOKY KETCHUP

MARINATE: PREFERABLY
1 DAY, AT LEAST 4 HOURS
PREPARE: 5 MINUTES
ROAST: 1 HOUR
SERVES 4 AS A MAIN
COURSE

for the chicken
3 tablespoons sea salt
10 tablespoons (150 ml)
    warm water
8 chicken thighs with skin
    and bone
3 tablespoons butter
about ⅓ cup (50 g)
    all-purpose flour
freshly ground black pepper

for the smoky ketchup
10 tablespoons (150 ml) rose
    hip ketchup (see page 138)
½ tablespoon smoked
    paprika
1 tablespoon red wine
    vinegar
1 teaspoon Worcestershire
    sauce
pinch of cayenne pepper or
    a drop of Tabasco sauce, or
    to taste
1 tablespoon nigella seeds
    (see page 12) or black
    sesame seeds

Prepare a *truly* succulent and crispy chicken, without use of a deep fryer. It can be done. In fact, it's so easy that you may never again prepare chicken any other way.

Make the chicken: In the morning, dissolve the salt in a large bowl with the warm water. Let the water cool somewhat and add the chicken thighs. Immediately pour in enough cold water to submerge the chicken. Cover with a plate or a lid and set aside in the refrigerator until closer to dinnertime.

Preheat the oven to 400°F (200°C).

Remove the chicken from the water and pat the thighs dry with a paper towel. Put the butter in a roasting pan large enough to fit the thighs side by side in a single layer (check this in advance) and place the empty roasting pan with the butter in the hot oven until the butter has melted.

Mix the flour with a lot of freshly ground pepper and pour it onto a deep plate. Dredge the chicken thighs through the flour until they are thinly coated on all sides. Pat off the excess flour.

Place the chicken pieces in the hot roasting pan, skin side down. Roast the thighs until golden brown, and crispy on the bottom. This should take about 40 minutes, sometimes a little longer, depending on the oven and the thickness of the chicken thighs. Turn them over carefully so that the other side can brown as well. Roast the chicken for another 15 to 20 minutes.

Make the smoky ketchup: Stir together all of the ingredients.

Drain the chicken thighs on paper towels and season with salt and pepper. Serve with the ketchup.

To balance out the dish, add a lot of greens. For example, the salad on page 175 with fava beans, asparagus, and cumber ribbons.

Mizen Head, West Cork

smoked mackerel at the farmers' market, Nieuwmarkt, Amsterdam

FISH & SEAFOOD

Fishmonger in Howth, Dublin

FISH FISH BURGERS WITH HOME MADE TOMA
FISH STICKS WITH A SPICY DIP, BANTRY BAY PR
SPICY COD CAKES & AVOCADO SALSA, EASY
THE GRILL, POACHED WHOLE SALMON WITH
ON A CUCUMBER & MANGO SALAD, DUTCH
MACKEREL WITH BAY LEAF, LEMON, BASIL &
WARM SMOKED FISH SALAD WITH ROMESCO

TO MAYO & KALE SALSA, HOME MADE
AWNS WITH SMOKY MAYO, TACOS WITH
MANGO SALAD, QUICK COCKLE POT FROM
CRAB, COCKLES & BUTTER SAUCE, MACKEREL
JAMBALAYA, KALE KEDGEREE, GRILLED
DRY SHERRY, SMOKING WHITE FISH,
DRESSING & MUSTARD CAVIAR

the West Cork coast

for the kale salsa
juice of 1 organic orange
  (reserved after adding zest
  to the burger patties)
¾ cup (50 g) very finely
  chopped kale
2 teaspoons good olive oil
sea salt and freshly ground
  black pepper

1 bunch (½ ounce/15 g)
  cilantro, finely chopped
1 red chile, seeded and finely
  chopped

also
4 brioche or burger buns
4 lettuce leaves
1 avocado, peeled, pitted,
  and sliced

tool
food processor

FISH BURGERS WITH HOME MADE TOMATO MAYO & KALE SALSA

PREPARE: 30 MINUTES
WAIT: 30 MINUTES
SERVES 4 AS A MAIN COURSE

for the fish burgers
1 tablespoon butter
1 onion, chopped
2 stalks celery, chopped
12¼ ounces (350 g) white fish (seasonal; look for the blue MSC label)
2 cups (200 g) breadcrumbs, home made or store bought
½ cup (125 ml) full-fat Greek yogurt
a few chives, minced
finely grated zest of 1 organic orange (reserve the rest of the orange for the kale salsa)
1 egg, beaten
sea salt and freshly ground black pepper
oil for shallow-frying

for the tomato mayonnaise
2 tomatoes, seeded and cut into very small cubes
½ teaspoon smoked paprika
9 ounces (250 g) home made mayonnaise (see page 129)
sea salt and freshly ground black pepper

Make the fish burger mixture: Melt the butter in a skillet. Add the onion and celery and cook, stirring, for about 4 minutes. Transfer the vegetables to a plate and let cool slightly. Chop the fish and mix it with the cooled onion-celery mixture, half of the breadcrumbs, the yogurt, chives, grated orange zest, and the egg. Season the fish burger mixture with salt and pepper. Shape into 8 balls. Slightly flatten the fish balls and dredge them in the remaining breadcrumbs, making sure that they are coated all around. Set the fish burger patties aside in the fridge for 30 minutes so that they can firm up somewhat.

Make the tomato mayonnaise: Stir the diced tomatoes and smoked paprika into the home made mayo and season with salt and pepper.

Make the kale salsa: Place the orange on a cutting board and use a sharp knife to remove the peel and separate the segments from between the membranes (see page 303). Collect the juice in the bowl. Cut the segments into cubes and set aside.

Add the kale to the orange juice, along with the olive oil and salt and pepper to taste. Massage the kale until it has softened and wilted. Add the cilantro, red chile, and diced orange and toss.

Cook the fish burgers: Heat a thin layer of oil in a nonstick pan over medium heat. Working in batches if necessary, add the fish burgers and cook for 8 to 10 minutes until golden brown, flipping them halfway through the cooking time. Drain on some paper towels.

Toast the burger buns, cut side down, in a dry, hot skillet.

Top the bottom half of each bun with a lick of mayo, a lettuce leaf, a quarter of the avocado slices, two fish burgers, and some salsa and cover with the top half of the bun. Serve right away.

FISH & SEAFOOD

HOME MADE FISH STICKS WITH A SPICY DIP

PREPARE: 20 MINUTES
SERVES 4 AS A STARTER

for the fish fingers
¾ cup (100 g) all-purpose
  flour
sea salt and freshly ground
  black pepper
2½ cups (200 g) panko
  (Japanese breadcrumbs)
  or fresh breadcrumbs
  (crumbled corn flakes also
  work)
3 eggs, beaten
1 pound 1 ounce (500 g)
  fresh, firm Arctic cod,
  haddock, Boston blue,
  Atlantic cod, or hake fillets
oil for frying or deep-frying

for the dip
2 tablespoons sunflower oil
½ to 1 red chile (to taste),
  seeds and membranes
  removed, minced
leaves of 1 sprig (8 g) basil,
  finely chopped
4 to 5 tablespoons (60 to
  75 ml) salty soy sauce
juice of 1 lime

also tasty
tartar sauce (see page 138)

handy
deep fryer (you can fry these
  in a skillet, but deep frying
  is preferred)

Making your own fish fingers is a piece of cake, and on top of that they're much tastier than those from the frozen food section of the supermarket. I'll give you more options for the type of fish to use. Choose a fish that's in season and truly fresh instead of sticking to the fish species mentioned in the ingredient list. This will prevent possible disappointments at the fishmonger. Fish can't be ordered to preference, it's a product of nature.

You can make fish fingers with any type of white fish except flat fish (such as sole or flounder). Haddock, Boston blue, cod, or hake are excellent, but Norwegian Arctic cod is my personal favorite. Always look for the MSC label, the stamp of approval for sustainably caught seafood. You can, by the way, also use frozen fish for this recipe.

Set out four deep plates: one with the flour mixed with salt and pepper, one with the panko, one with the beaten eggs, and one for the coated fish fingers.

Cut the fish into sturdy, long pieces, ¾ inch (2 cm) in width.

First, coat them with flour one by one, pat off the excess flour, then pass them through the egg and then through the breadcrumbs. Place them on the fourth plate and set aside.

Make the dip: In a skillet, heat the sunflower oil and sauté the red chile for 1 minute. Remove from the heat and add the basil, soy sauce, and lime juice. Stir everything together and pour the dip into a bowl.

Meanwhile, heat oil in a deep fryer to 350°F (180°C) or heat a generous layer of oil in a wok or cast-iron pan. Fry the fish fingers in batches of three or four at a time for 3 to 4 minutes. If you cook too many at the same time, the oil temperature will drop too quickly and instead of being crispy, the fish fingers will turn into soggy, fat-saturated sponges. Turn the fingers halfway through the cooking time. Using a slotted spoon, scoop them out of the oil and let them drain on paper towels. Continue until all the fish fingers are fried.

Serve with a generous salad, for example the radish and cauliflower salad with buttermilk dressing on page 157 or the broccoli salad on page 162, or the salad with fava beans, asparagus and cumber ribbons on page 175.

FISH & SEAFOOD

BANTRY BAY PRAWNS WITH SMOKY MAYO

PREPARE: 20 MINUTES
SERVES 4 AS A STARTER

16 langoustines (or large
   shrimp)
olive oil
pinch of chile flakes
pinch of salt flakes

on the side
smoky mayo (see page 130)

In the picture you can also
see charred lime. Briefly
roasting them in a skillet or
under the broiler warms limes
(or lemons) so you will be
able to squeeze more juice
out of them. They'll also taste
slightly sweeter, because the
sugars caramelize!

Our Irish home isn't too far from the small harbor town of Bantry, where
these langoustines are being caught daily. Over there, these aren't
as expensive or considered chic like they are in the Netherlands and
abroad. In the Netherlands they are only sold at top fishmongers. You
can replace them with large shrimp, as those are always available.

Clean the langoustines: Use a large sharp knife to halve them
lengthwise. Take a look at the cut halves: remove stuff you won't eat:
like the black intestine, or stringy parts that don't belong to the tail
meat. This sounds more complicated than it is, really: once you've cut
them open you'll see what I mean. Do this under a trickling stream
of cold water from the faucet. Then pat everything dry with some
paper towels.

Place the langoustines on a baking sheet, cut sides facing up. Drizzle
with olive oil and sprinkle the langoustines with chile and salt flakes.

Preheat the broiler to 400°F (200°C) or fire up the grill: the smoky
flavor of smoldering charcoal will make the langoustines even
more delicious.

Place them under the broiler or directly on the grill grate, shell side
down, and briefly cook them, no longer than a few minutes. The tail
meat should have just turned from transparent to opaque. It's fine if
they're still a bit raw: I really like that.

Serve with the smoky mayo. Provide plenty of napkins.

TACOS WITH SPICY COD CAKES & AVOCADO SALSA

PREPARE: 30 MINUTES
SERVES 4 AS A MAIN
COURSE; MAKES ABOUT
16 FISH CAKES

for the avocado salsa
1 avocado, peeled, pitted, and
  cubed
1 red onion, chopped
1 red chile pepper, roughly
  chopped
1 bunch (½ ounce/15 g)
  cilantro, leaves only (reserve
  the stems), coarsely chopped
grated zest and juice of
  1 organic lime
sea salt and freshly ground
  black pepper

for the fish cakes
1 pound 1 ounce (500 g) cod,
  fresh or frozen (or other
  white fish species, such
  as pollock, haddock, or
  whiting)
1 egg, beaten
2 cloves garlic, pressed
about ½ cup (50 g)
  breadcrumbs or panko, or
  more as needed
1 tablespoon red miso or
  pinch of salt
1 red chile pepper, roughly
  chopped
1 bunch (½ ounce/15 g)
  cilantro, stems only
4 sprigs of mint, leaves only
generous 1 cup (150 g) corn
  kernels
Oil for frying

on the side
12 to 16 small corn tortillas
  (see page 333), warmed
easy mango salad (at the
  bottom of this page)

tool
food processor

This entire dish is spicy. The fish cakes contain chiles, as does the salsa. If you find that too intense, you can leave them out. For the salsa you can also substitute chopped cherry tomatoes for the chile.

They're not listed in the recipe here, but I really like to add watermelon radish (look for it at farmers' markets) for a little crunch, and crumbled feta for a salty-creamy element. In fact, you can pair or top this with pretty much anything. I'll leave that to your imagination, or your fridge or pantry.

Make the avocado salsa: Stir the ingredients together and season with salt and pepper. Cover and set aside on the counter, allowing the flavors to meld.

Make the fish cakes: In a food processor, puree all the ingredients except the corn kernels, to a coarse mixture. Turn off the food processor and stir in the corn kernels by hand.

Shape the mixture into balls (using a wet ice cream scoop makes this fairly easy) and flatten them slightly with a wet fork.

In a layer of hot oil in a skillet, fry the fish cakes on both sides until golden brown. Drain the fish cakes on paper towels and place them in the tortillas. Top the cod cake tacos with the salsa. If you want, you can serve my easy mango salad on the side.

EASY MANGO SALAD

1 mango, peeled, pitted, and diced
2 scallions, sliced into fine rings
½ bunch (¼ ounce/7 g) cilantro, finely chopped
pinch of sea salt
juice of 1 lime

Mix everything together and serve immediately.

FISH & SEAFOOD

QUICK COCKLE POT FROM THE GRILL

PREPARE: 20 MINUTES
SERVES 4 AS A MAIN
COURSE, OR 4 TO 6 AS A
STARTER

1½ tablespoons butter
2 large shallots, chopped
4 cloves garlic, sliced
1 heaping tablespoon tomato
  paste
2 tablespoons harissa, or
  more to taste
1 bottle (about 10 ounces/
  300 ml) beer
about 20 cherry tomatoes,
  halved
1 can (14 ounces/400 g)
  black-eyed peas, rinsed and
  drained
2¼ pounds (1 kg) cockles (or
  small clams)
1 loaf of tasty sourdough
  bread, thickly sliced
3 to 4 tablespoons olive oil
sea salt and freshly ground
  black pepper
1 bunch (½ ounce/15 g)
  cilantro, coarsely chopped
grated zest and juice of
  1 organic lime
2 limes, cut into wedges

I'm willing to bet that if you've ever spent a day on the North Sea coast you (or one of your children) has stuck at the very least one beautiful shell in your pocket. And I'm also willing to bet that it was a cockle. The Netherlands is a cockle country, did you know? In fact we are pretty much one of the largest cockle-producing countries in Europe. Most of our cockles hail from the Wadden Sea. And do you know what we do with all those shells? We sell them to Spain en masse. And in return we buy vongole clams. They remind us of summer holidays. It's a bit bizarre. Our cockle is much cheaper, is available year-round, and most importantly: IT IS TERRIFICALLY DELICIOUS! And ready in 3 minutes. But the point is, I recommend giving whatever shellfish are local to your area a try!

Make sure the charcoal in your grill is sufficiently hot. Beautiful white ash-covered embers over which you can properly cook. Heat a heavy—preferably cast-iron—pan over the glowing charcoal. If you don't have a grill, or the weather isn't good enough for firing up the grill, you can of course also heat a heavy cast-iron pan over medium heat on your kitchen stove.

Melt the butter in the pan, add the shallots and garlic, and sauté for about 5 minutes, until soft. Stir in the tomato paste and harissa and cook for 2 more minutes, until the tomato puree starts to smell sweet. Deglaze the pan with the beer. Cook the sauce until it is reduced and thickened somewhat.

Stir the cherry tomatoes into the sauce. Cook to reduce the liquid by half. Stir the black-eyed peas and cockles into the sauce. Cover the pan with a lid or with aluminum foil and let simmer for 5 minutes. Turn the cockles over and cook, covered, for a few more minutes, until all the shells have opened. Remove any shells that won't open.

Move the pan to the side of the grill or heat a grill pan on the stove. Brush the sourdough slices with olive oil and toast them until golden brown. Season the bread with salt and pepper.

Sprinkle the cockles with cilantro leaves and season the sauce with lime juice, grated lime zest, and salt and pepper.

Place the pan on the dinner table, and serve with the bread and the lime wedges. Have everyone eat from the pan, breaking the bread and dipping it in the pan to mop up the sauce. Provide containers of lukewarm water and plenty of napkins for all those greasy fingers.

FISH & SEAFOOD

POACHED WHOLE SALMON WITH CRAB, COCKLES & BUTTER SAUCE

PREPARE: 40 MINUTES
SERVES 6 TO 12 AS A
MAIN COURSE

for the salmon
2 tablespoons olive oil
1 whole wild Alaskan salmon
  (for 12), or one side
  (for 6) with skin (ask your
  fishmonger)
¾ cup (200 ml) dry white
  wine (6½ tablespoons/
  100 ml for one side)
sea salt and freshly ground
  black pepper
1 bunch (½ ounce/15 g) dill,
  finely chopped
a few sprigs of tarragon,
  finely chopped

for the butter sauce
7 tablespoons (100 g) butter,
  at room temperature
1 tablespoon minced fresh
  tarragon
2¼ pounds (1 kg) cockles (or
  small clams)
6½ tablespoons (100 ml) dry
  white wine
3½ ounces (100 g) crabmeat,
  preferably fresh, otherwise
  canned
about 7 ounces (200 g)
  samphire
grated zest and juice of
  1 organic lemon
sea salt and freshly ground
  black pepper

on the side
2 lemons, halved

This is a fantastic festive dish. Serve with some salads and let everyone just dig in.

Make the salmon: Line a baking sheet with a large sheet of aluminum foil, or two sheets side by side, and place a sheet of parchment paper of the same size on top. Brush the parchment paper with olive oil and if using a side of salmon, place it in the center, skin side down. Drizzle the salmon with the white wine.

Sprinkle the salmon with salt and pepper and spread the chopped dill and tarragon on top. Fold the foil and paper sheets together and press the seams tightly so that no moisture will be able to escape.

If you decide, like me, to cook a whole salmon, fill the stomach cavity with the dill and tarragon, and use twice as much parchment paper, which you thoroughly seal with the help of some extra aluminum foil. The point is to prevent moisture from escaping, not that it looks good. The fish must be properly wrapped.

You can do this in advance; keep the wrapped salmon in the refrigerator until ready to cook.

Preheat the oven to 400°F (200°C).

Put the salmon package in the oven and bake a side salmon for 25 minutes or a whole salmon for 40 minutes. You can cook it longer too. If you do it will be well done, but I like it when the fish is still medium-rare.

When the fish is almost done, make the butter sauce: In a skillet, melt the butter with the tarragon, then add the cockles and white wine. Cover the pan with the lid, turn the heat to high, and shake the pan. Check if all the shells have opened. Remove and discard any cockles whose shells haven't opened after a few minutes.

Stir the crabmeat and the samphire into the sauce. Add the lemon juice and grated zest to taste. Season the sauce with salt and pepper. Make sure it doesn't come to a boil. Remove from the heat. >>>

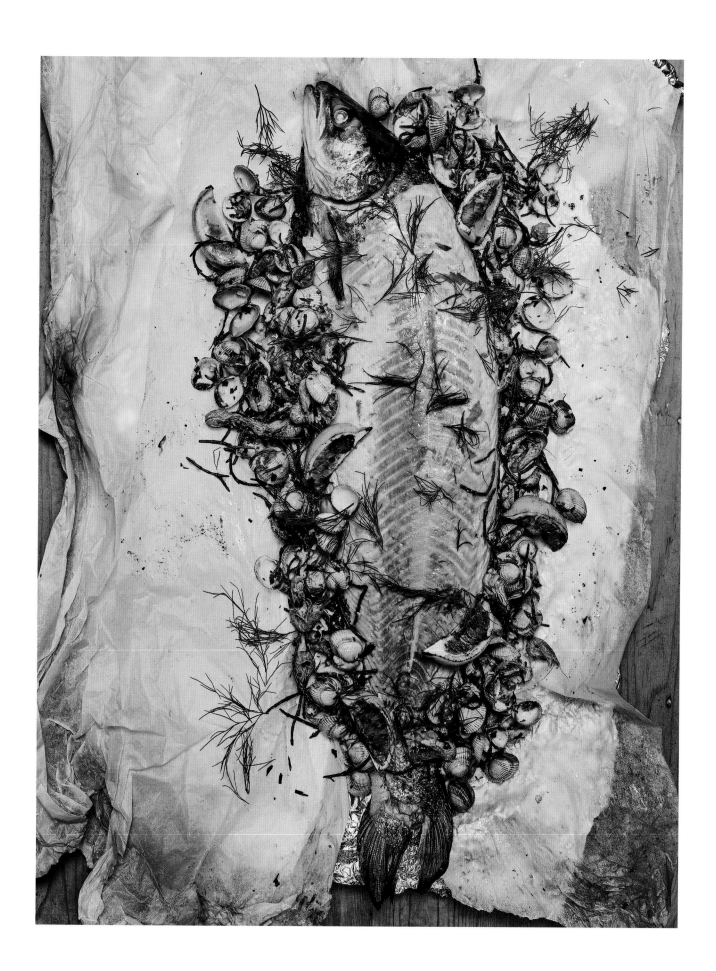

>>> In a dry skillet or a grill pan over high heat, cook the lemons, cut side down, until almost blackened. Set the lemons aside.

Open the wrapped fish. With the help of two extra hands, carefully transfer the package, paper and all, to a large tray or a cutting board, because nobody has a serving platter large enough to fit a whole salmon. Carefully pour out the cooking liquid over the sink. If you cooked a whole salmon, peel off the skin and spoon the cockle sauce over and next to the fish. Arrange the lemons halves to the side.

Place the board with the fish, the paper wrap, and everything at the center of the table. Which will look truly rustic and cool. That's how we've been doing it for years at our home.

MACKEREL ON A CUCUMBER & MANGO SALAD

for the dressing
2 tablespoons salty soy sauce
2 tablespoons rice vinegar or
  white wine vinegar
1 tablespoon sesame oil

for the salad
¼ red cabbage
juice of 1 lime
pinch of sea salt
heaping 1 cup (100 g) bean
  sprouts
½ cucumber
1 mango
1 red onion, peeled

for the mackerel
4 pieces (about 10½ ounces/
  300 g) fresh mackerel
  fillet with skin (ask your
  fishmonger)
sea salt
2 tablespoons sunflower oil
a few sprigs of cilantro
edible flowers (optional)

> Always eat mackerel
> immediately on the day of
> purchase: because it's such
> a fatty fish it can start to
> go bad quickly.

Mackerel is a real summer fish, so starting in May, and into June and July, you'll find the fattest mackerels at the fishmonger. Fat in the literal sense, as during that period right before they spawn their bodies contain about 20 percent more fish oil or fat than afterward. Use this to your advantage. Eating mackerel once a week is sufficient for getting your recommended daily dose of omega-3, so I'm told.

Make the dressing: Mix all the ingredients in a bowl.

Make the salad: Using a mandolin or a sharp knife, cut the red cabbage into razor-thin strips. Drizzle with the lime juice and sprinkle with a pinch of salt. Wash your hands and massage the cabbage with the lime juice and salt. Let stand for a while, so the juice and salt can soak in and the cabbage soften.

Rinse the bean sprouts under hot tap water, drain well, and gently pat dry in a clean kitchen towel.

Cut the cucumber into thin ribbons using a mandolin or cheese slicer. Peel the mango and cut the flesh into long wedges. Cut the red onion into thin rings. Drain the red cabbage in a colander.

In a bowl, combine all the ingredients for the salad, add the dressing, and gently toss everything together. Let the salad rest for 10 minutes.

Make the mackerel: Use a sharp knife to score the skin of each piece of mackerel a few times. Sprinkle the skin side with some salt. In a skillet, heat the sunflower oil, add the mackerel, skin side down, and fry for about 4 minutes (depending on the thickness) until crispy and just done around the edges. Turn the fillets over and continue to cook them for another 1 to 2 minutes.

Divide the salad among four plates. Place a mackerel, skin facing up, on each plate. Garnish the salad and mackerel with the cilantro leaves and, if you want, some edible flowers. Serve as a main course along with a bowl of steaming jasmine rice, or as a starter or lunch with a piece of crunchy bread.

FISH & SEAFOOD

DUTCH JAMBALAYA

1 tablespoon sunflower oil

2 onions, chopped

5 stalks celery, cut into small cubes

1 cup (200 g) basmati rice

1 teaspoon chile powder, or to taste

½ tablespoon paprika

1 tablespoon ground coriander

1 teaspoon fennel seeds, ground in a mortar

2 cans (14½ ounces/411 g each) whole peeled tomatoes, hand crushed (see page 266)

1⅔ cups (400 ml) vegetable stock

1 yellow and 1 green bell pepper, cut into small cubes

kernels from 1 ear of corn

2 cloves garlic, finely chopped

2 sprigs of thyme

sea salt and freshly ground black pepper

10½ ounces (300 g) shellfish (I use seafood from the North Sea: crab legs, a handful of mussels, squid rings and tentacles, and shrimp)

1 bunch (½ ounce/15 g) flat-leaf parsley, finely chopped

> No steamer pan?
> No problem:
> a strainer, placed over
> a large pan, a layer of
> water at the bottom, a lid
> on top also works.

We don't have to travel to the Mediterranean for frutti di mare; the entire North Sea is one big fruit basket. Partly due to the rising seawater temperatures, squid (though not octopus or cuttlefish) can be found swimming in our coastal waters in large quantities these days. The mussels on our plates also come from the North Sea, often from the Eastern Scheldt, where they grow up after having been cultivated in the Wadden Sea where the strong tidal system brings the mussels all sorts of nutrients. The North Sea crab season runs from January until September. Sustainable fishermen always release female crabs. If caught during the right season, North Sea crab even has a sustainable status. North Sea crab contains relatively little meat: no brown meat in the body, but they do have tasty white meat in the legs, which is why you often see those on display at the fishmonger. All you need to do is steam them, but that's super easy, I'll explain it to you below. We'll simply throw them in a pan, together with the cockles and shrimp: we're making Dutch-style jambalaya.

In a Dutch oven or a large skillet, heat the sunflower oil. Add the onion and celery and fry for a good 6 minutes, until soft. Add the basmati rice, chile powder, paprika, ground coriander, and fennel seeds. While stirring, cook the mixture for 2 minutes.

Pour in the hand-crushed tomatoes, rinse one tomato can with the vegetable stock, pour into the other empty can and pour the tomato stock water into the pan as well. Stir in the bell peppers, corn, garlic, thyme, and salt and pepper to taste. Bring to a boil. Cover the pan with a lid and simmer the jambalaya over low heat for about 18 minutes, until the rice is tender and almost all of the liquid has been absorbed.

In the meantime, in a steamer basket, steam the crab legs for 7 minutes, adding the mussels after 2 minutes. Crack open the crab legs by tapping them with a hammer so you can shell them. Serve them as is and let your guests do the rest of the work, or remove the crabmeat yourself beforehand.

In a skillet, sauté the squid in a splash of olive oil for a few minutes, until no longer translucent and light brown around the edges. Don't overcook them. Stir in the shrimp to heat them up.

Stir the shellfish and parsley into the jambalaya and serve immediately.

KALE KEDGEREE

PREPARE: 10 MINUTES
SERVES 2 FOR BREAKFAST
OR AS A MAIN COURSE

2 to 3 tablespoons butter
4 scallions, white parts only, sliced into rings
1 large onion, chopped
2 cloves garlic, finely chopped
1 green chile, sliced, seeds and membranes removed if you don't like food that is too spicy
1 teaspoon curry powder
seeds from 3 cardamom pods, crushed in a mortar
3½ cups (400 g) broccoli rice (or cauliflower rice)
1½ cups (100 g) sliced kale
squeeze of lemon juice
sea salt and freshly ground black pepper
4 eggs
9¾ ounces (275 g) smoked mackerel with pepper (pepper mackerel), at room temperature
handful of fresh flat-leaf parsley leaves

Kedgeree has an ancient history. It's believed to come from khichari, an Indian dish made with rice and lentils. Like in India, in Ireland it is served for breakfast. Irish people tend to eat a cooked breakfast meal that often includes smoked fish. They do, however, use different kinds of fish for smoking than we do in the Netherlands. Instead of fatty fish such as mackerel, salmon, or eel, the Irish often smoke white fish such as haddock, pollock, and cod.

Kedgeree is a humble and simple dish, made with leftover rice, stir-fried and flavored with curry and other fragrant spices. It generally includes some leftover vegetables, often peas, but anything is possible. For this recipe I use kale, the most popular Irish vegetable.

Kedgeree is served with a soft-boiled or nearly hard-boiled egg and smoked fish and is the best hangover cure I know.

When I see it on a breakfast menu in a restaurant or hotel, I order it right away: no kedgeree is the same, but this dish is always delicious. Zesty, spicy, and wholesome.

In a sauté pan, melt half of the butter, add the white part of the scallions and the chopped onion, and cook until the onions soften. Add the garlic, chile, curry powder, and cardamom. Add the remaining butter and the broccoli rice and stir-fry for 6 to 7 minutes, until al dente. Add the kale and while stir-frying, let it wilt for 2 minutes. Season the kedgeree with lemon juice, salt, and pepper.

Boil the eggs until nearly hard boiled, 6 minutes. Shock them under running cold water and peel them.

Spoon the kedgeree onto four serving plates. Break the fish into pieces and divide among the plates. Halve the eggs and place them on the top of the kedgeree. Generously sprinkle with parsley. Add more lemon juice if you like. Now that's what I call breakfast!

grilled mackerel with bay leaf, lemon, basil & dry sherry

Warren Beach, Rosscarbery, West Cork

GRILLED MACKEREL WITH BAY LEAF, LEMON, BASIL & DRY SHERRY

PREPARE: 20 MINUTES
WAIT: 1 HOUR
GRILL: 10 MINUTES
SERVES ABOUT 4 AS A
MAIN COURSE (DEPENDING
ON THE SIZE OF THE FISH)

2 whole mackerels, cleaned
¼ cup (60 ml) olive oil
grated zest and juice of
  1 organic lemon
1 bunch (½ ounce/15 g) basil,
  coarsely shredded, plus
  whole sprigs for garnish
at least 8 (fresh!) bay leaves
  (see below)
5 tablespoons (75 ml) dry
  sherry (or whiskey)
sea salt and freshly ground
  black pepper
1 lemon, half thinly sliced
  and half cut into 1-inch
  (2.5 cm) wedges

tool
butcher's twine or a fish
  grilling basket

For this dish fresh bay leaves
are a must. Bay leaf plants can
be bought in most nurseries.
And they grow in many
gardens (often unbeknownst
to their owners). I have also
spotted heaps of fresh bay
leaves at the farmers' market,
by the way.

I really can't make this recipe easier or the results more delicious. Don't skip the marinating part: it's essential for letting that special bay leaf flavor seep into the mackerel. A truly summery dish.

Score the mackerel's skin several times.

In a shallow bowl, combine the olive oil with the lemon zest and juice, half of the basil, 4 bay leaves, the sherry, and salt and pepper to taste. Thoroughly rub the fish with the mixture. Cover the mackerels and let them marinate in the fridge for at least 1 hour, but preferably longer.

Fire up the grill. Once the charcoal is smoldering and coated in white ash, you can start grilling the fish. Or heat a grill pan on the stovetop until piping hot.

Remove the fish from the marinade, saving the marinade for later. Stuff the cavities of the fish with the remaining basil, some extra fresh bay leaves, and the lemon slices. Tie up the fish with butcher's twine or place them in a fish grilling basket.

Pour the marinade into a saucepan, bring to a boil, then remove from the heat.

Grill the mackerels for a few minutes on each side. Drizzle the mackerels with a bit of the boiled marinade from the pan and serve, with the wedged lemon, basil sprigs, some crunchy bread—also from the grill!—and a green salad.

SMOKING WHITE FISH

I know, a smoker can be pretty pricey, but you can make your own indoor smoker at home for next to nothing.

Always first brine the fish for 10 minutes: fill a container with cold water and add so much salt that it no longer dissolves. The brine is perfect if you can feel some salt lying on the bottom of the container when you stir it with your hand.

Make sure you do use actual smoking wood dust. You can buy it in a cooking supply shop, although most supermarkets also carry it these days. Look in the barbecuing or outdoor section. Use the fine kind that's like sawdust, as you want everything to catch fire quickly.

Line a flameproof roasting pan, large old casserole pan, or deep baking sheet with a layer of aluminum foil (to protect the bottom) and sprinkle with a layer of smoking wood dust about ⅓ inch (0.75 cm) deep. Place a loose sheet of aluminum foil on top. This sheet will protect the smoldering wood dust against the drippings from the fish.

>>>

Howth Harbour, Dublin

>>> Place a grill grate or similar rack over the roasting pan. You can use an oven rack, one from the microwave oven, or a metal trivet, as long as it's heat resistant. (One of those old-fashioned elongated fish pans with a removable rack is also suited for this: chances are that a grandmother or an older aunt has one of these in a kitchen cabinet somewhere.)

Place the fish on the rack, put the roasting pan on the stovetop, and turn the heat to high. Wait for the wood dust to start smoking, reduce the heat, then thoroughly cover the roasting pan with aluminum foil or a fitting lid.

Smoke the fish for about 12 minutes (depending on size and thickness). Check to see if it's done by piercing it with the point of a knife and looking. If the fish meat is still translucent, it needs to smoke a little longer.

WARM SMOKED FISH SALAD WITH ROMESCO DRESSING & MUSTARD CAVIAR

PREPARE: 25 MINUTES
WAIT: 10 MINUTES
SERVES 4 AS A MAIN-DISH
SALAD

romesco dressing (see
    page 153)
4 tablespoons (60 ml)
    mustard caviar (see
    page 139)

for the fish
1 piece (about
    1¾ pounds/800 g) of cod,
    Norwegian Arctic cod,
    white pollock, or another
    kind of white fish
3 to 4 handfuls of salt

for the salad
10½ ounces (300 g) haricots
    verts (or green beans)
10½ (300 g) baby spinach
1 bunch (¾ ounce/20 g) flat-
    leaf parsley, leaves only
2 scallions, thinly sliced
splash of olive oil
squeeze of lemon juice
sea salt

tools
smoker, or follow my simple
    instructions to make one
    yourself (see pages 390–91)
3 handfuls of fine smoking
    wood dust
aluminum foil

You need a smoker for this salad. If you don't have one, you can make one yourself with little effort: the easy instructions can be found on the previous pages.

Ask your fishmonger which fish is in season. You can often get my favorite: skrei (Norwegian Arctic cod) by the end of January. A piece of white pollock is also great, though, and remember: you can't order fish—it's wild food, a product of nature. So it's always exciting to see what a trip to the fishmonger will yield!

Place the fish in a brine of cold water and the salt (see the previous pages for how to do this) for 10 minutes.

Prepare the romesco dressing and mustard caviar and set aside until ready to serve.

Remove the fish from its brine bath. Pat it dry with paper towels. Smoke the fish using the method on pages 390–91. You should be able to gently break it into nice pieces with a fork.

Make the salad: In a saucepan, bring water to a boil and cook the haricots verts for 6 to 8 minutes, until al dente. Drain and rinse with cold water immediately. Combine the haricots verts with the baby spinach, flat-leaf parsley, and scallions, drizzle the vegetables with a little olive oil and lemon juice, and sprinkle with salt.

Divide the romesco dressing among four plates. Arrange the salad next to the dab of dressing and partly cover with the fish. Spoon some mustard caviar to the side of the vegetables and serve immediately.

FISH & SEAFOOD

DESSERT

FROZEN DESSERTS

Frozen desserts come in many varieties. They can be made with sugar, fruits or vegetables, milk or cream, and yogurt or eggs. They have many different names too.

There really is no reason at all for you to buy an expensive ice cream maker. With a little patience you can make perfect ice cream by hand. If it turns out you find home made ice cream crazy delicious and fun to make, you can always ask for one of those nifty devices for your birthday.

Actually, it is faster using an electric ice cream maker. The ice will become creamier too, because the constant churning while the ingredients freeze will result in finer ice crystals. But let's not nitpick. Whenever I'm being served hand whisked ice cream, I get an enormous sense of love and respect for the maker. And those who don't feel like whisking by hand can make semifreddo. That's even easier.

SORBET

Sorbet is a nicely refreshing and sweet frozen dessert. It's based on water, which makes it less heavy than ice cream. The sweet flavors of fresh fruits such as lemon, strawberry, or melon lend themselves best for making sorbet. Vegetable sorbets are also possible: tomato, celery, or cucumber, for example, are good ingredients for making the kind of refreshing ice that satisfies your craving on a hot summer day.

Add fresh herbs for tasty combinations.

SHERBET

Sherbet is actually very similar to sorbet, except that the water is replaced with milk or cream. This creates a slightly creamier version. If you make sherbet with orange (as in the recipes below), it actually tastes the same as an orange Split (aka Creamsicle)!

E SHERBET, ROSEMARY LEMON SHERBET,
Y OGURT PARFAIT WITH RASPBERRIES, MINT ICE
ERMELON GRANITA WITH ORANGE BLOSSOM
E NOISETTE—ALMOND MILK ICE CREAM,
LT, SUPER-EASY BANANA ALMOND ICE CREAM
CHED PEARS IN WHITE PORT & FENNEL SYRUP,
ELNUT TWIST WITH FRIED BACON FRUIT BAKED
ROSÉ JELLY WITH RED FRUIT, CANDIED LEMONS,
CHOCOLATE CUSTARD WITH CINNAMON,
CHESTNUT (& LIQUOR)

FROZEN DESSERTS CUCUMBER SORBET, ORANG
STRAWBERRY, HIBISCUS & ROSE SHERBET, FROTH
CREAM OR PARFAIT, HONEY TEA GRANITA, WAT
WATER, RHUBARB & RICOTTA ICE CREAM, BEURR
CHOCOLATE OLIVE OIL ICE CREAM WITH SEA SA
BAKED DESSERTS ALMOND CARAMEL TART, PO
FENNEL SEED ALMOND CAKE, CHOCOLATE HAZ
PINEAPPLE WITH HONEY & CHILE, VERMOUTH &
LEMON & DATE BARS **SWEETS** MARSHMALLOWS
MAKING CARAMEL, CHOCOLATE TRUFFLES WITH

Night falls over the Irish house, West Cork.

ICE CREAM

Ice cream consists of a custard base, which is made from egg and milk and/or cream. The cream custard gets its flavor from vanilla or other rich flavorings. Chocolate, nuts, and spices are well suited for this. Also fruit with a richer taste is very suitable. I'd rather make banana ice cream than banana sorbet.

Can you feel the difference?

PARFAIT/SEMIFREDDO

In a nutshell, semifreddo is ice cream that hasn't been stirred. By agitating the ice the ice crystals will be constantly broken up, making the ice cream smooth and easier to scoop. A semifreddo is poured into a mold and frozen. Super easy, therefore, especially if you don't own an ice cream maker or don't feel like whisking your ice cream every other hour as it freezes. I make my semifreddo extra frothy by folding in whipped cream and/or beaten egg whites. This will make the semifreddo easier to cut as well as softer when fully frozen.

GRANITA

Granita is a fresh dessert originating in Sicily. It looks like sorbet, but is made with less sugar, and the ice is served semi-frozen. Because it contains less sugar, larger ice crystals form during production, making granita extra refreshing. This semi-frozen dessert is nicely cooling and, like sorbet, also lends itself very well to savory flavors like tomato, cucumber, or tart green apple!

SIMPLE FROZEN DESSERTS

CUCUMBER SORBET

PREPARE: 15 MINUTES
FREEZE: 4 HOURS, OR ABOUT 15 MINUTES
WITH AN ICE CREAM MAKER
MAKES ABOUT 2 PINTS (1 L)

1 whole cucumber (about 1 pound
   1 ounce/500 g), peeled
tiny pinch of sea salt and freshly ground black
   pepper
1 cup (200 g) granulated sugar

tools
blender or food processor
1-quart (1 L) freezer-safe container
ice cream maker (optional)

In a blender or food processor, puree the
cucumber with salt and pepper to a pulp. In
a saucepan, bring the sugar to a boil with
2 tablespoons water and simmer for a few minutes
until dissolved. Let the syrup cool slightly.

Pour the sugar syrup into the cucumber pulp.
Thoroughly stir the cucumber mixture and
pour into a 1-quart (1 L) freezer-safe container.
Freeze the cucumber sorbet and whisk the ice
cream every hour for 4 hours until smooth. If
you have one, you can make the sorbet in an
ice cream maker. If you do, thoroughly chill the
cucumber mixture in the refrigerator, then churn
it until frozen.

ORANGE SHERBET

PREPARE: 15 MINUTES
COOL: 1 HOUR
FREEZE: 4 HOURS, OR ABOUT 15 MINUTES
WITH AN ICE CREAM MAKER
MAKES ABOUT 2 PINTS (1 L)

¾ cup (150 g) granulated sugar
2½ cups (600 ml) orange juice
¼ cup (60 ml) lemon juice (from about 3 lemons)
10 tablespoons (150 ml) whole milk

tools
1-quart (1 L) freezer-safe container
ice cream maker (optional)

Bring the sugar with the orange and lemon juices
to a boil and stir until the sugar has dissolved. Let
the syrup cool to room temperature

Stir in the milk, then pour the liquid into a
1-quart (1 L) freezer-safe container. Freeze the
sherbet and whisk the ice every hour for 4 hours
until smooth. If you have one, you can make
the sherbet in an ice cream maker. If you do,
let the orange mixture thoroughly cool in the
refrigerator, then churn it until frozen.

ROSEMARY LEMON SHERBET

PREPARE: 15 MINUTES
COOL: 1 HOUR
FREEZE: 4 HOURS, OR ABOUT 15 MINUTES
WITH AN ICE CREAM MAKER
MAKES ABOUT 2 PINTS (1 L)

¾ cup plus 1 tablespoon (200 ml) lemon juice
   (from about 5 lemons, at room temperature)
1¼ cups (250 g) granulated sugar
2 to 3 large sprigs of rosemary
1⅔ cups (400 ml) heavy cream or milk

tools
1-quart (1 L) freezer-safe container
ice cream maker (optional)

Bring the lemon juice with the sugar and rosemary to a boil and stir until the sugar has dissolved. Let the syrup cool to room temperature.

Strain out the rosemary and beat in the heavy cream or milk. Pour the mixture into a 1-quart (1 L) freezer-safe container. Freeze and beat every hour for 4 hours until smooth. If you have one, you can make the sherbet in an ice cream maker. If you do, let the lemon-rosemary mixture thoroughly cool in the refrigerator, then churn it until frozen.

STRAWBERRY, HIBISCUS & ROSE SHERBET

PREPARE: 15 MINUTES
COOL: 1 HOUR
FREEZE: 4 HOURS, OR ABOUT 15 MINUTES
WITH AN ICE CREAM MAKER
MAKES ABOUT 2 PINTS (1 L)

1 pound 1 ounce (500 g) strawberries, tops
  removed
1¼ cups (250 g) granulated sugar
2 tablespoons dried hibiscus (tea)
juice of 1 lemon
2 tablespoons rose water
1 cup (250 ml) heavy cream or milk

tools
blender or food processor
1-quart (1.2 L) freezer-safe container
ice cream maker (optional)

In a blender or food processor, puree the strawberries along with the sugar to a smooth pulp. Pour the strawberry puree into a saucepan, add the hibiscus, and bring to a boil. Remove from the heat and let the flavors steep while the puree cools.

Strain the strawberry puree, discarding the solids. Stir the lemon juice, rose water, and cream or milk into the liquid. Pour the strawberry mixture into a (1 L) freezer-safe container. Freeze and

whisk every hour for 4 hours until smooth. If you have one, you can make the sherbet in an ice cream maker. If you do, let the strawberry mixture thoroughly cool in the refrigerator, then churn it until frozen.

FROTHY YOGURT PARFAIT WITH RASPBERRIES

PREPARE: 25 MINUTES
COOL: 1 HOUR
FREEZE: OVERNIGHT

3 eggs, separated
¾ cup (150 g) granulated sugar
¾ cup plus 1 tablespoon (200 ml) whole milk
2 teaspoons vanilla extract
¾ cup plus 1 tablespoon (200 ml) heavy cream
¾ cup plus 1 tablespoon (200 ml) yogurt
9 ounces (250 g) raspberries

tool
loaf pan with a volume of 1–2 quarts (1.5 L)

Line a loaf pan with plastic wrap and let the edges hang over.

Beat the egg whites with half of the sugar until stiff peaks form and you can hold the bowl upside down without the egg whites falling out.

In a saucepan, bring the whole milk with the vanilla extract to just under a boil. Remove from the heat and let cool for 10 minutes.

Beat the egg yolks with the rest of the sugar until foamy. While stirring, slowly pour the hot milk into the yolk mixture, then pour the custard back into the pan. Keep stirring over low heat until the custard thickens; never let it boil. If you do, the egg will coagulate and you'll need to start over. The custard should get so thick that it sticks to the back of a spoon. Remove the pan from the heat and pour the custard into a bowl so it will cool faster. Let cool completely.

>>>

Whip the heavy cream until stiff. Carefully fold the whipped cream and yogurt into the cooled custard. Gently fold in the egg whites and carefully pour one-third of the mixture into the cake pan. Arrange half of the raspberries on top. Repeat previous steps until all of the mixture and raspberries are used. Tap the loaf pan on the countertop a few times, allowing any air bubbles to escape.

Cover the semifreddo with the overhanging foil. Place the cake pan in the freezer and let the semifreddo set overnight.

Before serving, carefully lift the semifreddo out of the mold and unwrap it. Cut into slices and serve right away.

MINT ICE CREAM OR SEMIFREDDO

PREPARE: 15 MINUTES
COOL: 1 HOUR
FREEZE: 4 HOURS, OR ABOUT 15 MINUTES
WITH AN ICE CREAM MAKER
MAKES ABOUT 2½ PINTS (1.2 L)

1 large bunch (1¾ ounces/50 g) mint
1¾ cups (425 ml) heavy cream
1¾ cups (425 ml) milk (preferably whole!)
2 teaspoons vanilla extract
5 egg yolks
1 cup (200 g) granulated sugar

tools
blender or food processor
ice cream maker (optional)
6½-cup (1½ L) freezer-safe container

Pick the mint leaves from the stems and place them in a blender or food processor along with the heavy cream. Puree into a smooth soft green cream. In a saucepan, bring the mint cream, milk, and vanilla extract to a boil. In a bowl, whisk the egg yolks with the sugar until frothy. Strain the cream mixture into a clean saucepan, discarding the mint. Whisking continuously, slowly pour half

of the cream mixture into the bowl with the egg mixture. Pour the egg-cream mixture back into the other half of the strained cream. Reheat the custard, keeping it just under a boil. Never let it boil. If you do, the egg will coagulate and you'll need to start over. Keep whisking until the sauce thickens to the consistency of thin custard.

Transfer the custard to a clean bowl and let cool. Stir occasionally to prevent a skin from forming. As soon as it has cooled to room temperature, put the custard in the fridge in order to get really cold.

In an ice cream maker, churn the custard until frozen. Don't have an ice cream machine? Make a semifreddo instead! Pour the mint cream custard into a freezer-safe container or loaf pan (which you have lined with plastic wrap, leaving the edges overhanging) and freeze overnight. Turn the semifreddo out onto a plate, unwrap, slice, and voilà: mint semifreddo!

HONEY TEA GRANITA

PREPARE: 5 MINUTES
WAIT: 2 HOURS
FREEZE: 4 HOURS, OR ABOUT 15 MINUTES
WITH AN ICE CREAM MAKER
MAKES: ABOUT 500 ML

1 tablespoon Earl Grey tea leaves
1¼ cups (300 ml) boiling water
5 tablespoons (100 g) honey
½ cup (100 g) sugar
1 organic lemon, sliced

tools
ice cream maker (optional)
freezer-safe container

Put the tea in a heatproof bowl, add the boiling water, honey, sugar, and lemon slices. Stir until the sugar has dissolved. Let the sweetened tea stand for 2 hours.

Strain the tea, discarding the solids.

Pour the tea into a freezer-safe container and freeze it. Beat the granita with a fork every hour for 4 hours until it has become a nicely crystallized, coarse ice. Or churn it in an ice cream maker until frozen.

WATERMELON GRANITA WITH ORANGE BLOSSOM WATER

PREPARE: 5 MINUTES
WAIT: 2 HOURS
FREEZE: 4 HOURS, OR ABOUT 15 MINUTES
WITH AN ICE CREAM MAKER
MAKES ABOUT 2½ PINTS (1.2 L)

2¼ pounds (1 kg) peeled and seeded watermelon
½ cup (100 g) granulated sugar
juice of ½ lemon
1 tablespoon orange blossom water
1 teaspoon ground cinnamon

for garnish
basil

tools
blender or food processor
ice cream maker (optional)
freezer-safe container

Put the watermelon in a blender or food processor and puree. Bring 6½ tablespoons (100 ml) water to a boil. Stir in the sugar until dissolved, then let the syrup cool completely. Combine the syrup with the watermelon, lemon juice, orange blossom water, and a pinch of cinnamon.

Pour the watermelon mixture into a freezer-safe container and freeze. Beat the granita with a fork every hour for 4 hours until smooth. You can also churn it using an ice cream maker until frozen, about 15 minutes.

Garnish the granita with a basil leaf and serve immediately.

RHUBARB & RICOTTA ICE CREAM

PREPARE: 25 MINUTES
WAIT: 2 HOURS
FREEZE: 4 HOURS, OR
ABOUT 20 MINUTES WITH
AN ICE CREAM MAKER
SERVES 4

14 ounces (400 g) rhubarb,
    cut into 1-inch (2.5 cm)
    cubes
1 cup (200 g) granulated
    sugar
9 ounces (250 g) ricotta
    cheese
6 tablespoons (90 ml)
    Campari

tools
ice cream maker (optional)
freezer-safe container

In a saucepan, toss the rhubarb cubes with 3 to 4 tablespoons water and half of the sugar. Cook over low heat until the rhubarb has turned soft. This will take 12 to 15 minutes.

Let the compote cool completely on the kitchen counter, then refrigerate for at least 2 hours, allowing it to thoroughly chill.

Beat the ricotta with the Campari until frothy. Beat in the rhubarb compote and the rest of the sugar, up to ½ cup (100 g). Don't add all of the sugar at once. Depending on the acidity of the rhubarb, you may not need all the sugar. It's okay if the mixture tastes a little sweeter than you'd prefer, because once ice cold, the rhubarb's intense sweetness will mellow out a bit.

If using an ice cream maker, churn the composition (a technical term for "the mixture") until frozen. Otherwise, pour the mixture into a freezer-safe container and beat the ice cream with a fork every hour for 4 hours until smooth.

BEURRE NOISETTE–ALMOND MILK ICE CREAM

PREPARE: 30 MINUTES
WAIT: 2 HOURS TO 1 NIGHT
FREEZE: 4 HOURS, OR
ABOUT 20 MINUTES WITH
AN ICE CREAM MAKER
MAKES AT LEAST 10 SCOOPS

14 tablespoons (200 g) butter

3 cups (750 ml) almond milk

6 egg yolks

scant 1 cup (200 g) superfine sugar

½ teaspoon sea salt

about 6 tablespoons almond nougatine or almond crisp (see page 433), or generous ½ cup (75 grams) blanched almonds, briefly toasted in a dry skillet, chopped

tools

blender

ice cream maker (optional)

1-quart (1 L) freezer-safe container

MAKE AN AFFOGATO

Put one scoop of this ice cream in a glass and pour a shot of hot, freshly brewed espresso over it. Serve right away.

This ice cream goes well with a slice of almond caramel tart (page 413).

In order to get a more intense almond flavor I use almond milk in this recipe. Be extra careful when making the custard, however: eggs will coagulate above 140°F (80°C), and nut milk can't really withstand heat that well either. So do not overheat the custard. Make sure the eggs are just about cooked, then remove the pan from the heat and immediately transfer the custard to another bowl so it will cool down more quickly. In a blender set to high speed, beat the brown butter in with the mixture so everything will set properly. It all sounds more complicated than it is, really. Most of all it's criminally delicious.

Begin by making the beurre noisette: Melt the butter over medium heat. Preferably use a heavy, thick-bottomed pan that heats up evenly. Warm the butter until it turns the color of tea and begins to smell somewhat like caramel. Pour the butter through a fine sieve (make sure that the dark solids remain in the pan). Set the beurre noisette aside.

In a heavy-bottomed saucepan, heat the almond milk, careful not to boil it. Meanwhile, beat the egg yolks with the superfine sugar and salt in a mixing bowl until frothy and light yellow.

While beating, slowly add the hot almond milk to the egg yolks. Return the egg-milk mixture to the pan. Heat the custard over low heat while stirring—do not let it boil, or the egg will coagulate!—until it is thick enough to not slide off the back of a spoon. Have patience: sometimes it will take as long as 12 minutes. Remove the pan from the heat and pour the custard into a blender.

With the blender motor running, pour in the beurre noisette through the hole in the lid and blend with the custard until smooth and creamy. Pour the custard into a 1-quart (1 L) freezer-safe container and let cool to room temperature. Chill in the refrigerator for at least 2 hours or until very cold, then churn the custard in an ice cream maker until frozen. Or put the custard in the freezer. In that case, beat the ice cream with a fork or a mixer every hour for about 4 hours until smooth.

After about 2 hours (if freezing in the freezer), or halfway through churning (in the ice cream maker), add the almond crisp or chopped almonds to the ice cream mixture.

CHOCOLATE OLIVE OIL ICE CREAM WITH SEA SALT

PREPARE: 30 MINUTES
WAIT: 2 HOURS TO
OVERNIGHT
FREEZE: 4 HOURS, OR
ABOUT 20 MINUTES WITH
AN ICE CREAM MAKER
MAKES AT LEAST 10 SCOOPS

2 cups plus 1 tablespoon
(500 ml) whole milk
¾ cup plus 1 tablespoon
(200 ml) heavy cream
6 egg yolks
⅔ cup (125 g) superfine
sugar
½ teaspoon fine sea salt
7 ounces (200 g) dark
chocolate (at least 70%
cacao), finely chopped
1 heaping tablespoon cocoa
powder
6½ tablespoons (100 ml)
best-quality olive oil, plus
extra
pinch of salt flakes (Maldon,
for example, or *fleur de sel
de Guérande*, which I find
the most delicious)

One time in a tiny hole-in-the-wall restaurant in Barcelona I tasted this dessert, more or less—it technically wasn't ice cream, by the way, but a kind of very stiff mousse, or rather a fudge. It was so amazing that I returned the next day to eat it again. The following year, when I found myself in Barcelona again, I went again and they still had the small chocolate dessert with olive oil on the menu. Unforgettable. This ice cream is an ode to that humble desert.

Pick the ingredients you use for this recipe with care. For this simple ice cream it matters a great deal.

In a heavy, thick-bottomed saucepan, bring the whole milk and heavy cream to a boil. In a bowl, beat the egg yolks with the superfine sugar and fine salt until frothy and light.

While whisking, slowly pour the hot milk-cream mixture into the egg yolks and then return everything to the pan. Heat while whisking—do not let it boil, or the eggs will coagulate!—until the custard is thick enough that it won't slide off the back of a spoon. After running your finger through it, the trace shouldn't disappear. Have patience: sometimes it will take as long as 12 minutes. Remove from the heat.

Add the dark chocolate and stir until melted.

Sift the cocoa powder over the pan and stir it in as well. Let the custard cool to room temperature. Stir the olive oil into the custard and refrigerate until ice cold. Preferably overnight, but 1 to 2 hours is fine.

Churn the custard in an ice cream maker until frozen. Or put it in the freezer to freeze. Stir with a fork or use a hand mixer to break the ice crystals every hour for 4 hours until smooth, thus making nice smooth ice cream by hand—it really isn't that difficult.

Serve 1 scoop per person, topped with a drop of olive oil and sprinkled with a few flakes of sea salt.

FROZEN DESSERTS

YOU CAN REPLACE THE ALMOND PASTE IN THE ICE CREAM WITH ONE OF THE INGREDIENTS LISTED BELOW:

1 tablespoon cocoa powder
3 tablespoons peanut butter
handful of blueberries or other berries or chopped stone fruit
pulp of 2 to 3 passion fruits
2¾ ounces (75 g) white, milk, or dark chocolate, finely chopped
½ cup (50 g) toasted pecans, hazelnuts, or pistachios, coarsely chopped
⅓ cup (50 g) sesame seeds
4 crisp cookies or sweet biscuits, crumbled

TOPPINGS

caramel syrup, dulce de leche, or maple syrup
melted chocolate
marshmallows from page 429 (roasted or not)
frozen custard or custard
toasted coconut

frozen Lake IJsselmeer, the Netherlands

SUPER-EASY BANANA ALMOND ICE CREAM

CUT 4 BANANAS INTO SLICES.

PUT IN A FREEZER-SAFE CONTAINER AND FREEZE FOR 4 HOURS TO OVERNIGHT.

THE NEXT DAY, BLEND THE FROZEN BANANA AND 1¾ OZ (50 G) ALMOND PASTE UNTIL SMOOTH IN A BLENDER.

ALMOND CARAMEL TART

PREPARE: 25 MINUTES
WAIT: 1 HOUR 15 MINUTES
BAKE: 2 X 20 MINUTES
MAKES 8 TO 12 SMALL
SLICES

for the dough
1 cup plus 3 tablespoons
(150 g) all-purpose flour,
plus extra
⅓ cup (75 g) cold butter,
cubed, plus extra for the
pan
scant ⅓ cup (60 g) superfine
sugar
pinch of sea salt
1 egg yolk

for the filling
2⅓ cups (225 g) sliced
almonds
1 cup plus 1 tablespoon
(250 grams) butter
1¼ cups (250 g) superfine
sugar
½ cup (120 ml) milk
2 tablespoons Chinese
five-spice powder or
pumpkin spice mix

tools
food processor (optional)
9-inch (22 cm) round
cake pan, preferably a
springform pan
dried beans or weights for
blind baking

A divine little pie that will last quite a while because you really need to cut it into small pieces. However, having this, with an espresso: heaven.

Make the dough: In a food processor, grind all the ingredients except the egg yolk to a crumb, or do it by hand. Beat 1 tablespoon cold water with the yolk to loosen it up. Then pour the egg into the crumb, drop by drop, until the dough is just coherent. Form into a flat ball, cover, and refrigerate for 1 hour to rest.

Thoroughly butter the cake pan and cut a sheet of parchment paper to fit the bottom. Butter that as well and place it in the bottom of the cake pan.

Roll out the dough and press it into the pan, forming an even, thin crust on the bottom and up the sides. Prick the entire bottom with a fork. Place the pan in the fridge for 15 minutes, allowing the dough to firm up.

Preheat the oven to 400°F (200°C).

Blind bake the crust: Line the bottom and sides with a sheet of parchment paper and cover with uncooked dried beans or rice or blind-baking weights. Bake for 15 minutes. Remove the parchment paper and weights and bake the crust for another 5 minutes in the oven, until just dry.

Make the filling: In a skillet, toast the almonds over medium heat, stirring until golden brown. Transfer to a large bowl.

Heat the butter, sugar, and milk in the same pan. Stir in the five-spice powder (or pumpkin spice mix) and keep stirring until the sugar has dissolved and the butter has melted.

Cook the caramel for another 2 minutes, or until it starts to smell like caramel and spices. Pour half of the caramel into the almonds and mix well to coat them. Turn off the heat under the remaining caramel sauce. Pour the almond-caramel mixture over the prebaked pie crust.

Bake the almond tart for 15 to 20 minutes, until evenly golden brown. Reheat the saved caramel sauce until it liquifies. Drizzle the tart with it. Let the tart cool completely before cutting it.

BAKED DESSERTS

poached pears in white port & fennel syrup, with fennel seed almond cake

firewood stash for the Irish winter

POACHED PEARS IN WHITE PORT & FENNEL SYRUP

PREPARE: 40 MINUTES
BAKE: 45 MINUTES
MAKES 10 PEARS

10 small stewing pears
(preferably Bartlett), peeled
but left with the stems,
blossom removed at the
bottom
½ organic lemon, scrubbed
and sliced
3 to 4 bay leaves
2½ inches (6 cm) fresh
ginger, thinly sliced
2 cinnamon sticks
2 tablespoons fennel seeds
⅓ cup (75 g) granulated
sugar
1 bottle (750 ml) white port
7 tablespoons (150 g) honey

Place the pears side by side, upright in the bottom of a wide pan.
Add the rest of the ingredients except the honey and slowly bring
the liquid to a boil. Reduce the heat, cover with a lid, and let the
pears simmer for 25 minutes.

Preheat the oven to 350°F (180°C).

Carefully spoon the pears into a deep baking dish that they fit in
snugly.

Cook the remaining liquid in the saucepan until somewhat reduced.
Stir in the honey, then strain the sauce over the pears in the baking
dish. Place the pears in the oven and allow them to continue
cooking. Open the oven briefly every now and then to baste the
pears with the caramel sauce or to turn them over so they cook
evenly. This is easiest using two spoons. Be careful not to damage
the pears.

The pears are done when you can effortlessly pierce them with a
sharp knife. There should be no friction. This will be after about
45 minutes.

Let the pears cool a bit. Transfer them to a beautiful glass bowl.
Drizzle with the sauce from the baking dish and serve with the
fennel cake from the adjacent page or with some cheese, which is
also a really good idea.

FENNEL SEED ALMOND CAKE

PREPARE: 10 MINUTES
BAKE: 40 MINUTES
SERVES 6

1 cup (125 g) all-purpose
  flour, plus extra for dusting
¾ cup plus 2 tablespoons
  (100 g) almond flour
¾ cup (150 g) superfine
  sugar
1 teaspoon baking powder
pinch of sea salt
½ cup (125 ml) whole milk
1 tablespoon fennel seeds

on the side
lightly sweetened whipped
  cream and/or poached
  pears (page 416), but you
  can also use another fruit
  compote

tool
8- to 9-inch (20 to 22 cm)
  springform pan or tart pan
  with removable bottom

Preheat the oven to 350°F (180°C). Grease the springform pan or tart pan, dust with a little flour, and tap out the excess flour.

In a mixing bowl, combine the all-purpose flour with the almond flour, superfine sugar, baking powder, and a pinch of salt. Make an indentation in the center and pour in the milk; stir with a spatula to make a smooth dough. Stir in the fennel seeds. Knead the dough and press it out in the springform pan. Smooth the top. Bake for 40 to 45 minutes, until the cake springs back when you press it gently with your fingers.

Let the fennel seed almond cake cool on a wire rack, then cut into wedges and add whipped cream and/or stewed pears or fruit compote.

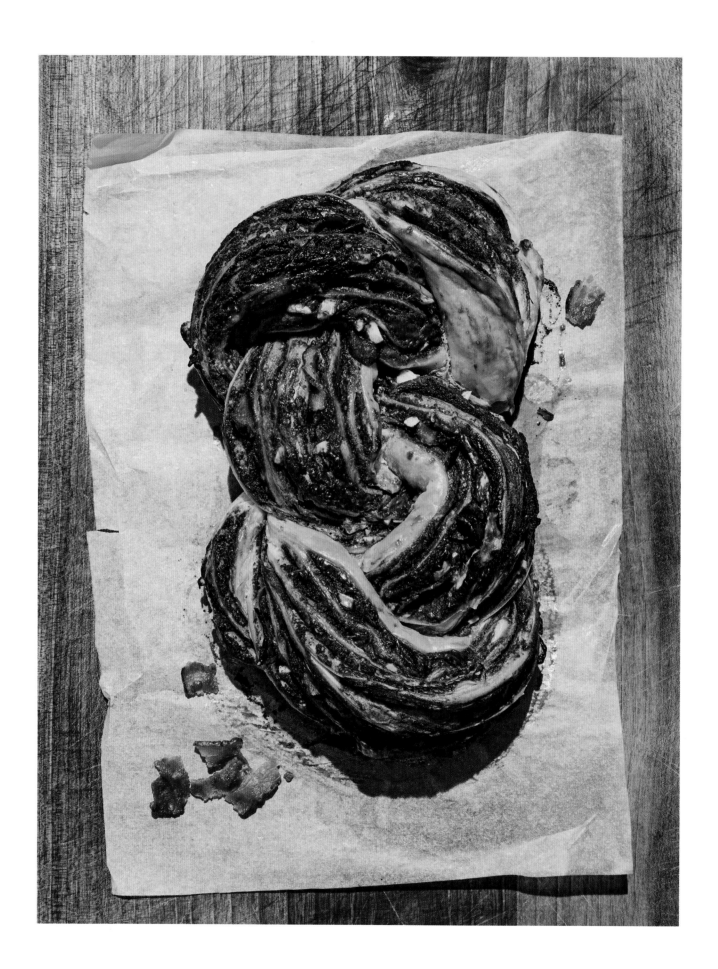

CHOCOLATE HAZELNUT TWIST WITH FRIED BACON

PREPARE: 20 MINUTES
REST: 30 MINUTES
BAKE: 25 MINUTES
SERVES 6

10½ to 14 ounces (300 to 400 g) frozen puff pastry, thawed

small handful of all-purpose flour

scant 1 cup (300 g) hazelnut chocolate spread (see page 65)

¾ cup (100 g) blanched almonds, briefly toasted in a dry skillet, coarsely chopped

2 slices bacon, fried, cooled, and crumbled

1 egg, beaten

This may seem like an odd combination, but it's so delicious. The sweet and salty pairing is super addictive! Serve the twist with coffee, or use it as part of a dessert and add a scoop of ice cream—the easy-to-make banana ice cream on page 411, for instance, or the beurre noisette and almond milk one on page 407.

On a flour-dusted counter, roll out the dough to a rectangle with the thickness of 2 millimeters. If it already is that thin, you don't need to roll it out. It should measure about 14 by 10 inches (35 by 25 cm).

Spread the puff pastry sheet with the hazelnut chocolate spread, leaving a margin of ½ inch (1.5 cm) all around. Sprinkle the hazelnut chocolate spread with the almonds and the crumbled bacon.

Roll up the puff pastry from the long side so that you have a long, flat roll about 2½ inches (6 cm) thick in front of you. Cut the roll in half lengthwise. This works best with a pizza slicer, but a large chef's knife works fine too. Wrap one strand around the other, keeping the cut side facing up so that the inside with the hazelnut chocolate spread remains visible.

Place the twisted pastry loaf on a parchment paper–lined baking sheet. Refrigerate for 30 minutes. That way the twist won't collapse in the oven.

Preheat the oven to 400°F (200°C).

Brush the puff pastry with the beaten egg. Bake for 25 to 30 minutes, until golden brown and crispy. Serve the chocolate hazelnut twist warm.

BAKED PINEAPPLE WITH HONEY & CHILE

PREPARE: 20 MINUTES
MARINATE: 15 MINUTES
SERVES 4

1 pineapple
½ cup (100 g) loosely packed
  dark brown sugar
pinch of chile flakes
3 tablespoons honey
6½ tablespoons (100 ml)
  orange juice
scant 1 cup (200 g) crème
  fraîche or Greek yogurt
heaping ½ cup (75 g)
  unsalted shelled pistachios,
  briefly toasted in a dry
  skillet and coarsely
  chopped
small handful of fresh mint
  leaves

Pictured at left you can see us roasting the pineapple over open fire. We suspended the fruit in a basket that Oof fashioned from wire. Using this method the pineapple takes a little longer to roast: 30 minutes at least. It truly is delicious: the hint of smokiness really complements this dessert.

Oooh, this is finger-licking good. Serve with some yogurt or crème fraîche. Although I can also imagine how amazing this would taste with the cucumber sorbet on page 400 or the mint ice cream on page 402.

Peel the pineapple. Cut off enough so you remove all of the eyes and seeds as well. Quarter the pineapple lengthwise and remove the tough core. Halve the quarters lengthwise once more so you end up with 8 wedges.

Preheat the oven to 400°F (200°C). Line a large baking sheet with parchment paper, letting the edges stand up.

In a large bowl, stir the brown sugar, chile flakes, and honey with the orange juice until the sugar has dissolved. Swirl the pineapple chunks through the orange juice and let them marinate for 15 minutes.

Remove the pineapple from the marinade and place the wedges on the baking sheet with the outer edges facing up, cored sides down. Roast in the oven for about 15 minutes. While roasting, brush the wedges with the remaining marinade several times to glaze the pineapple.

Let cool slightly. Serve the roasted wedges with a generous spoonful of crème fraîche on the side and sprinkle with chopped pistachios and mint leaves.

FRUIT

CANDIED LEMONS

With a sharp knife, cut an organic lemon into razor-thin slices and remove the seeds.

Bring 1 cup (250 ml) water to a boil and add 1¼ cups (250 g) superfine sugar and the lemon slices. Stir until the sugar has dissolved. Slightly reduce the heat and cook the lemon slices over very low heat, until the white part of the rind looks translucent, about 35 minutes.

Using a fork, lift the lemon slices out of the syrup and arrange them, somewhat spaced apart, on a sheet of parchment paper. Allow them to dry a bit.

Cook the syrup until reduced to a jelly.
Delicious on a pancake or a slice of bread.
You can also turn the syrup into lemonade by reducing it less, letting it cool, and pouring in sparkling water.

Store them divided by layers of parchment paper in the refrigerator; they will keep for a few months (if they last that long!).

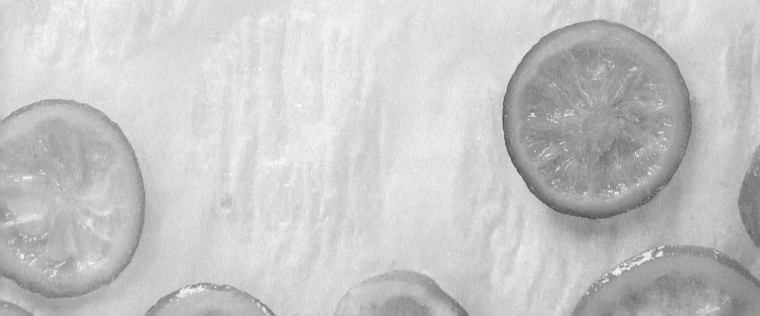

lemon & date bars

VERMOUTH & ROSÉ JELLY WITH RED FRUIT

PREPARE: 20 MINUTES
WAIT: AT LEAST 4 HOURS
SERVES 4 TO 6

12 sheets gelatin, or
  3 (¼-ounce/7 g) envelopes
  powdered unflavored gelatin
2 cups plus 1 tablespoon
  (500 ml) red vermouth
2 cups plus 1 tablespoon
  (500 ml) tasty, dry rosé
1 cup (200 g) granulated sugar
1 pound 1 ounce (500 g)
  locally grown berries such
  as raspberries, currants,
  blackberries, and small
  strawberries
edible white violets (available
  at some supermarkets and
  farmers' markets), untreated
  rose petals or flowers from
  the garden (optional)

tool
mold or bowl with a capacity
  of 1 quart (1 L)

Be careful when adding other
fruits: raw pineapple and
kiwi, for example, contain
an enzyme that prevents the
gelatin from solidifying! I once
made this painful mistake
myself, so I'm passing it along
to avert further suffering.

You'll never take the child out of me. I grew up on jelly desserts. It was the same story each birthday party, and you couldn't make me any happier. I've grown a little older by now, so this is going to be a more adult version of that treat from my youth. It is, by the way, one of the few ways I like rosé: as a dessert. In combination with this dish I don't mind pouring a glass too, just this once.

If using gelatin sheets, soak them in a bowl of cold water until softened, then drain and squeeze out excess water. If using powdered gelatin, sprinkle it over about ¼ cup (60 ml) cold water and let stand until it's absorbed the water.

Make a syrup: In a saucepan over low heat, heat the vermouth, rosé, and sugar and cook until the sugar is dissolved and the syrup is reduced slightly. Remove from the heat and add the squeezed or reconstituted gelatin, stirring until it is dissolved. Set aside and let cool to lukewarm.

Clean the fruit.

Pour the vermouth-rosé mixture into the mold. Add the fruit and, if you want, the flowers. Briefly tap the mold on the counter to allow any air bubbles to escape. Cover with plastic wrap and refrigerate for at least 4 hours, until the jelly is set.

To easily turn out the jelly, fill a washing-up bowl with hot water. Briefly hold the mold in the hot water so that it heats up. Not for too long, because in that case the jelly will melt. Be careful not to let any water leak into the mold!

When you see the edge of the jelly separate from the side of the bowl, remove the bowl from the water and cover it with an upside-down plate. Turn the whole thing over. The jelly should slowly come out of the mold. If it doesn't work, hold the bowl in the hot water again.

Serve the jelly straightaway, plain or sprinkled with more edible flowers. Serve with a glass of chilled rosé, naturally.

FRUIT

~ 423 ~

LEMON & DATE BARS

SOAK: 30 MINUTES
PREPARE: 50 MINUTES
BAKE: 1 HOUR (IN TOTAL)
COOL AND SET: AT LEAST
2 HOURS
MAKES 12 BARS

for the filling
2 cups (250 g) Medjool
    dates, pitted
1 cup (250 ml) boiling water
1¼ cups (250 g) granulated
    sugar
3½ tablespoons (30 g)
    all-purpose flour
½ teaspoon sea salt
4 eggs
grated zest of 1 organic
    lemon
⅔ cup (175 ml) lemon juice
    (from about 5 lemons)

for the crust
⅔ cup (150 g) cold butter,
    cubed, plus extra for the
    baking pan
1¾ cups (225 g) all-purpose
    flour
¾ cup (75 g) sifted
    confectioners' sugar,
    plus extra
½ teaspoon sea salt

tools
9-inch (23 cm) square baking
    pan or dish
blender

Start the filling: Put the dates in a heatproof bowl, pour the boiling water over them, and soak for at least 30 minutes (but preferably longer).

Make the crust: Butter the baking pan and line the bottom and two sides with parchment paper, letting the paper overhang a bit. Butter the parchment paper as well.

In a bowl, combine the flour with the confectioners' sugar and salt. With clean fingers, rub in the butter until the dough just holds together when you pinch it. If necessary, add a few drops of water. Press the dough into the baking dish, forming a nice, even layer, and put the baking sheet in the freezer for 15 minutes to let the dough firm up.

Preheat the oven to 350°F (180°C). Bake the crust for 25 minutes, or until nicely golden brown. Let cool on a rack. Leave the oven on.

Make the filling: Drain the dates over a bowl and keep the soaking liquid. Puree the dates in a blender, adding some of the soaking liquid if necessary, until the date puree is a spreadable paste.

In a bowl, combine the granulated sugar, flour, and salt.

In another bowl, beat the eggs with the lemon zest and juice. While stirring, pour the egg mixture into the flour-sugar mixture in a thin stream and stir into a smooth batter without lumps.

Spread the date paste over the prebaked crust in an even layer. Bake the date layer for 5 minutes. Reduce the oven temperature to 325°F (160°C). Pour the lemon mixture over the dates and bake for 20 to 25 minutes, until the lemon layer has just set.

Let the cake completely cool on a wire rack. After 20 minutes, run a sharp knife along the edge of the baking sheet to loosen the filling and crust. Transfer to the refrigerator to chill and firm up.

Lift out of the baking pan using the parchment paper. Dust with confectioners' sugar and cut into evenly sized squares. If you want, decorate the bars with candied lemon slices (see page 425).

FRUIT

MARSHMALLOWS

PREPARE: 30 MINUTES
DRY: 8 TO 12 HOURS
MAKES ABOUT 20
MARSHMALLOWS*

4 sheets gelatin, or
  1 (¼-ounce/7 g) envelope
  powdered unflavored gelatin
6 tablespoons (125 g) golden
  syrup or honey (see below)
2 cups (400 g) granulated
  sugar
pinch of sea salt
handful of cornstarch

tool
food processor or stand mixer

*Depending on the size you
cut them.

GOLDEN SYRUP

My great love: there really is
no substitute, such an addictive
flavor!

This thick amber syrup is made
from refined cane sugar. It's
sold at some supermarkets
as well as online; search for
Lyle's brand.

Substitute with honey; it tastes
a little different but has a
similar color. Or feel free to
use corn syrup.

P.S.: Golden syrup and salted
butter, melting over freshly
baked crumpets (see pages
28–29): JUST MAKE THEM.

Making marshmallows is easy, provided you have a stand mixer and a *lot* of patience, or a large family willing to take turns whisking.

The syrup can be flavored any way you want, by the way: substitute a floral or herbal tea for the water, or add a drop of extract or oil (almond extract, peppermint oil) if you want to add a flavor to your marshmallows. Anything goes.

The hotter the syrup, the dryer and tougher the foam will end up being. If the temperature of the syrup is too low, however, the marshmallow won't set. Use a candy thermometer if you have one. I often make marshmallows without using one, though of course that requires some level of experience.

If using gelatin sheets, soak them in a bowl of cold water until softened, then drain and squeeze out excess water. If using powdered gelatin, sprinkle it over about 2 tablespoons cold water and let stand until it's absorbed the water.

Bring ¾ cup plus 1 tablespoon (200 ml) water to a boil, along with the golden syrup or honey, the sugar, and salt. Let the liquid continue to boil over low heat for at least 7 minutes, until you have a thick golden syrup at 240°F (116°C).

Put the gelatin sheets or reconstituted gelatin in the mixing bowl of a stand mixer fitted with the whisk attachment and set to medium speed. While whisking, pour in the hot syrup in a thin stream. As the mixture turns whiter, you can switch the mixer to a higher setting.

Continue to whisk until a thick white foam forms and the bowl feels lukewarm to the touch (this will take about 10 minutes).

Place a sheet of parchment paper on a cutting board or serving tray. Using a spatula, spread the whipped foam over the paper into a layer about 2 inches (5 cm) thick and dust the marshmallow slab with cornstarch. Let dry for 8 to 12 hours.

Cut the slab into diamonds, squares, or whatever shape you want. If you use cookie cutters, always dip them in the cornstarch before pushing them into the marshmallow slab. Dust all the cut out shapes with cornstarch and tap them to remove excess. This way they won't stick together as easily. Store the marshmallows in an airtight container for up to 3 weeks.

SWEETS

CHOCOLATE CUSTARD WITH CINNAMON

PREPARE: 20 MINUTES
CHILL: AT LEAST 1 HOUR
SERVES 4 TO 6

2 cups plus 1 tablespoon (500 ml) whole milk
1 teaspoon vanilla extract
½ cup (100 g) granulated sugar
2 tablespoons all-purpose flour
pinch of sea salt
3 egg yolks, plus 1 whole egg
3½ ounces (100 g) dark chocolate (at least 70% cacao), grated or chopped, plus extra to garnish
2 tablespoons butter
½ teaspoon ground cinnamon, plus extra
½ cup (125 ml) heavy cream

I grew up in Ireland, the land of custard. The Irish eat custard over—or with—everything. When I moved to the Netherlands, at age ten, the children in my class ate *vla* for dessert, but I'd never had that. When I asked my mother if we too could try *hopjesvla*, she firmly retorted: "No! Vla is factory processed, it's disgusting." She didn't like to make custard herself, for fear of that gruesome milk skin.

I taught myself to make custard and found that my mother was right. Home made custard truly tastes a thousand times better than the processed version. A container of Jell-O Pudding is no match for this chocolate custard with cinnamon. When you close your eyes, there's a distant resemblance—but it's very, very, distant.

In a saucepan, heat the whole milk and vanilla extract to just below the boiling point. Remove from the heat and let the vanilla milk steep.

In a bowl, combine the sugar with the flour and salt and add the egg yolks and the whole egg. Beat the egg mixture until frothy and the sugar and salt are dissolved. While whisking, slowly pour the hot milk mixture into the egg mixture and then return everything to the pan. Heat over low heat while whisking—do not let it boil, or the eggs will coagulate!—until the custard is thick enough that it won't slide off the back of a spoon.

Remove from the heat, stir in the dark chocolate, butter, and cinnamon, and let the custard cool to room temperature, stirring regularly to prevent the forming of a skin and allowing the chocolate to melt evenly.

Pour the custard into four to six glasses and refrigerate for an hour or more, allowing the custard to firm up and cool.

Whip the heavy cream until stiff. Top each glass with a dollop of whipped cream and serve the chocolate custard decorated with a sprinkle of grated chocolate and a pinch of cinnamon.

SWEETS

MAKING CARAMEL

Because making caramel really isn't that difficult, but has many pitfalls nonetheless, I will explain exactly what you need to do to make a beautiful caramel.

Keep children and pets away from the kitchen while you work. Sugar gets scorching hot: please be extremely careful and don't get distracted.

Spoon the superfine sugar into a pile in the center of the bottom of a heavy-bottomed saucepan, carefully. Make sure no sugar touches the wall of the pan because it will crystallize. This will ruin the caramel and force you to start over again.

Pour 2 tablespoons water drop by drop onto the center of the sugar heap. Let the water run in a slow trickle. Don't turn up the heat too much—slightly below medium-high—and without stirring, let the sugar melt into a golden brown caramel.

Only once the edges begin to brown, you can swirl the pan gently so that the sugar melts evenly.

Stop when the caramel has the color of weak black tea. You can add a pinch of sea salt to the caramel, but it isn't mandatory.

If you do spot any crumbs of sugar around the wall of the pan, you can clean them off using a moistened pastry brush.

CHOCOLATE TRUFFLES WITH CHESTNUT (& LIQUOR)

PREPARE: 30 MINUTES
WAIT: 3 HOURS
MAKES ABOUT 20 TRUFFLES

7 ounces (200 g) dark chocolate (at least 70% cacao), finely chopped

6½ tablespoons (100 ml) heavy cream

3 tablespoons chestnut puree, or 1¾ ounces (50 g) precooked chestnuts plus an extra 3 tablespoons cream

2 tablespoons whiskey or rum (optional)

about 6 tablespoons (45 g) cacao nibs,* chopped; or 6 tablespoons chocolate sprinkles

for the crisp

½ cup (100 g) superfine sugar

pinch of sea salt (optional)

heaping ⅓ cup (50 g) hazelnuts or almonds, briefly toasted in a dry skillet

tool

food processor or blender

* Sold online, in the health-foods aisle of some grocery stores, and in organic food stores.

This is a base recipe for truffles. You can throw in any ingredient and coat them with all sorts of crunchy stuff. I like the bitter bite of cacao nibs, but perhaps you prefer crunchy caramel nuts instead. You can also grate a bar of white chocolate and dredge the truffles through it. Just indulge yourself and get loose.

Put the chopped chocolate in a large heatproof bowl. Warm the heavy cream and the chestnut puree (or the whole chestnuts and splash of extra cream) until just below the boiling point. (If you used whole chestnuts, puree the hot cream and chestnuts in a blender, then reheat the mixture to just under a boil.) Pour the hot chestnut cream over the chopped chocolate. Let stand for 3 minutes, then stir until the chocolate is completely melted. If you're using liquor, now is the moment to add a splash. Let the chocolate-cream mixture cool to room temperature.

Now put the ganache (that's what the chocolate-cream mixture is called now) in the fridge for at least 3 hours to firm up.

Make the crisp: For this you'll need to make caramel with the superfine sugar and optional salt. Make sure to work with careful attention. See the previous page for more detailed instructions.

Line a baking sheet with parchment paper. Arrange the roasted hazelnuts or almonds on top in a single layer. Pour the hot caramel over the nuts on the baking sheet. Allow the caramel to harden for 1 hour. Break the caramel slab into pieces, then grind these pieces in a food processor or blender to a nice crumb. Spoon the caramel nut crumbs onto a plate. Spoon the cacao nibs or chocolate sprinkles onto another plate.

Shape the ganache into balls using a moistened small ice cream scoop or two spoons. Make them as round and smooth as you can using your wet hands. Work swiftly so the mixture heats up as little as possible and doesn't melt. Dredge the balls through the caramel nut crumbs or the chopped cacao nibs.

Let the chocolate balls firm up in the refrigerator until ready to serve. Offer them when coffee is being served or wrap them up nicely as a gift.

SWEETS

Hughie, our Parson Russell terrier

FOR OUR PETS

LITTLE CHICKEN BONES

**PREPARE: 20 MINUTES
BAKE: 25 MINUTES
MAKES ABOUT 80 DOG
BISCUITS**

7 ounces (200 g) chicken,
   cooked until tender and
   cooled, cooking liquid
   reserved
½ cup (100 g) cooked
   brown rice
½ cup (120 ml) chicken
   cooking water or low-salt
   chicken stock
1 egg
2⅓ cups (300 g) all-purpose
   flour, plus extra

tools
food processor or blender
bone-shaped cookie cutter
   (any other small cookie
   cutter will work fine too,
   of course)

Dogs aren't allowed to eat *actual* chicken bones because of the danger of splinters but rest assured, these "chicken bone" biscuits are safe. These cookies made from thoroughly cooked chicken meat are merely *shaped* like bones. Hughie is nuts about them!

Preheat the oven to 350°F (180°C). Line a baking sheet with parchment paper.

Puree the chicken, chicken cooking water, rice, and egg in a food processor or blender into a thick paste. Using a spatula, fold in the flour until you get a firm dough. Place the dough on a flour-dusted counter, knead the dough a few more times, and add a pinch of flour or a drop of cooking water if necessary.

Dust the counter with flour again. Roll out the dough into a sheet with a thickness of a little less than ¼ inch (5 mm) and cut out dog biscuits. Sweep the scraps together and roll them out again to cut out more biscuits. Continue until you've used all the dough.

Place all the biscuits on the prepared baking sheet and bake for 20 to 25 minutes, until they are a beautiful light brown.

Store the chicken biscuits in an airtight container in the fridge or freezer.

THE DOG

BANANA DOGSICLES

PREPARE: 10 MINUTES
FREEZE: 4 HOURS
MAKES ABOUT 12

2 cups plus 1 tablespoon
   (500 ml) yogurt
2 bananas
4 tablespoons (60 ml)
   peanut butter
splash of olive oil, for
   greasing
about 12 elongated dog
   biscuits (store bought or
   home made; see previous
   page), for the "popsicle
   sticks"

tools
blender
muffin pan

On a hot day, dogs need to cool down, too.

In those moments, giving him or her a "dogsicle" isn't such a bad idea. My dog loves ice cubes. You can give those to your dog as well. But whenever I have a little time, I make my dog real popsicles. Especially if there happens to be an overripe banana in the fruit bowl.

Dogs shouldn't eat nuts, but peanuts are legumes, not nuts. Some dogs are allergic to peanuts, so if yours is, omit the peanut butter from this recipe. Dogs are just like people, aren't they?

Puree the yogurt, bananas, and peanut butter in a blender until smooth.

Grease the cups of a muffin pan or several separate small cups with olive oil. A silicone pan works even better, because you'll be able to easily remove the banana ice and silicone doesn't need to be greased.

Pour the banana mixture into the cups and put them in the freezer. After about 2 hours, stick the dog biscuit "popsicle sticks" into the ice, which will be frozen firm enough to prevent the sticks from sinking.

Allow the popsicles to freeze for at least 2 more hours, until solid.

Harrie, the cat next door

HARRIE'S MOUSE COOKIES

PREPARE: 12 MINUTES
BAKE: 40 MINUTES
MAKES ABOUT 75 CAT
COOKIES

1 can (about 5¼ ounces/
 150 g) fish (salmon,
 sardines, etc.)
1 egg
about 1⅔ cups (200 g)
 whole-wheat flour or
 regular all-purpose flour

tool
small mouse-shaped cookie
 cutter (optional)

Harrie is his official name,
but he is commonly called
Hallie. His two-and-a-half-
year-old mistress thinks the
r is too difficult a letter to
pronounce. In order not to
embarrass her, we say Hallie
too, whenever she's around.

Harrie is our cat next door. He's a little younger than our dog Hughie and doesn't want anything to do with him. Hugh, on the other hand, *really* wants to make contact with him. This sometimes results in war—after which we are obliged to broker a peace by way of a home baked present.

Preheat the oven to 400°F (200°C). Line a baking sheet with parchment paper.

Drain the fish. Mash it with a fork and stir in the egg. Stir in the flour until you have a dry dough.

On a flour-dusted counter, roll out the dough and cut out tiny biscuits. Arrange the cookies on the prepared baking sheet and bake for about 40 minutes, until just light brown.

Let the cookies cool and store them in the refrigerator in a sealable container.

THE CAT

Lower East Side, New York

INDEX BY RECIPE

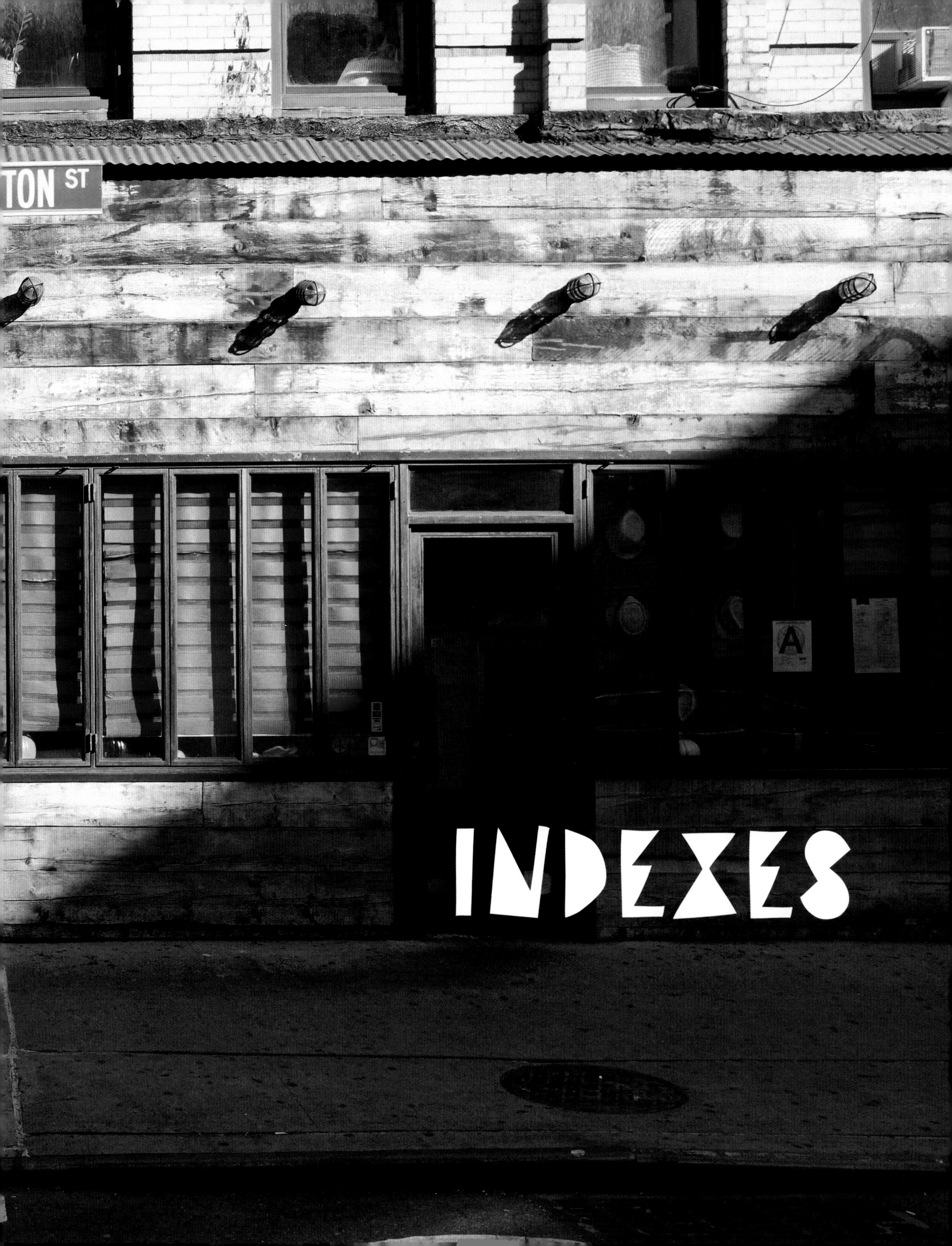

INDEXES

Hughie & Jaap, Inchydoney, Ireland

INDEX BY INGREDIENT

the River Amstel, Amsterdam

breakfast at Katz's Deli, New York